TOO SOON TO PANIC

TOO SOON TO
PANIC

GORDON FORBES

LYONS & BURFORD, PUBLISHERS

Printed in the United States of America

Design by Jennifer Corsano

10 9 8 7 6 5 4 3 2 1

Excerpt from "The Waste Land" in *Collected Poems 1909–1962* by T. S.
Eliot, copyright 1936 by Harcourt Brace & Company, copyright © 1963,
1964 by T. S. Eliot, reprinted by permission of the publisher.
Excerpt from "Burnt Norton" in *Four Quartets*, copyright 1943 by T. S. Eliot
and renewed 1971 by Esme Valerie Eliot, reprinted by permission of
Harcourt Brace & Company.

Library of Congress Cataloging-in-Publication Data

Forbes, Gordon, 1934–
      Too soon to panic / Gordon Forbes.
        p.   cm.
      Sequel to: A handful of summers.
      Originally published: New York: Viking, 1995.
      ISBN 1-55821-566-2 (cl)
      1. Forbes, Gordon, 1934–   . 2. Tennis players—South
Africa—Biography. I. Title.
GV994.F67A36 1997
796.342'092—dc21
      [B]   96-52805
                                                          CIP

To Jean,
Who travelled with me
When we were young
And played the game
With such finesse;
Who read me words she liked
And never stopped persuading me
To write some of my own—

CONTENTS

ACKNOWLEDGEMENTS

I would like to thank Frances Forbes, Gavin and Venetia Forbes, Sean and Ashley Godfrey, Jamie Forbes, Alison Lowry, Jenny Archibald, Jacques and Rhona Sellschop, Des and Dawn Lindberg, Mark Miles and the others at the ATP Tour, Richard Evans, Chris Gorringe and the committee of the All England Lawn Tennis Club, Philipe Chatrier, Patrice Clerc, Georgina Clarke, Lee and Claude Frankel, Clive Menell, Sir Robin Renwick, Sir Peter Ustinov, the players with whom I shared these adventures, and the young players of today who continually take the game onwards and upwards to greater perfection; the friends who have been generous in their encouragement; and all those members of the sports media whose writing, comments, and humour over the years have been of life-sustaining inspiration. And Ray Cave and Mark McCormack, who would not allow me to give up.

I acknowledge, too, the great writers and poets of whom my sister Jean enabled me to get glimpses, and whose lines I have used; Sammy Cahn, Axel Stordahl, and Paul Weston, writers of the music and lyrics of the song "I Should Care," which has been in my head ever since I can remember; Allen Fox and W. Timothy Gallwey for their philosophies on the playing and winning (and sometimes losing!) of tennis matches.

FOREWORD

Walls come tumbling down on Gordon Forbes. Nightly, as you will learn, he fights the Battle of Jericho in his pajamas. Alone, without even Joshua as a supportive doubles partner. This has been going on for years, and Forbsey has come through the nocturnal deluge of bricks remarkably well. And it's lucky for us tennis degenerates, because nobody has ever written about the game with such joy and good humor, as well as the neat brush stroke of a perceptive observer.

He passed this talent along to delighted readers in *A Handful of Summers* and, happily, is at it again in *Too Soon to Panic*. Presumably Forbsey either has a very hard head or successfully assumes a defensive fetal cover-up amid his cataclysmic nightmares, because he doesn't seem to have suffered much brain damage, and—hurrah!—his typing fingers remain unimpaired.

Many of those unsuspecting readers who, perhaps fortuitously, first came across *Summers* nearly twenty years ago wondered who Gordon Forbes was. They hadn't noticed his name thrown around in discussions of Wimbledon greats, and understandably were unfamiliar with the peregrinations of the South African Davis Cup team. Whenever anybody asked me, I would report having seen him play on the lawn of Boston's

Longwood Cricket Club in 1962, and spoiling the tournament for most of the spectators, that is, those who wanted to see much more of the admirable Aussies—Rod Laver and Fred Stolle—in the U.S. doubles championships.

In a monster of a quarterfinal ending at dusk, Forbes and his future brother-in-law, Cliff Drysdale, elicited a chorus of groans from the gallery by breaking Stolle's serve in the last game to win, 4-6, 12-10, 2-6, 11-9, 17-15. Ninety-two games. One of the longest matches ever perpetrated in a major championship, an atrocity made obsolete eight years later by the introduction of the tiebreaker. Moreover, after all that, the wrong guys won.

Laver and Stolle took it better than the customers who gathered around them in commiseration at the clubhouse bar. (The setback did nothing to set back their thirst.) Laver went on to become a double Grand Slammer and the greatest player. Drysdale and Stolle went on to become a very good television partnership in tennis commentary. None of the three ever had to go to work for a living.

Alas, for poor Forbsey . . . there was no alternative. Sad to contemplate, though sadder for him, of course. Selling lighting fixtures is no occupation for a writer able to illuminate the world of tennis with his prose. But there is the imperative of eating.

The knowledge is cheering that he has pulled the plug on that career and is back on the scene to regale us here, and, I trust, further. And he brings along his pal, Abe Segal, a picaresque character whom Forbes, even with all his skill, couldn't have made up.

Long may they wander, and long may Forbsey stand up to the collapsing walls with notebook in hand.

—Bud Collins

THE LAST LETTER

At first it had seemed an ordinary sort of Friday, and I had gone fishing. In the sunlit mists of the eastern Transvaal mountains the streams run clean and cold, falling in cascades towards the low country. You walk the grassy banks, lost in a world of your own, listening to the river and casting for trout in the shadows. The streams are peaceful beyond words. It was here, on a place called Three Falls Farm, that I got the telephone call from Texas—that evening just after dark in the middle of a storm—pitch black, rain in sheets, lightning, wind, and suddenly Cliff Drysdale's voice, empty and far away. I can hear it to this day.

"Gordon, Jeannie's in trouble."

"What kind of trouble?"

"She's very sick."

A fleeting sense of relief. How sick could she be?

"How sick?"

"Gordon, listen. She's not sick. She's dying."

I had a pad that I'd taken along to make notes on fishing—I still have it, and on the front cover is scribbled the word "meningiococcaemia," which I'd written down as Cliff spelt it out. "A kind of toxic shock," he said. He was in despair—I could hear it in the usually imperturbable voice that hurled such easy insults and teased people about their golf. That was at about eight o'clock. At three the next morning he phoned again to say that she had died.

The storm had gone. In the absolute quiet of that African night I went back to bed and listened to the sound of the river, and the feverish darkness was filled with glimpses of her life—fleeting images of my sister in all the old familiar places—the smiling urchin face, the jaunty walk, the cross-court forehand, the happy laugh.

Jean had married Cliff in the summer of 1967. He was the prince of South African tennis—handsome, assured, and so talented that it didn't seem quite fair. I'd known then that it was only a matter of time before they would leave us and move to the United States, and I was right. After a year or two they went to live at the Lakeway World of Tennis near Austin, where Cliff was to be resident pro.

We would write letters to each other. Sometimes I would go to visit them there, and for a while there was this promising place in our lives—the Lone Star State, the Hill Country, cottonwoods, bluebonnets, the Cowtown Barbecue, a little limestone creek. The spirit of Texas. There, with her two children, Jean made a new home while Cliff played his tennis. Sometimes she was lonely. She never actually said so, but you could tell from her letters—innuendos tucked between lines full of news and gentle humour. She was a prolific writer and a natural scholar of the English language, a talent that had enabled her to become one of the youngest lecturers at the University of the Witwatersrand.

More images: On the campus with her hair tied back and

an armful of books; at her graduation, self-conscious in her gown and mortarboard; at a lectern, glancing up with the little tongue-in-cheek smile that made her students love her so. A laugh in her voice: "Why should we learn, you ask? The use of knowing things is they help you get on, Mr. Forster says. And we all want to get on, I am sure. . . ."

Every now and then she would take upon herself the task of trying to polish up my awareness of literature. "You might dip into that," she would say, throwing a book on the table. "Perhaps some of it will rub off . . . ," and I'd find some little classic, the relevant pages marked with slips of paper and cryptic messages:

"Byzantium = Holy City of the Imagination!—(could be useful if only we could find it!)."

Or: "'Things fall apart; The centre cannot hold;' do you think Yeats also played mixed doubles?"

Scraps of poetry were often tucked into my sister's conversations. It was she who first read me the lines that open the first chapter of this book, she who smiled at my tennis articles as she edited them, and she who encouraged me to write an account of our tennis travels, which we decided to call *A Handful of Summers*. For her, the tennis circuit was just another stage on which people could play out their lives.

Above all, she loved people. No heart could be softer than hers. She was patient, tolerant, kind; the perfect listener, the great observer of life, the incomparable friend.

"Enough!" I hear her say, as clearly as if she were sitting beside me, here, now. "Enough! It's the others I want to hear about. Tell me about them! Tell me what I've been missing!"

A few weeks before she died I received what was to be her last letter. She must have been in a deeply reflective mood when she wrote it. Things weren't going as well as they might, she wrote. Her life was at a crossroads.

"Perhaps I am in what old T. S. called 'the bewildering minute!'—something about giving yourself up and then recovering yourself—and the self recovered is never the same as the self before! Complicated, hey? Oh, well, never mind. I'm sure my two selves will get to know each other quite well . . . !" Which was typical of my sister—to embark on a profound bit of philosophy then suddenly deflate it with a rueful aside.

I carried that letter around with me for a while, then put it carefully away, then found it again. And one day long afterwards, in that kind of mood, I sat down under one of the trees in Paris that we'd sat under before, and began to answer it.

Dearly Beloved [this was one of the traditional beginnings]:
I've been meaning to write for quite a while, now—to tell the truth, for over ten years! I'd actually begun to reply to your last letter when, suddenly, out of the blue, you went and died—an act that, of course, was simply unforgivable. Never a day goes by when we don't think of you. I'm in Paris, at Roland Garros with tennis all around me. I drink a glass of wine at lunchtime and then wander round the outside courts (of life, you used to say) and watch the matches. Sometimes I hear your voice, and your shadow hides round every corner.

Life and tennis! Do you remember how you once told me, when I was feeling low, that the game of tennis was just a smaller version of the game of life—both of them full of line calls and let cords, some good, some bad, and you simply had to play them as they came along, and keep trying. "Be sure to keep trying," you'd always tell me. "It's the only comfort. That and a nice cup of tea; oh, and if you can help it, don't miss too many of the easy volleys of life. They get more difficult as life goes on."

Well, I wish I'd paid more attention.

And talking of games, you would never believe what has happened to our old game. Most of the simple things are gone—white balls, afternoon tea, the blind old British umpires who used to write things down in pencil after calling "Mr. Worthington to serve," and then forget which one was Mr. Worthington.

Tennis is now populated by young millionaires and their coaches, managers, families, lovers, friends, etc. If in our time it was a game of grace, it is now ablaze with light and colour, worldly-wise, awash with money, and, as Hamlet would have put it, "Words, words, words."

Behind "all the crap" (as Abie says—he's a bit cross because there was no money when we played), there is still the game itself—handsome as it always used to be, overflowing with young talent—the pure style of Pete Sampras, Edberg's backhand volley, the quirkish genius of Andre Agassi, a German girl called Steffi Graf with long legs. Gabriela Sabatini! One talks of grace! Well, then. . . .

Every now and then you get a glimpse of our old world. Kenny Rosewall's backhand still glides and Rodney George Laver's game remains so pure one could weep. Nails Carmichael is now a coach—as are Niki Pilic, Ray Ruffels, Bob

Brett—supercoaches with superpupils. Fred Stolle has a son called Sandon, who is about the closest any of the ex-stars have gotten to having their children follow in their footsteps. Fred likes to coach Sandon, but Sandon won't listen to him anymore, so Fred has to tell Tony Roche what to tell Sandon, except Tony forgets exactly what Fred has said and often tells Sandon other things, so Fred spends a lot of time rolling his eyes upwards and grumbling to himself! The older players have tended to become a little testy about the money. You'd like them. Abie says the whole thing's like a friggin' circus.

Anyway, I thought you might like to know about it. After all, it is still about people—people and places, and so I've tried to put it all down for you. One thing is for sure. I would not have written anything without your inspiration, so please accept these notes as the good-bye that I was never able to say; or, if you like, just a last, cloudy glass of cold white wine. One for the road!

SEARCHING FOR

SOMEWHERE

Footfalls echo in the memory
Down the passage which we did not take
Towards the door we never opened
Into the Rose-garden.
—T. S. Eliot

On the farm where we were born, our father built what he called an antheap tennis court out of the termite mounds that dotted the plain above the house. His theory was that whatever technology termites used to bind the surface of their mounds would also serve to bind the surface of our court, and he was right. If we rolled the court after every rain, the surface became hard and smooth and the lines could be marked with whitewash. Eventually, after a lot of play, the antheap powdered to a fine clay that mixed with the limedust of the lines, and in the gloaming at the end of the day, when we served the odd ace or two, there were very satisfactory explosions of white dust where the balls bounced. It is the white dust I remember most of all.

There was the one slight hiccup in the history of that old antheap court. During one of the very dry spells that afflicted our farm, our father used it as a paddock to feed orphaned calves and lambs, and the surface became impregnated with manure. When the rains finally came he restored it, but he could never quite get rid of the manure, and from then on the surface seemed to have become somewhat slower.

"I suppose you could say it has a bit of grass in it," said our father, always passionate about the courts at Wimbledon, "so it should be a better surface!"

"It's an unusual sort of surface," said our mother, ever helpful.

"It was a *shit* surface!" cried Abe Segal delightedly, much later on, when I told him about it. And thereafter, in the locker rooms of the tennis circuit, when the conversation got around to court surfaces and who played well on what, and the players made remarks like "Neale Fraser is great on grass" or "Nicola Pietrangeli is a genius on clay," Abie would let it be known that Forbsey was "world class on manure"—a dubious claim to fame, but one that I decided would have to do until something better came along.

When we got a little older, our father turned the antheap court into a cement one and the explosions of dust were gone forever; but according to Abie, my game, and especially my backhand volley, would forevermore show signs of an early basic training on manure.

Abe was my companion and doubles partner all through

our playing days, and he quite frequently drove me crazy with his impulsive deeds. He often felt that by rights we should have won Roland Garros or Wimbledon, or both, if this, that, or the next thing had or hadn't happened. Sometimes I agreed with him, but at other times I was not so absolutely dead sure. Tennis, like life, can be a hard taskmaster. Usually, in an odd sort of way, you get only what you deserve. It's a very profound equation. . . . But I am going too fast!

It was Jenny, I think, who asked our father the question that for the rest of our lives would give us so much food for thought. Tennis intrigued all four of us children. Jack, the eldest, was open and optimistic, with a cheerful, no-nonsense game that could always be relied upon; I, the second child, had my patches of brilliance, my off days, and my tantrums; Jean surprised first us and later the entire tennis world by achieving at a very young age a tennis game of such instinctive ability, courtcraft, and maturity that at times it verged on pure genius. And Jenny, who arrived late, regarded tennis with a suspicious eye, never seeming quite to trust its intentions. She cared, though—more than we ever realised. Thus, I suppose, the reason for her question.

Our father was the driving force behind our tennis. He would devise clever schemes to get us on the court, and once we were there he would walk up and down giving us his range of broad-spectrum instructions—eye on the ball, follow through, forward on the shot, etc.—always egging us on to work harder, to try harder, to fight harder. We would never get anywhere unless we did, he would always say. Dad was a great one for "getting somewhere." For him life moved either forwards or backwards—it never stood still. Our notion of a comfortable, shady limbo where we could laze about and dream our teenage daydreams existed only after it had been earned through sweat and blood, and then only briefly before the next bout of striving. "Taking the strain," Jack used to call it. I can hear him even now. "Come along, Gordon, we better go out and take the strain"—whenever there was a big job to be done.

On the day of Jenny's question we'd just finished one of our challenge sets, and hadn't played too well. Our father had been in full cry all afternoon, and as we walked off the court we could sense a major lecture coming on.

"Still not enough effort!" The usual stuff. "Not enough will to win! How many times do I have to tell you kids that you will never get anywhere unless you wake up?"—and we looked at our feet, gloomily contemplating the extent of our idleness.

"Where is anywhere?" asked Jenny suddenly, and the penetrating look she gave him somehow suggested that she was talking about much more than just tennis.

The question stopped him in his tracks for a moment, because above all he was a fair and thoughtful man. "It's where you get if you make proper use of all your talents and opportunities," he said at last, taking refuge in logic. But I realised even then that an "anywhere" for him would never be the same as an "anywhere" for her.

In every life, I suppose, comes a moment when the carefree days of youth are suddenly over, and life is clouded by the need to "get somewhere." For me, Jenny's question and its answer was a turning point. From that moment on I was conscious of a need to strive—to find a satisfactory somewhere of my own that somehow met the demands, not only of our father's words, but of some other more obscure duty—to myself perhaps, or even to life itself.

It was tennis that first showed me an open road, a road full of promise, which I took without even knowing where it might lead.

"Who cares where it leads!" said Abie when I told him. "The worst that can happen is that you have a good time on the way!"

A lot of Abie's endeavours began with only this very brief contemplation of their ultimate downside—the "how bad can it be?" approach to life, which I would get to know so well. ("Upside is no problem, Forbsey. We can easily handle upside.") On the subject of journeys, I found it easy to agree with him.

These notes are more to do with journeys than destinations—with the fun of the game more than the winning of it. Sometimes they pause to regard wistfully those who seem to have reached their destinations; but mostly they tell of the many who simply tried the best they could and somehow lost the way—all with their own particular ambitions, their private dreams, their secret fears—taking the outside courts of life to prove some point, if only to themselves, and afterwards dropping into some little pub to drink a pint or two and talk it all away.

A racket, a ball, an opponent; lines, a net, a set of rules; the urge to compete, the will to win, the fear of losing. The old man who hit the shot to win Wimbledon in 1934 now watches quietly while the young man hits the shot in 1994, and it is the same shot, and all the effort and emotion are the same. There is a timelessness about these things; a simple ebb and flow; a turning of the wheel.

A ONE-ANT

TOWN

DIARY NOTES, OCTOBER 1954

After London, our little town seems to have gotten even smaller; the country is lonelier; the silence is deeper; the road is dustier. On my first day home I drove the Chev into town. You cross the railway line, climb the hill, pass the station, the trading store, the butcher shop, and after the road crosses the little bridge over the dry riverbed it becomes the main street— swept gravel with old cypress trees. Churches, general dealer, post office, café.

I parked outside the chemist shop and Mr. Hall was standing in the doorway, as he had been when I last saw him.

"Hello, Gordon," he said. "How was your trip?"

"It was very nice, thank you, Mr. Hall," I replied.

"Did you go to the British Museum?" he wanted to know.

"Yes, we did," I said. How can you explain to people that a game like tennis can change your entire life?

Tennis came into our lives very early on—so early, in fact, that to me it seemed always to have been there, materialising from the shadows of my first memories along with other things like the smell of bread baking, the lowing of cows at sunset, the sound of thunder or a tumble of collie pups.

There was a cupboard in the passage of our farmhouse where the tennis stuff was stored—white balls in cardboard boxes, hats and caps, a bag of resin, a few hanks of catgut (my father's usage), and various rackets in wooden presses, one of them called a Prosser Phenomenon and another a Red Devil. The cupboard had a certain smell, the kind of smell that you never forgot, a smell that had about it everything to do with tennis.

There were tennis parties on Saturday afternoons. The cars would pull up, crunching the swept gravel, grown-ups in cable knits and white cottons would get out, and the tennis court, with its background of poplar trees, would echo to the tap and thud of balls, and the bits of conversation that go with that kind of tennis.

"Rats, how feeble!"

"Duncan, you dirty dog! Don't cut!"

"What does that make it?"

"Thirty to the poor and needy."

"Ting-a-ling! It's set point!"

"If I double-fault I'll have a fit!"

"Hang on, partner, all is not lost."

They all had their styles and methods. Kingsley Hall from the chemist shop had a service that started with such a jerk that he sometimes put his back out and had to sit in the shade and take an aspirin. Louis Light, the general dealer, always bandaged both his knees, although he had injured only one of them in a school rugby match over twenty years before.

"God forbid they should ever give in," he sometimes used to say, with the variation other times that "God willing, they should see me through this life on earth!" except that he said "dish life on eert," which always made Jack and me laugh.

One of my mother's friends served gently underarm but began with an heroic overhead flourish. Another broke crisp little winds when she ran for short balls, and yet another had a bosom so vast that when she moved to hit a ball at anything more than a walk she had to take hold of it with her left arm to prevent a sort of pendulum effect that would nearly throw her off her feet.

DIARY NOTES, 1945

Mr. Light's shop and Mr. Hall's shop face each other across the street. Quite different smells come from their doors. Mr. Light's name used to be Mr. Lichtenstein, but he changed it He told my father that it took people so long to say "Hello, Mr. Lichtenstein" that he got "tired vaiting." Mr. Light and Mr. Hall stand in their doorways when they're not busy and tease each other across the street. Mr. Hall has this stutter. He says things like this to Mr. Light:

"N-n-n-n-nice p-p-p-pile of hi-hi-hides you have there Lou-Lou-Louis. P-p-p-pity you can't k-keep the s-s-s-s-smell on your si-si-si-side of the st-st-st-street!"

"There's no extra charge for de smell, Kingsley," says Mr. Light. He has the edge because he can say things much quicker.

Mr. Light's wife's name is Girlie, and Mr. Hall's wife's

name is Brownie. This morning Girlie baked Louis a lemon cake for his tea, and Louis offered Kingsley a slice. "Girlie a vonderful vife in the home," said Mr. Light, but Mr. Hall was not to be outdone.

"Well, B-B-Brownie is a ba-ba-ba-ba-boon in the shop," he said.

"Louis's not a bad old stick when you come to think of it," said our father. "And neither is Kingsley."

Our father played tennis in long flannels and had a self-proclaimed "whip" service of great speed, and also an illusive "twist" that puzzled everyone. When one of his twists came off, he would tap his temple the way he had seen Bobby Riggs do that afternoon in Queenstown while he was beating Donald Budge. He had also once watched Fred Perry win Wimbledon and had been profoundly affected by what he saw. It was Perry's dauntlessness that had gotten his blood up.

"He was afraid of nothing!" he often told us children. "He had the will to win! Perry's the one you ought to watch if you want to get anywhere!"

I suppose it was the "Touring Americans," as our father called them, who really made us want to be tennis players. They had come to play in Queenstown on a hot, windy Tuesday. In our father's opinion, of the four of them only Donald Budge was great. Bobby Riggs he had read of as being "a bit too cocky, and only in it for the money," and he referred to him as "that Riggs fellow." Carl Earn and Welby van Horn, who completed the foursome, were quite unknown to him, although he told us round the supper table that if they were in

"the Budge circus" they couldn't possibly be "complete duds."
Whatever his views, we'd all looked forward to the matches
for months.

"The fact that they're playing on a Tuesday means that
they don't think much of Queenstown," Jack would say.

"The fact that they've even heard of Queenstown is a miracle," said Jean.

"Queenstown's not a bad sort of town," said our father.

"We'll take a picnic lunch," said our mother.

DIARY NOTES, BARCELONA, 1994

*Veterans' doubles against the Italians! Abie, yet again.
While we wait, I tell him about Budge playing Riggs in
Queenstown in 1946. A thoughtful look.*

*"Jesus!" he says, "imagine Agassi and Becker going all the
way to Queenstown on a Tuesday afternoon to play tennis in
the wind."*

"They'd want a few million dollars each," I agree.

*"Which is more than Queenstown's worth!" he says.
"They could buy the whole town."*

*"You think they'd want Queenstown?" I ask. It's a very idle
conversation.*

"I want you to study Budge's drives," our father told us when
the big day finally came and we were driving the Chevrolet
down the hundred miles of dusty road to Queenstown. "They
say that his backhand is a very pretty stroke."

It was. I had never believed that a backhand could possibly
be so splendid and assured. As it turned out, Riggs ended up

beating Budge, backhand and all, but for me the result didn't matter one iota. I wanted a tennis game that looked like Donald Budge's.

For each one of us that Tuesday afternoon had been unforgettable.

For our father it had been Budge's elegance and his long cream flannels that somehow translated themselves into all that was good and noble about the game that he loved.

For Jack it had been the power. He had never imagined such pace, and the excitement of this new actuality deeply impressed him, causing him to go out onto the court and practise serving with all his might.

"Don't lose control," our father would advise when the thuds of his services could be heard up at the shearing sheds, but for Jack power was the key. "Theoretically," he would say, "if you can serve hard enough you can never lose to him." (In our young lives all the opponents whom we might ever have to take on at anything were always referred to as one vast, collective 'he.')

For our mother it had been the family picnic before the matches in the hot, resinous shade of the pine trees with the little table unfolded and its white tablecloth arranged.

For Jean, then about eight, it had been the chance to wear her new dress and to add to the dreams she dreamed of one day playing on "the centre court" and winning "the cup" for her father.

For me it had been the elegance and harmony of Don Budge's tennis. But there was also the dropshot that Carl Earn played with so much backspin that it bounced back over the net to his side. He had shaped up for a hard approach then suddenly played that dropshot.

"Van Horn nearly pulled a muscle just standing and watching," I said in one of our endless postmortems of the matches.

"A muscle in his mind!" added Jack.

"He nearly pulled his whole body!" said Jean.

For me, all the provocations of the game were wrapped up in that little shot—all the guile and artistry, the different ways and means, lay somewhere at some centre point between the majesty of Budge's backhand, the rocklike steadiness of Riggs's attitude, and the mischief and deception in Carl Earn's dropshot.

We had talked about tennis all the way back to the farm while the Chevrolet rumbled over the corrugated gravel and the fine dust seeped in through the door seals. At midnight, when we finally reached the farm gates, the night sky was brilliant with stars, the silence was immense, and I felt enveloped by well-being and a quite new awareness of an anywhere that, in my dreams, allowed me to play magnificent backhands on the centre court at Wimbledon.

For a while after that memorable day, there was a purity in the tennis that we played on the old court with its traces of manure—a oneness with the game itself that consisted simply of a racket, a ball, the dust of the court, the moods of the weather, and the dreams and images that we held tight in our minds.

We played, and as we played we improved, and as we improved our horizons expanded to competitions and tournaments, which in turn introduced all the other ingredients— excitement, anxiety, conflicts and tensions, the yearning to win and the fear of losing—a whole competitive mix that would finally overshadow the pure sensation of hitting a ball with a racket. Never again would we quite achieve the keen simplicity of playing tennis only for the fun of it.

Coming from the seclusion of that lonely farm we had a lot to learn. We progressed gradually from the small local tournaments to the bigger ones. It was at the Border championships in East London, years after we had seen the Touring Americans, that we got our first glimpse of the then top South African stars, and I clearly remember the new impression that they made. Tennis suddenly became more technical, more precise, more disciplined, and more serious than we had ever believed it could be. We were badly beaten, and not even by the best of them, so that we had to adjust our thinking and set up new goals and standards.

It was also in East London that we got our first glimpse of the nineteen-year-old Abe Segal.

Our farm was situated deep in the interior of the country near a small town called Burgersdorp on the edge of a dry region called the Karroo. Queenstown was the nearest medium-sized town, and East London was not only the nearest big town, it was also our favourite town, as it was there that we always spent our seaside holidays. This, anyway, was the ranking that had existed in our minds in those days, until one day Abe Segal had let it be known that East London was "the most one-horse town" he knew. He made the statement in the clubhouse at the Selbourne Park courts one rainy Sunday during the Border championships, and having said it, and after driving round the whole town in search of "something open," without success, he returned to the sodden little tennis stadium to add: "And what's more, its one horse has friggin' well died!"

It was the first time we'd heard this rather tired line, and also the first time we'd come in close contact with Abie, and his choice of words alone left us wide-eyed.

Abie lived in Johannesburg, which he then considered to be a multihorse town. Later, when he became a tennis star and thus familiar with places like London, Paris, and New York, he would refer to even Johannesburg as a "one-horse town." But meanwhile, that Christmas in East London, he'd deeply upset all three of us children by demolishing our number-one-ranking town in one short phrase.

"If East London is 'one-horse,'" I remember saying that evening at our little hotel, "then what is Burgersdorp?"

"One dog!" Jack suggested.

"One ant!" I piped up.

"Abe Segal is a one-fart person," Jean said. She was about nine at the time, and hated bad language.

"He's a multifart person," said Jack. "You should just hear him in the locker room after he's had his lunch. . . ."

"Now then, children!" our mother said, genuinely angry. "For the love of Mike, behave!"

"As far as bad language goes," Jack said to Jean and me, later on, "'for the love of Mike' is just about the best that Mom can do."

But from that day onwards we always felt a little on the de- fensive about living near a one-ant town on the edge of the Karroo.

Our mother used to dislike blasphemy so much that it seemed actually to pain her. It was even worse if the Lord's name was involved. To be on the safe side we thus always referred to Him as Pete or Mike. In addition to "for Pete's sake" or "for the love of Mike," which were standard phrases, we would sometimes say things like "thank Pete that he missed a sitter at match point," or "let's pray to Mike that our serves are working."

It was all part of the somewhat strange relationship that our family had with religion. My father's family had been deeply religious, and until he was about eighteen my father had gone along with them. Then one day he had suddenly changed, disliking what he called "the trappings of religion," and never again attending formal religious services.

"When I was a child," he always told us, "we had to go to church every Sunday morning of our lives. We'd get up at daybreak, hitch up the cart and horses, and go into town. After the service, which seemed to take a very long time, we would go to Uncle Harry's farm for lunch. Everyone was very quiet and serious. There didn't seem to be much one could do on a Sunday without offending Old Pete."

As a child our father had been an avid collector of birds' eggs. Then came the Sunday on Uncle Harry's farm when he had been walking quietly in the fields and a nightjar flew out from under his feet. To his great delight he saw two mottled brown eggs nestling in the gravel. Nightjars were very rare and finding their eggs, even rarer. He had to have them, but he was afraid that Uncle Harry might object. So where to put the eggs for safekeeping? His Sunday clothes were tight and had very small pockets.

"And so I decided to put the eggs in my mouth," my father told us. "Trust in God, they were always saying, so that's what I decided to do. Excepting that old Aunt Ellie was very affectionate, and when she said good-bye that day she squeezed my cheeks with her fingers as she kissed me. The eggs broke and I had to swallow them. My precious eggs! I don't think that I ever quite forgave Him for that!" he added, with a twinkle in his eye, so that we were never sure whether the incident had had any real effect on him.

It was about six years later, he told us, when he was eighteen and had left to join the Royal Flying Corps, that he'd come to a decision.

"I decided to make an arrangement with God," he said. "I told Him that I would try to manage on my own. If I needed Him, I would contact Him. If He needed me, He should contact me. In that way I could get on with my work and He could devote more time to the meek!"

There was another twinkle in my father's eye when he told this story. There was always a twinkle in his eye where religion was concerned. He never spoke of it much, and never interfered with the beliefs of others. But his arrangement with Pete lasted for the rest of his life, and he never wavered from it.

"If you simply add another *o* to the word *God*," he would say to us with a wink, "things tend to become much simpler!"

DIARY NOTES, FLORENCE, 1959

In our doubles match today against Pietrangeli and Sirola I played badly, and kept saying sorry to Abie.

"Why do you keep saying sorry?" he wanted to know when

we were changing ends. "Don't be so friggin' meek and mild!"

"The meek shall inherit the earth," I said (stupidly).

"Well they won't keep the friggin' thing for too long," he said, sounding quite irritated.

Abie also had his own ideas about religion, but he never mentioned making any actual arrangements in that regard. It was in fact he who gave me a different angle on the philosophy of making the important line calls of life from that given me by my father.

Aged about ten and twelve, my brother and I had one day played one of the competitive sets that we often played against one another, and it turned into a very close game that he eventually won. I behaved badly, disputing several line calls, arguing about the score, complaining about the setting sun, throwing my hat on the ground, and finally, in desperation, when one of his shots took the very outer edge of the baseline on a vital point, simply calling the score in my own favour.

Unbeknownst to us, my father had watched the whole set through a window of the house that overlooked the court. He was waiting for us at the gate of the tennis court after the game and had the deadly quiet look in his eyes that made my throat go dry.

"Follow me," he'd said, and took us into the study. "Sit down," he went on, "look at me, and listen very carefully, because I am going to say this only once. There are three things you will never do while playing tennis. Never, for as long as you live. You will never behave badly; you will never make excuses; and you will never cheat."

Here I dropped my eyes, but again he insisted that I look up.

"The first two are simply bad sportsmanship and bad manners," he'd said quietly, "and I will tolerate neither one. But cheating is quite another matter. If I ever catch either of you cheating —deliberately cheating—then you will never again play tennis on this farm. Do you both understand what I have said?"

We'd replied very clearly that we understood, because we knew that when our father spoke thus, a clear reply had better be made at once. From that day on I cleared from my mind the temptation to make dubious calls. Accepting the way the ball bounced became almost a way of life. But one day Abie had given me an alternative view of things.

"Tell me what you mean by a bad call and I'll tell you if I make them," he'd said to me. We were playing a tournament in Italy. That afternoon he had played an early-round match on the slow clay against a low-slung Italian player who scurried about the court so fast that the red dust crept up over his shoes, into his socks, and on towards his knees. Spurred on by his hometown supporters, Abie's opponent went into a sort of a high-level trance and hardly missed a ball; Abie ended up just winning an unbelievably tight match by a hair's breadth. What was memorable about the match was the fact that at about 7-6 for Abie in the final set, he had gotten a match point at 30-40 and handled the situation in a very creative way. With the memory of my father's words still in my head, I asked Abie about it afterwards.

The said point had started quite normally, with Abie chipping his return to the backhand side and coming in to net (for about the six hundredth time, as he put it), but then, what with his opponent's accuracy off the ground and a few dropshots and lobs thrown in, the rally developed into what Abie used to call "an off-road fuck-up"—meaning that he'd had to cover an awful lot of ground in a scrambling sort of way. On about the fifteenth stroke of the rally, his opponent hit a very hard, deep cross-court backhand that Abie couldn't quite get to. He did, however, arrive on the scene fractionally after the ball had bounced, having travelled all the way from the other side of the court at high speed, his body obstructing the view of the line judge and his forwards momentum causing him to go into a monumental slide that completely wiped out the mark made by the bouncing ball.

I was watching the match with Claude Lister, and I fancied that I'd seen the ball mark in the damp clay just inside the baseline, before Abie's slide had buried it in a fountain of clay. There was an expectant murmur from the small crowd of spectators. The umpire hesitated and looked at the line judge, who indicated that he was unsighted. He then looked at Abie, who, still maintaining the heroic pose bequeathed him by his slide, met his eyes and gave the slight finger action that he'd perfected to deal with balls that were out, but dangerously close to the line. Then he got to his feet and trotted towards the net with outstretched hand.

"Game, set, and match to Mr. Segal," said the umpire very firmly, impassively ignoring the protests of the crowd and the eruption of despair unleashed by Abie's opponent.

"But didn't you think the ball was in?" I asked Abie afterwards.

"Who knows exactly where it bounced, Forbsey?" he replied.

"Doesn't it worry you a bit?"

"I'll get over it," said Abie. "In fact, I'm already over it. It took about five seconds. With a wanker like that, that's about how long it takes."

"But how did you know?" I persisted.

"Know what?"

"That the umpire would call the point for you?"

"He looked like he was on my side," said Abie. "So I figured it was worth a try. How wrong could I go?"

"I don't know whether I could have managed that," I said, adding wistfully, "I'd never have gotten away with it, for a start."

"We seem to have two issues here," said Claude Lister, always the mediator. "The first is whether one ought to have the point. The second is how to get away with it! Abie, I must say, performed very well in both departments." There was a silence while we all digested these facts, then Claude went on in his careful way.

"I must admit," he said, "that fellow Abie played had it coming to him. His actions earlier on were very unsporting indeed. In my book, he owed Abie a number of points. And after all, how could Abie be sure? He'd been running a long way, d'you see?"

"A shit of a long way," Abie agreed.

I've often wondered what my father would have said about that. He had died by then, so I could never ask him. But one day, long afterwards, when I told the story to a venerable old lawyer whom I had gotten to know, he listened carefully with closed eyes and said, *Fiat justitia et ruant coeli.*"

I waited patiently, and in good time was rewarded by the

translation—"Let justice be done though the heavens fall"—
which has always seemed to me a very satisfactory way to close
the case. I am sure Claude Lister would have agreed.

On a summer's day at Roehampton in 1954, I won the final
qualifying match for the Wimbledon singles and part of the
first journey had been made. Although I lost in the first round
to a Canadian named Bob Bedard, the fortnight was filled with
promise. On finals day I sat in the competitors' enclosure and
watched Jaroslav Drobny win the title by beating Ken Rosewall
in four sets. The surge of emotion I felt when at last he won the
final point was one that, I later discovered, came only at such
rare and particular times.

And my emotions were made keener that day by a strange
feeling that somehow a part of the moment was my own, and
that one day it would be me who would be standing on that
centre court, holding up the cup.

THE VERB
"TO PANIC"

My father once mentioned that as a family we tended to take life too seriously. We children agreed, but decided amongst ourselves that it was perhaps his eternal quest for anywhere that was the chief cause. He was passionate about Scotland, being of the firm opinion that to be born a Scot gave one a slight edge over everyone else on earth. Periodically he would take down the two heavy volumes called the *Histories of the Scottish Highlands* and we would look up our ancestors, finding in our blood hundreds of years of adversity—fire and sword, hunger, freezing weather, mountain fastnesses, clans falling upon each other in the middle of the night, plunderings, lootings, sackings.

"Not to mention spillage of blood and rapine!" Jack once remarked, looking up from the book with a crooked smile.

The colour plate showing our tartan was nearly worn through—as was the part about us being a powerful clan, and

the very first page where "one Ochanchar," having slain a fero-
cious bear, stood on top of it and with a great shout took
the name of "Forbear." (In spite of the fact that he'd only slain
Onebear!)

"He obviously had the killer instinct," Jean once remarked.

"A born net-rusher," Jack agreed.

"You had to be strong then, as you have to be strong now,"
explained our father, "for if the trumpet makes an uncertain
sound, who would prepare himself for the battle?"—although it
wasn't often that he used lines from the Bible to make
his point.

One day much later on, while waiting to play a doubles
match, I told Abie about our ancestors. To my surprise I found
him to be interested.

"Fire and sword, hey?" he said musingly, liking the sound
of it.

"Plus the rest!" I said. "So although it all happened about
eight hundred years ago, it's no wonder that as a family we're
still a bit twitchy."

"Never mind twitchy," Abie said. "On tight points you
completely crap yourself!"

"But not on every tight point," I objected. "Sometimes
pressure makes me play brilliant shots."

"Or complete frig-ups," he said gloomily. "And what's
more, a man can get a heart attack waiting to find out," said
Abie.

DIARY NOTES, BERLIN, 1962

It's a Monday and we're at the Rott-Weiss Tennis Club in

Berlin. Davis Cup versus the Germans. The place smells of coffee and cigars, Abie wears his raincoat all the time as though he's one of Smiley's People. He'd love to be a spy except he doesn't know exactly who to spy on. Drysdale keeps disappearing with beautiful women, and neither he nor Abie seem aware that I am still in shock after nearly losing the deciding match against the French.

We have the centre court at twelve for practise, and as we arrive the German team is just coming off, relaxed and laughing as though they have already won the match. Bungert, Kuhnke, and Buding and about twenty coaches carrying liquids in jugs.

"They have more jugs than we have," I say.

"A bunch of wankers," says Abie.

He gives the trumpet blasts, but it is Drysdale and I who have to play the singles. We only have one coach, who also acts as manager, travel agent, doctor, physio, psychiatrist, ball boy, etc. Claude Lister of Bathgate Road, Wimbledon SW 19, cheerful, courageous, and British to the core—which is just as well. Stability is what we need.

We start out with drills, all three of us, then Drysdale collapses in the shade and has to have milk to drink, which means that he's been doing things in the night. So Abe and I play singles, and it turns into one of those days. Heavy, humid, and windy. The balls feel like lead and two of them fluff up so much that Abie throws them to Claude and tells him to get others as we aren't playing "friggin' badminton." I have no centre to my racket, thus no touch, thus waves of irritation and bad behaviour. Also, there are these poplar trees behind the courts that give off fluffy seeds.

"Friggin' things float about like they own the place!" says Abie. *"A man goes up for a smash and ends up hittin' a floater. . . ."*

"Come on, chaps," says Claude. *"Everything's going to be all right."*

When Abie wins the set I throw my racket at the fence, which, at this precise moment, seems to be a reasonable thing to do. Because it's that kind of day, the racket hits a pole and falls to pieces.

"Crap-almighty, Forbsey!" says Abie. *He comes over to my side and takes me by the shoulders. "Listen,"* he says. *"What day is today?"*

"Monday."

"Right," he says. *"Monday. The match starts Friday."*

"So what?"

"So it's too soon to panic," he says. *"Just be with me. I'll tell you exactly when to panic."* And somehow after this I begin to play better.

Tuesday: Better balls and more strings in my racket. Even more seeds today. "It's the mating season for trees," says Abie. *After we practise, he announces that he wants to see the Berlin Wall.*

"You want to hit against it?" Drysdale wants to know.

"Take him away," Abie says to Claude. *"Put him in his cage and feed him."*

Abie regards Cliffie as a minor and usually talks to him via someone else. If Cliffie says, "You want to hit some balls at three?" Abie will say to me, "Tell him I only play with juniors in the mornings." Meanwhile Cliff is getting tougher and tougher to beat, and Abie knows it.

Wednesday: Lost a practise set to Drysdale. Then Drysdale lost to Segal. Then Segal lost to me. "That means that you're all in good form!" says Claude Lister, although I'm not sure how he works that out. My forehand is still playing up. Abie says it's still too soon to panic (and still the seeds come down).

Thursday: Beat Drysdale. **Killed Segal, 6-2.** *("Frig you, Forbsey," he says. "You're supposed to be crappin' yourself, remember?") My whole game has come back by some mira-cle—a huge turnaround. But can it last? ("Of course it can," says Claude, but how does he know?)*

Friday: We're bitterly disappointed. "Now I've seen every-thing!" is all that Abie says. Drysdale leads two sets to love against Buding and loses in the fifth. I lead 4-3, 40-30 in the fifth against Bungert and lose. Too cautious. A precious point that could have changed everything. Claude says we put up a jolly good show. "They had the run of play on the day," he says. Meanwhile we're down two to nothing, with three to go. A miracle is needed, and miracles are in short supply.

Saturday: The doubles. Abie and me against Bungert and Kuhnke. In the locker room Abie adopts his philosophical atti-tude: "What can I tell you, Forbsey?" he says. "A man can only do what a man can do," but I'm as scratchy as the devil. A strange mood. I'm prepared to try my guts out, except I don't feel a win in the air, no matter how much I grope about for one. Later, just before we walk on the court, he stops me and grips my shoulders again.

"Listen, Forbsey," he says. "Listen. So what's the worst thing that can happen today? What's the worst, most crap-

defyin', shit-forsaken thing that can possibly happen to us?
We could lose the match, right?"

"Right," I mutter.

"So we've lost matches before, right?" he asks.

"Right."

"So we'll have a glass of beer," he says. "It's not like they
don't make beer in Germany, is it? And we won't actually get
the death sentence, will we?" And he lets go of my shoulders
and picks up his rackets and walks off.

Play starts at three. The court is packed with spectators
come to witness our demise. By quarter to six it's two sets all.

"Another saga," I say to Abie at changeover.

"Like the book that Russian guy wrote," he mutters. We're
standing next to the umpire's seat, towelling off. "Who was
that Russian guy again, Forbsey?"

"Tolstoy," I say, a bit absently.

"Right, Tolstoy," he says. The Germans are discussing tactics and we're discussing literature.

The fifth set goes on dead even. At 4-3 for us, on Bungert's
service, out of the blue we find ourselves with a break point at
40-30, same situation as in my singles. I'm on the left court and
I realise that I have to make a return, and what flashes through
my head is the return I made in the singles that was too careful. So I walk in a bit of a circle, hoping for a mental glimpse of
something more attacking while the crowd quiets down.

Bungert gets ready to serve and the court goes dead quiet.
As he's about to serve, Abie holds up his hand and stops play.
Bungert waits, and Abie walks over to me, and puts his lips
right next to my ear.

"Okay, idiot," he says, "panic now!" and in spite of everything I have to laugh.

The Germans think we've got some terrific play worked
out, so that when my return goes down the middle they're
busy watching the lines.

"Game, South Africa," says the umpire. It's 5-3 for us, final
set, Segal to serve (thank God).

"Listen, Forbsey," he says as we walk back together. "This
is the last game, right? Enough is enough. I don't care if we
have to catch the ball in our teeth and spit it back. Just hold
onto your ass and watch the lobs!" and sure enough we hold
his serve and win the set 6-3.

Afterwards in the locker room Abie tells Claude Lister that
he's finally figured out a way to make Forbsey panic on schedule.

On the final day, tennis did one of its celebrated tricks. The
clouds lifted, I beat Buding and Drysdale beat Bungert, and we
won the tie 3-2 and were able to bask for a while in the warmth
that envelops one after such events. The diary notes recapture
the anxiety that I used to feel—senseless now, but at the time,
devastatingly real. They also remind me of Abie's inspired
improvisation on the use and timing of the verb "to panic."

I came upon the Berlin notes some time ago when we were
moving house. They were in an old tennis bag, tucked into an
envelope with other notes yellow with age and stained with
what might have been coffee. The first portion was written on a
paper napkin marked CAFÉ HEINZ—so faded that I had to under-
take some restoration and rewriting.

I am not sure when or why it was that I first began writing things down. Perhaps the habit came from my mother, who also made notes—simple comments on farm life—the animals, the crops, the changing seasons. The long winter evenings we spent in front of the fire must have encouraged us to read and write, for all of us children kept diaries at times. My own note-keeping habit has stayed with me on and off since childhood, and I've ended up with boxes full of papers, some yellow with dust and smelling of time past, some so cryptic that they stir only the vaguest of memories. For some periods I actually kept formal diaries, but often I simply wrote things down on any available scrap of paper. Sometimes the notes were lost, and sometimes they simply petered out, leaving promising notions leading nowhere.

DIARY NOTES, DEAUVILLE, 1954

Lew Hoad told me that Ken Rosewall said that Mervyn Rose had heard Frank Sedgman telling Ken McGregor that Harry Hopman had told him that if you could serve a big-enough service deep enough, and then get to net fast enough to make a deep-enough first volley (to the backhand, usually), so that he (the other guy) was kept under enough pressure for enough of the time, then you'd never have to mess about with backhands and forehands from the back of the court, which makes life a heck of a lot easier . . . etc., etc. . . . . When I told that to Abie he said, "Yes, but it's got to be one hell of a friggin' big serve, Forbsey!"

Occasionally I go through the old notes and relive the memories.

"To be a tennis player," I found in one old notebook dated 1959, "you need something to eat, somewhere to sleep, somewhere to play, someone to make love to, and somewhere to have your laundry done"—hardly a profound statement, but one that quite accurately described the simplicity of the tennis circuit as it then was.

Yes, we were a family of note makers, and it was one of the notes made by my mother when I was still a boy that made me realise I had always been a nervous sleeper.

"Gordon has dreams," she wrote. "He sits bolt upright in bed and shouts out 'Who are you?' very loudly in the middle of the night. And last night he leapt on top of his brother and told him that there was a 'terrible thing' in his bed—all of which can be quite alarming, especially if you're not expecting it."

"Friggin' alarming!" cried Abie when one day I told him what my mother had written. He'd had to put up with quite a number of things that went bump in the night. Ever since childhood I have been a victim of these hallucinations, which come out of the blue so suddenly and so vividly that I instinctively leap out of bed and take action.

Broadly speaking, my dreams could be divided into about five categories, involving (but not restricted to) such things as:

1. surprise attack by man or beast;
2. suffocation by poison gas or shortage of air (or both);
3. awakening (or rather believing myself to be awake) and not having the slightest idea where I am—knowing only a terrifying and empty blackness;
4. floods, eruptions, and deluges;

5. collapsing walls. In my youth, these were my most frequent nightmares, and the ones that required the fastest action. The wall behind my bed would begin to fall on top of me. Action would depend upon what stage the falling wall had reached. If it was just beginning to topple, I would jump onto my bed and try to heave it back into place with my shoulder. If the collapse had reached an advanced stage, I would leap sideways out of bed with a great shout: *"Wall's falling!"*

Abie eventually became quite used to my concern about the state of the walls. But the first time I shouted "Wall's falling!" he, too, had leapt sideways out of bed, "just to be on the safe side," as he'd told me later. After several false alarms, however, he took things more calmly.

"Leave it, Forbsey," he would say sleepily. "Let the friggin' thing fall over if it wants to," and for the few seconds before I awoke I'd get really angry with him.

Finally, to stay sane, as he put it, he would give me a checklist before we went to sleep. "Walls cemented down," he would say. "No-one in the cupboards, windows open, bath taps tight shut, floorboards nailed down, animals all in the zoo, birds in the trees. Crap-almighty, Forbsey! I can't believe we have to do this!"

I might go for a week or two sleeping like a child and then suddenly run out of air or have a wall or two fall over. To this day I am unable to pinpoint their exact causes. The tensions of competitive tennis must certainly have been a contributing factor, as many dreams occurred during my playing days.

Finally I simply accepted them as permanent fixtures. There was nothing I could do about them, I decided, except make notes. And sometimes, tucked into the notes, I am now able to detect veiled reference to my fears, hidden as they were beneath the layers of my youthful nonchalance.

FEAR IS A
TERRIBLE THING

There is a tennis court at the British embassy in Pretoria that is sometimes the setting for surprisingly tense, though sometimes technically iffy, tennis matches. One end of the court has a background of purple bougainvillaea, the other a long view of the lovely Union Buildings—in November set about with purple jacaranda trees.

One day the British ambassador, Sir Robin Renwick, in a cunning alliance with the Greek ambassador, Lucas Tsilas, challenged the U.S. ambassador, William Lacy Swing, and me to a doubles match—to the death, they said, no quarter asked or given. After some deliberation the United States and I decided that, as several categories of honour were at stake, there was nothing for it but to accept. But almost at once, I felt a certain tension beginning to build.

The Anglo-Greek alliance considered its challenge to be one of great tactical shrewdness. If they lost, they would be able to say, "My dear chap, what do you expect—the United States was playing with a Wimbledon champion?" Whereas if they won, word of their victory would echo down the corridors of embassies throughout the free world.

The United States, on the other hand, would be under the worst kind of pressure. If she lost, all the blame would rest squarely on her shoulders, whereas if she won, others could say, "Well, what do you expect? She was playing with a Wimbledon champion!"

I, of course, never quite won Wimbledon. But on such occasions I often find my tennis exploits tend to become amplified—to the extent that Abe Segal and I were once actually awarded two Wimbledon titles by a pair of businessmen who nearly managed to win a set from us while we played along with them in the fond hope that they would give us some inside information on the stock exchange.

"This is-a the big time," said Lucas Tsilas that Sunday morning as we walked on the court. He'd said it to his partner in a confidential voice, but he made sure that his words carried to the United States, adding, in an even more dramatic way, "Is good we gh-have strong nerves! Fear is a terrible thing!" I had never before heard this complex circumstance so effectively abbreviated.

Lucas was small and robust, with sturdy legs and a compact swing that suggested steadiness and reliability. As if that was not enough, he talked nonstop as we warmed up ("Gh-we make-a big surprise, Partner! Like Pearl Harbor"), while William Swing studiously ignored him and concentrated fiercely on getting his somewhat low-key game into gear.

Sir Robin playing the backhand court was the epitome of all those images evoked by the term *Cambridge Blue:* an elegant waif in threadbare tennis garb, tall and slender, his loose-jointed limbs suggesting a stylish but fickle batting technique at cricket, but causing me to wonder whether his tennis game could actually withstand the pressure of international play.

"Enough of practise!" announced Lucas. "I have found-a the middle of racket. Now we make toss," and he spun his racket with a flourish, crying out, "Gh-what-a you say?" to the United States. When we won the toss he said, "Mean nothing. Sun-a no problem. In Gh-Athens we gh-have-a sun like *fire!*" and walked off to receive, leaving me to serve first in the direction of the Union Buildings.

Feeling that I should try to establish some sort of mental edge early on, I decided to go for an ace, and managed to slide a slice to the forehand side that curved fiercely away into the fence, leaving Greece temporarily surprised and stranded.

"Verrry fast ball!" he said. "But first point only. Plenty more, Partner!"

My first experimental kicker to Sir Robin's backhand confirmed my suspicions. I could virtually see the urgent instructions being dispatched from his brain, and his limbs begin to take up their positions—all of which had to be frantically re-adjusted when my serve kicked high and to the left. His return went over the side fence and nearly upset the tea tray that was all laid out under the trees.

"How paltry!" said Sir Robin.

"Bad bounce!" announced Greece, firmly. "England must-a

put new surface!" He kicked contemptuously at the court with his shoe.

We held my first-service game without much trouble, but then Lucas, with a cry of "ace warning!" proceeded to produce a series of low-level topspin serves followed by fiery advances to net, ending the game with a minor smash that went "right through me," as William Swing put it sombrely.

"Early days," he added gamely, although the intensity of the Greek assault had clearly rattled him. He collected the balls to serve and out of the corner of my eye I caught a glimpse of him shaping up with a heroic McEnroe-like left-handed stance, while Lucas bounced up and down on the receiving court saying things like "this our chance, Partner," and "time for big attack!"

I stood waiting at net in the ready position and after a while there was the merest whisper of sound behind me and a tennis ball came drifting past my head to land at the feet of Lucas, who gave a deafening call of "out," before moving farther in for the kill. Presently a second ball arrived with even less fanfare, this time hitting the net with a sigh and rolling to an apologetic halt

"What I tell you? Love-fifteen," cried Lucas gleefully. "United States in trouble. Fear is a terrible thing!"

On the love-15 point Sir Robin, still under the influence of my kickers, was standing well back to receive when America's first ball, struck with the same mystifying gentleness as before, just cleared the net. It faded away into the alley long before Sir Robin's mental instructions got anywhere near his feet, so that the best he could manage was a sort of galvanic start that, if anything, sent him staggering a half-step backwards rather than in the direction of the service.

"How spastic!" he said.

"United States trick!" exclaimed Lucas.

And so on. Play continued with steadily rising tensions. The Anglo-Greek alliance pounded America while I hovered about trying to poach without seeming to try too hard.

"Let's lob Greece," I remember suggesting to William Swing at some stage (Lucas virtually touching the net with his nose). At another Great Britain suddenly produced an alarming series of wristy drives that went whistling "through America," while Greece continued to make oral contributions. ("Gh-what you think? Gh-we lie down and die?") The score became 5-all. More alarming was the fact that a little collection of wives and other spectators had gathered round the tea things. Lady Renwick, unaware of the critical state of our match, walked to the netting fence and asked Sir Robin to call a halt for tea.

"Things are at rather a delicate stage, dear," he said.

"Never-a mind!" cried Lucas, "Gh-we play-a tie-break! Sudden death!" This notion seemed to appeal to him so much that he repeated it specifically to William Swing as we changed ends. "Sudden death, Mr. Ambassador! Sudden death! Remember! Fear is a terrible thing!"

At four points to three for us, Sir Robin got an unexpected backhand smash, and in spite of a last-minute rearrangement of arms and legs it got lost in the sun and he missed it altogether.

"How pitiful!" he exclaimed. Throughout the game he had complained (unjustly, I thought) about certain of his efforts, proclaiming them to be such things as "lamentable," "woe-ful," "timid," or "thoroughly abominable." This time, though, he looked particularly stern, and to my surprise William Swing looked at him with a twinkle in his eye and said: "Fear is a ter-rible thing!"

At 6-5 for us, set point, William Swing put up a high and cautious lob that hung for a while in the noonday sun, so that both Britain and Greece had time to get underneath it. There was a great clash of rackets, and the ball fell to the court untouched.

"What a shambles!" said Sir Robin. "Sorry, Partner!"

"Not-a your fault," said Lucas. "They have-a all the lucky breaks. No, we-a gh-have a nice cup-a tea."

Which, of course, is the ultimate weapon of all natural competitors like Lucas. They dispense with the need to panic. Having stuck their necks out, done their best, and failed, they put the failure right out of their minds and have a cup of tea!

DIARY NOTES, HAMBURG, 1963

When I was young, there was no dividing line between nervousness and excitement. Whether I won or lost, there was no fear—only a feeling of great expectation, as though at any moment it might be my turn. Now that I am old [I was twenty-nine at the time] I have to search for the expectations, and watch out for the fear. It's always knocking at the door. Today in my match against [Edison] Mandarino, it slipped in the back way. I should beat Mandarino. But the big points come up and seem to melt away before I am ready. . . .

I now realise that my father's emphasis on our Scottish ancestry was meant to give us confidence. We would sit in front of that lonely fire on winter evenings, turning the creamy old pages of the *Histories*, smelling the leather, listening to the deep voice exalting Scotland, and feeling a sort of comfort while we counted the pages given to each clan, secretly suspecting that the stronger the clan, the more pages their story would be given. The Forbeses had seven. The MacGregors had about nine, but the Campbells and the MacDonalds had over twenty each.

"Too oft met with," our father would say, having no such doubts. "Too many of them about. We are the more exclusive," always with that particular twinkle in his eye.

Some clans, like the MacBeans, the Duffies, and the MacQuarries, had less than a page each, and we felt an indulgent sort of pity for them.

"Only just clans," Jack would say.

"Clanlets," Jean would agree, while looking up the ancient mottoes on their coats of arms and reading them out: "Truth Conquers." "Royal is My Race." "Endure with Strength." Our ancient motto was "Grace Me Guide."

"A civilised sort of clan," our father used to admit.

One day Jean discovered that the motto of the Drummond clan was "Gang Warily."

"They knew!" she cried delightedly. "Those Drummonds must have been a smart clan!" And from then on, whenever danger threatened, we would adopt the Drummond motto.

On the tennis circuit Jean almost never left for the courts without throwing a book into her tennis bag. Mostly they were ordinary novels—she liked anything from, say, *The Saint* to Alastair McClean or Bertie Wooster—but occasionally Shakespeare would get an outing. One day at the tennis court she nudged me in the ribs and gave one of her fruity chuckles.

"Look what happened to Horatio when he saw Hamlet's father's ghost!" she said, and read me the part where the ghost came within a truncheon's length of Horatio and was "distilled almost to a jelly with the act of fear." "You see!" she said. "They had the same problems as we do, except they had truncheons instead of rackets!"

We were sitting in the stands of some or other tournament as we'd done a hundred times before, watching someone win or lose, waiting for our match, and idly chatting away. Match temperament was an eternal topic. On occasion we had all watched players "choke," "get the elbow," "freeze," "seize up," or simply "blow it." We'd done it ourselves and knew how it felt. You'd go into the locker room, and for a while you'd hate yourself, living the moment over and over again in your mind, promising yourself it would never happen again. As you got better, it became ever more important:

a) not to choke, or
b) if you did choke, not to show it.

To be devastatingly cool under pressure was the right thing—like Pancho Gonzales, or Lew Hoad, or John Newcombe. (The match point comes up, they calmly serve an ace, then lope up to net, hand outstretched, a big grin.) Later on, of course, we were to find that the fear syndrome applied to more things in life than tennis!

I have watched chief executives who have nerves of steel in boardroom meetings completely miss an easy smash or a short putt simply because, say, a pretty woman happens to appear at the critical moment. I have heard top academics lose their place in public speeches and retire in disarray. Charlie Brown never makes the catch when the little red-headed girl is watching.

"What is this thing called fear?" we must all have asked ourselves many times over. "How exactly does it all work?"

DIARY NOTES, 1957

Abie has this Australian—friend, I suppose you could say, but really he's more like a trainer-cum-mentor—who travels with us and keeps Abie out of trouble. His name is Wally Wolfe, but Abie calls him "Doc." Doc has certain rules that Abie has to follow—like exercising regularly, trying not to blaspheme, avoiding chocolate, and having to have his Eno's Fruit Salts every morning at six-thirty. Doc has a thing about bowels. "If your bowels don't move," he says, "nothing moves." Someone should inform Doc that when it comes to this kind of movement, Abie wrote the book.

Here in Copenhagen, being his roommate, I also get handed a foaming glass of Salts every morning. I have to sit up half asleep, trying to swallow and nearly suffocated by bubbles. Maybe that's why last night I had one of my poison-gas nightmares.

Sometime in the middle of the night I was convinced that my whole duvet was full of poison gas. I had to hold my breath while I decided what to do about it, which didn't give me much time. Finally, nearly dying from not breathing, I leapt out of bed, rolled up my duvet, snatched Abie's off his bed just in case, ran to the door of our room, opened it, and hurled both duvets out into the corridor of the hotel. Then I slammed the door and leaned against it, taking great gulps of air.

Of course Abie woke up at once. "Holy crap-almighty, Forbsey!" he said, "what have you done with our bedding?"

"I threw it out the door," I explained peevishly, realising that he had absolutely no idea of the crisis that I had just averted.

"He threw it out the door," Abie said, sitting up in bed and talking to his feet. "Nothing wrong with that. I mean, why would we want our bedding?" He turned back to me. "Why don't we want our bedding?" he asked.

"It's full of poison gas," I said, angrily. But already I was beginning to have doubts.

"Come on, Forbsey," said Abie. "Have a heart!"

So of course I had to open the door and go out into the corridor to get the duvets back. Luckily there was no-one about. When I put Abie's back on his bed, he gave it a sniff or two.

"And the match only starts on Friday!" he said to his feet. "We got to get Forbsey a shrink."

I suppose that my nightmares were part of the anxiety. Something about playing the Danes, in combination with Doc Wolfe's Fruit Salts and Abie's explosive mornings in the bathroom, must have preyed on my mind. Often now, in later life, I think back to those days of contest and wonder about fear, and the "why" comes up again: why some people are distilled to jellies while others seem able to take things in their stride; why on some days I felt good, yet on others tentative; why I had not found some better way to handle my own rebellious temperament.

DIARY NOTES, PARIS, 1957

In our doubles match today, I had to have three match points before being able to make a good-enough return to win the match. I was playing left court, the theory being that if we have two forehand volleys in the middle we will strike fear into the hearts of our opponents. Sometimes the theory works, but the bad part is that it leaves me to play the ad points on the backhand side. After today's match Abie said that for a change maybe he should have a go on the left court.

"That way, when the ad points come up, I can at least give them a bit of a crunch," he said, forever of the opinion that even if a point was to be lost, it was better lost via a crunch than a chip—which was what usually happened on my backhand side.

Doc Wolfe then stepped into the breach and said that when I get a big point, I should first visualise the shot in my mind very carefully. [In those days, this was a new concept.] Then, his theory continued, if I allowed my body to simply "roam free," (as he put it) I would play the same shot in reality. Although the thought of my body roaming free on big points was a bit alarming, I told Doc Wolfe I would give it a try. Now I even practise by visualising big returns wherever I go. For example, this morning I hit a great low backhand in the

Metro on the way to the courts.

Anyway, today we had to play Budge Patty and Herbie Flam, which was a pretty tough match. Finally, sure enough, up comes the dreaded 30-40 set point, so it's time to put Doc Wolfe's theory to the test. I visualise like mad, and come up with a great cross-court angle that in my mind has Patty groping. But his serve hits the tape of the line, leaps sideways, hits the throat of my racket, and goes flying past the umpire's head. Feeling stupid, I say to Abie: "Sorry, Abie. Would you believe I played a great shot in my mind?"

"Crap almighty, Forbsey!" he says, "don't listen to Doc! Next time, just screw it up in your mind and play a great shot on the court!"

So it's not as though we didn't *try* to deal with our fear! In those days there were no such things as sports psychologists. We had to fend for ourselves and learn from experience—the trouble being that experiencing too many disappointments in the learning process eventually sapped all but the strongest hearts.

How can you describe those long minutes when the victory that you so badly want hangs in the balance? When you can actually feel it in your hand—and yet the needling of fear is still there. When what you most need is patience, yet every instinct cries out for haste—end the point! Win the game! Finish the match! Get off the court! *Escape!* And without even realising it, everything begins to speed up. You walk faster, play faster, think faster; you begin to snatch at the ball instead of stroking it; your head moves, your timing goes, and you don't know why. "Escape!" your mind is crying, yet the only escape is victory itself. The burden of winning must be borne. If you give in for even an instant and listen to that other voice—the one that tells you there will always be another chance, that after all it's only a game—then you are lost forever. The sublime moment when the win is truly yours will never come around.

Watch carefully in almost any match in any sport and you will see the things that players sometimes do to escape the tension of the big point that must be won. If they go for a winner that's too big, a passing shot that's too risky, a dropshot too small, you can be sure that their actions are in part an escape. The rationale is that if the shot comes off, they win the point. If it fails, then they can say, "Too bad! At least we went for it!" But the fundamental truth is that the agony of a long point under pressure is at that moment just too hard to bear. It has to be avoided at any cost.

In his book about the psychology of tennis competition, Allen Fox, player, author, scholar, coach, and strategist, writes:

> If you are not tough enough on the big points, if your resolve collapses when match point looms, then it is your self-image that takes the punishment. Your worst fears are realised. Your character is flawed. You are a loser, and that is frightening. There is no place to hide!

The fear of losing? Or the fear of becoming known as a loser? Or, worst of all, the fear of knowing yourself to be a loser.

The fear of fear itself! And so at last the condition named "fear" begins to define itself.

DIARY NOTES, 1957

A metaphysical entity has crept into our doubles partnership. It began the other day when I was tired from playing singles, doubles, and mixed doubles all on the same afternoon. Our next-round doubles opponents then wanted to know whether we would play them that evening, as one of them had to leave the next day. Abie was fresher than I was and all set to play.

"Come on, Forbsey, we may as well beat their asses today instead of tomorrow," he said.

Caught off guard, I replied with one of my father's pet phrases. "The spirit is willing," I said, "but the flesh is weak."

Abie doesn't much like "intellectual bullshit," as he calls it, so my answer was enough to set him off.

"Oh, really," he said, talking to his tog bag as he put away his rackets. "Forbsey's flesh is weak. Well, fuck me! Maybe I should be playing with his spirit! Maybe his spirit doesn't panic so much! And who says it doesn't have a better backhand return than his flesh?"

So now he goes about telling people that he's about to team up with "Forbsey's spirit." "His body," he says, "can stay at the friggin' hotel!"

And talking of dualities, there is another intriguing book that deals with these and other aspects of the mental approach to playing tennis. It's entitled *The Inner Game of Tennis*, and written by W. Timothy Gallwey. In it he discusses (amongst many other things) what he calls "the two selves" that he believes exist in every tennis player, and in fact every sportsman. The first self, the "I," is the conscious self who gives the instructions:

"Watch the ball! Get your first serve in!" "You clumsy ox! My grandmother could have done that better!"

The second self is the "doer," the one who must take the criticism and carry out the instructions. The problem is that at the *moment critique*, the conscious instructions of the first self play no part in the action. It is the unconscious, instinctive actions of the "doer" self that either make the shot or miss it.

Gallwey goes on to visualise the two selves as two separate people, the first self constantly urging the second to do better and reminding it to concentrate, as though it has a short memory, or is stupid or inept. Such urgings only serving to add tension to the already tense relationship.

"Leave it to the second self!" is his conclusion. "He is more competent than you think!"—thus adding a whole new set of dimensions to the question of performing under pressure.

DIARY NOTES, 1993

At lunch in Mark McCormack's tent at Wimbledon, we talk about the effects of fear. Today amongst the guests are Dame Kiri te Kanawa and Placido Domingo, and the British women's golf star Micky Walker.

Dame Kiri doesn't look to me like someone who would "get the elbow" while singing at La Scala. Both her selves could probably do it beautifully, but I ask her about it anyway: "Don't you sometimes worry that you will—well—lose your place, or forget the words, or something?"

"If you are properly prepared, you feel confident," she says. "Sometimes, I suppose, at the very back of the mind there are always some small thoughts. . . ." The lovely face is thoughtful for a moment, then she says, "Sometimes in rehearsals, when you know that a very difficult passage is coming, you shy away from it. You stop, and ask the conductor to do it over. Then, when you know that you are prepared, well, then you feel a sense of comfort. . . ."

Expertise, the practising of skills, proper preparation! Ask any great competitors and they will tell you that this is the only real way to counter nerves. Margaret Court, one of the greatest women players of all time, once told me that she liked to feel that on the practise court she was at least twice as good as she needed to be in matches. And Tony Trabert told me that the only time he felt uneasy was when he felt that he was not ready for a match.

"If I was satisfied that I had done all that I could, I never felt nervous," he said. "After all, what else was there? I could do no more!"

But, I found, there was more than just one kind of fear.

DIARY NOTES, BAASTAD, 1963

[Having beaten the French and the Germans, we arrived in Baastad to play our semifinal match against the Swedes.]

It's high summer, the weather is warm, the food is good, and the beach is full of Nordic girls with long legs and blonde hair. I should be having a good time—Segal and Drysdale seem to be. Maybe it's this tooth that's getting me down. It's been

*aching like the devil, so today instead of practising I went to
see a Swedish dentist.*

*"Now vitch vun is it?" he asked. "Vitch vun is de sensible
one?"—and in a singsong Swedish way he eventually found
the sensible tooth and gave it a nerve treatment. I should have
told him that my* whole body *was sensible and needed a nerve
treatment!*

Baastad remains one of my worst tennis memories. Both
in 1962 and 1963, our Davis Cup team—consisting of Abie,
Cliff Drysdale, and me—reached the semifinals of the European
zone, only to lose to Sweden in Baastad. For some reason the
Swedes in general, and Jan-Erik Lundquist in particular, proved
to be my black beast.

In 1962 the encounter began well enough. Drysdale, playing
the first match, beat Ulf Schmidt in four sets. Then I took the
court against Lundquist and was in trouble from the word go.
Nearly all players have certain other players whom they hate to
play. My list included Nicola Pietrangeli of Italy, Manuel
Santana of Spain, Pierre Darmon of France, and, in doubles,
Bob Hewitt and Frew MacMillan. In my mind, however, none
of these were as bad as Jan-Erik Lundquist. I simply could not
read his game. I would be bombing down my biggest serves and
volleys, and he would be strolling about on his side making
what seemed to be casual, last-minute strokes that invariably
caught me on the wrong foot—the kind of immobility that
comes at the moment your instinct tells you a ball is going
one way and it suddenly goes another. There is a great clang
inside, and you are unable to move!

I took the court against Lundquist and sprained an ankle at the start of the second set, having spent a thoroughly miserable time losing the first one 6-2. The sprain occurred when I changed direction on the service line and my foot slipped on the tape. The ligaments gave with an audible crackle, and down I went. And even as the knifelike burn shot up my leg (I had never before sprained an ankle), I felt a sort of desolate relief at this unexpected intervention by fate. Segal and Drysdale played the remaining matches and lost them all. Our dream had slipped away.

The following year we again reached the semifinals to play Sweden and arrived in Baastad in good spirits despite my sensible tooth. After all, it was another year, we were playing well, and who could say what fate held in store?

What made me even think of starting the chess game against Jan-Erik I cannot imagine. The tennis club was pleasant and self-contained, and we saw quite a lot of the Swedish team. Jan-Erik would often sit in the lounge, poring over a chessboard and various books on openings. As children on our farm, we too had played chess on long winter evenings, and I have always been intrigued by the game. Naturally enough, I suppose, I stopped to look down on Jan-Erik's game, and we began talking of chess.

"Would you like to play?" he asked, unexpectedly, and I heard myself agreeing that I would, even though the formidable array of books that he was studying made me uneasy. We set up the pieces and began a game. While I had a reasonable feel for openings, I knew none of them by name, and certainly was unprepared for the Sicilian defence with which he met my standard P-K4. After seven or eight moves, which seemed to me to be perfectly safe, he suddenly sat back and said: "You know, Gordon, you have already lost the game!"

"Why?" I asked.

"Because you cannot play this opening the way you have. You are already at a disadvantage."

Suddenly, stupidly, I had no stomach for the contest. His (to me) slightly supercilious words struck a raw nerve and I got up, saying something like, "Well, Jan-Erik, if you are so sure of that, then we may as well leave it," and I left.

Whether Jan-Erik was, in fact, an expert chess player, I never found out. Whether he would really have routed me, or whether his invitation was merely a clever ploy, will also remain a mystery. What I do know is that I have cursed myself many times since then for not simply playing—quickly, unorthodoxly, a skittles game such as Jack and I played many times in front of our fireplace at home. I might just have fluked a win— or I might have been badly beaten. I will never be sure. What I *am* sure of is that the outcome, whatever it was, could not have been worse than the way it turned out.

The incident haunted me. I never told the others—would not have dared tell Abie—and at the draw later that week I watched with fascination as my name was drawn with Lundquist's for the first match, which I lost in straight sets. We lost the tie by five matches to zero, so my lone singles loss was not the deciding factor. But the circumstances surrounding it left me badly shaken.

There was a week in early April 1990 when I sat alone in

the quiet of my living room in Johannesburg watching the last round of the Masters golf tournament, played at Augusta, Georgia. Perhaps it was the quiet of the night—the telecast reached South Africa after midnight—perhaps the beauty of the course, or the uncomplaining courage of the players. Or perhaps it had to do with my own introspective mood. The fortunes of those golfers ebbed and flowed for hours and seldom have I been so moved by an outcome in sport.

The tournament had unfolded like the pages of a book being slowly turned over. From the start of that final round I had the ever-increasing feeling that there was some transcendent force evolving in support of Nick Faldo. Lagging at first, he slowly pulled back into contention as though the moods of destiny were taking him by the elbow and leading him forwards. Inexorably my feeling grew, until at the end of the eighteenth hole he and Scott Hoch had played an equal number of strokes.

And so to the play-off. On the tenth green, Scott Hoch stood over a three-foot putt for a victory that could change his life. Was this, I asked myself, another of destiny's tricks?—to lead Faldo by the hand all this way, then suddenly abandon him? But as Hoch shaped up to putt, there suddenly seemed all kinds of dangers in the air surrounding him—a treachery almost tangible in the stillness.

The record books show, of course, that Hoch missed the putt. Heaven knows how many times since then he has relived the moment—that instant in time when he must actually have felt the trophy in his hands, felt the green jacket going about his shoulders.

But his ball slipped past, and finally, on the eleventh,

Faldo's twenty-five-footer rattled into the hole. For Hoch the moment had passed, perhaps never to return.

Read a detailed account of that (or any!) Masters event and you will find hundreds of small interventions by fate, an ever-increasing quantity of ifs and buts, contingencies piled one upon another, right down to, say, the position of a divot on the approach to the thirteenth green! If the third shot on the second hole of the first round had only missed the divot. . . . On and on—a weaving of uncertainties as fragile as a spider's web.

Why, then, did Faldo win? Why he, out of all the others? What power sits in judgement, controlling such things? Or is it, at the death, all just arbitrary? A throw of dice? The question has gone through my mind a hundred times, not least when one of my own shots, which might radically have changed the course of things, bounced badly, or just missed, or hit the tape and fell back.

"Pete or Mike, after all?" I sometimes mused. Perhaps my father was wrong. Perhaps his long-ago arrangement with God needed updating. There certainly are, and have always been, a number of great sportsmen who claim that God has been with them during their victories.

"You just have to trust your luck and give it a full go," says Abie. "It's all there inside you! You start shaking in your pants and your luck goes straight out the winder!" Abie always says "winder" instead of window.

"Hard work and positive thinking!" I can hear Gary Player's voice, with its undertones of Dale Carnegie. "The harder you practise, the luckier you get!"

All part of the answer, I suppose, but to me there always

seemed to be more to it than that.

It was long after midnight when Faldo's final putt went into the hole, and in the silence of that dawn I seemed to come close to another part of the answer. It had something to do with devotion to winning—a personal dedication to a private cause, a dedication more profound than any I had ever really known. Something to do with a balance between giving and receiving, the serving of time, the paying of dues. Poetic justice, perhaps! That same evening I looked up the lines by Pope in one of Jean's books:

> Poetic justice, with her lifted scale;
> Where, in nice balance, truth with gold she weighs,
> And solid pudding against empty praise.

Solid pudding! Perhaps that was it. Abie, anyway, would be sure to agree. For him there has always been a great deal to be said for something as tangible as solid pudding . . . !

REMEMBERING

A B I E

While we waited to play our doubles matches, Abie and I would talk of many things. I was often surprised by the wide range of subjects that interested him—anything from, say, shearing angora goats to planes disappearing in the Bermuda Triangle. When I told him about our Scottish ancestors, he listened more carefully than I expected him to.

"A family tree!" he exclaimed. "Ours was more like a friggin' bush!" going on to say that at least we knew who we were, and that he wasn't at all sure about his friggin' ancestors, and that there was no way that anyone could trace them, and it was probably a good thing because he didn't think they'd paid their taxes that meticulously.

"And I sure don't remember any of us slayin' a bear!" he added.

Abie's sayings often had profound philosophies hidden in their depths.

DIARY NOTES, LONDON, 1969

"What are you doing on Monday night?" asked Manny Simchowitz.

"Nothing special," replied Monty Wolpe.

"Well," said Manny, "if you know of two beautiful, intelligent, single women, we could take them along to see Hamlet."

"I'll see what I can do," said Monty.

"You don't have to be beautiful, intelligent, and single to see Hamlet," said Abie. "All you need is friggin' tickets!"

The three of them had been running in Hyde Park. Monty and Manny, two of Abie's cronies, were very elaborate bachelors at the time, ran every morning, and generally lived life to the hilt. Abie was married and a bit out of shape, so that he was: a) very short of air; and b) put out by not being considered a contender for the *Hamlet* excursion. Not that he would actually have gone to see the whole of *Hamlet* enacted on a London stage.

"I once saw a bit of the movie with that Olivier guy, Forbsey," he said to me, "and I'll tell you one thing. Too much of that stuff can make a man phone up his shrink." Abie had a mythical "shrink" whom he considered phoning (but never did) when in his opinion things were getting out of hand.

But of course this all happened much later on, after I had become more accustomed to his methods. In the beginning I had to go through a very long apprenticeship before I even began to get used to him.

DIARY NOTES, JOHANNESBURG, 1954

After practising today, Abie took me in his father's delivery van to his mother's flat to eat lunch. His mother is a v small person, almost all energy and hardly any mass (Einstein would have been pleased), and it was v surprising to think that an object as large as Abie could possibly have sprung from her loins.

"Vere have you been?" she shouted out when we arrived.

"Playing tennis, Ma."

"Does your father know of dish?"

"Sure he knows, Ma."

"And who is dish?"

"Forbsey, Ma."

"Vhy he so tin? Like an umbrella?"

"That's the way he is, Ma."

"Must eat. Too many bones." And with two large spoons in her hands she stationed herself at a large stove covered with pots, seeming about to play them like a timpanist plays drums. She then proceeded to remove dripping objects from the pots and put them on plates while Abie gave a cryptic commentary:

"Chicken livers; herring in cream; mince pies; fish balls; dumplings."

His mother got more and more agitated at the unfamiliar Anglo-Saxon terms, muttering interjections like, "Perogen, already! Gehakte fish!" Or "Kreplach! Kreplach! Kishka! Gefilte fish! Eat mit kichel!"

Abie's mother, I discovered, fed him like a zookeeper feeds dolphins—she put things in his mouth and he simply swallowed them—so that by the time he had finished his lunch, I was still picking gingerly at an arrangement of internal chicken parts, having managed a portion of gehakte fish with kichel and two small kneidel.

"Eat!" Mrs. Segal kept saying. "It's no vunder. Dish boy has been starved." I wondered what my mother would have said to that, thinking of the brown bread, peanut butter, bananas, and honey washed down with milk that we'd often had for our lunches on the farm.

I finally got to know Abe Segal better during the first Davis Cup trials played at Ellis Park, Johannesburg, in 1954. Before that, as a somewhat introspective junior I had merely observed him from a safe distance—this big, dark-haired, paganlike youth with a voice like a foghorn and a tennis game consisting of a range of wild and frightful strokes in which raw power ruled with an iron hand.

By far his biggest weapon was his service, a monumental, left-handed affair struck from a great height with a wrist of steel and a grip so far round to the backhand side that the gut of the racket used to bite into the ball with a ripping sound, sending it egg-shaped and curving to leap off the court either this way or that in a brand-new orbit, still curving, ever curving, until finally its passage was interrupted by something impenetrable.

I maintain even now that of all the left-handed serves I have ever seen, Abie's had the biggest sting in its tail. Of other notable left-handed serves that come to mind, Rod Laver's was the smoothest, Neale Fraser's had the best disguise, Mervyn Rose's had the sharpest angles, John McEnroe's was the most vicious, Jimmy Connors's produced the least result from the biggest effort, Goran Ivanisevic's was the most blinding, but Abie's had the biggest sting in its tail—the *tail* of a service being defined as the last six feet that the ball travels before it reaches the racket of the receiver.

I clearly remember Abie playing Rex Hartwig on the centre court at Wimbledon and twice in succession hitting him in the chest with second serves. Hartwig tried to run round Abie's service, but the ball just kept curving into his body until he was forced to catch it with his left hand next to his chest.

One of Abie's main early philosophies was that if you gave the ball enough of a crunch, you would eventually conquer. This philosophy was finally extended to cover almost everything in life, and became known as the "crunch factor." Even when I first met him, naive though I was, I sensed that Abie was destined to cut a wide swathe through the fields of life, leaving in his wake a fair selection of well-crunched objects.

At Ellis Park that year I would arrive at the courts early and establish myself in the quietest corner of the locker room. On the first day, apart from telling me that I was like a mouse, Abie paid very little attention to me. It was on the second day that I was to be properly exposed to his ways.

I had an old-fashioned, vermiculite tennis suitcase designed to hold one racket and one set of clothes. There was also a compartment that was supposed to take damp clothing, but that my mother had persuaded me to use for all the things she felt I might need to survive long matches—salt and glucose tablets, Band-Aids, a sweatband, resin for the racket grip, lip ice, sun lotion, aspirin, a comb, foot powder, etc., even a toothbrush. Although I seldom used most of them, the sight of this neat pharmaceutical array gave me a feeling of security against the tensions of tournament play that cities the size of Johannesburg used to evoke in my heart.

I had nearly finished changing when Abie barged into the room. Even today he enters places by barging—but that day he was late for his match, and as soon as I saw him I had a feeling that I was in trouble, for the only space left in the room was on the bench next to me. Sure enough, it was there that he threw down his tog bag and his three battered Dunlop Maxplies, while simultaneously hurling insults about the room at the other competitors.

"Jesus Christ, Woodroffe, what's happened to that chest of yours? Friggin' thing's disappeared! You gonna have to advertise in the newspaper for a new chest!"

Brian Woodroffe was Natal's number-one player. He was a thin man with wide shoulders and a very narrow side elevation that almost never escaped Abie's comment. "Now you see him, now you don't!" he would usually say. "How does your doubles partner ever figure out where you are?" This time, though, he said, "Listen! If there was a wind blowin' and they tied a string to your belly button a man could fly you like a kite!"

"Screw you, too, Abie," said Woodroffe, a bit lamely, but Abie had already moved on.

"Hey, Mrs. Hurry's little boy!" (John Hurry was a thoughtful and canny player who was studying history at the time and often referred to himself as "Mrs. Hurry's little boy, John.") "All that crap you're learning has softened up your mind! Who cares who conquered who in 1066? Today's the real problem,

Professor! Today you're gonna need more than that Conqueror guy to save you!"

When Hurry ignored him, as he always did, Abe turned his attention to Johan Kupferburger, whom he had drawn to play in the first round.

"Kupferburger!" he said, "how's your ass today, buddy? Don't forget to bring it along, because sure as sour nuts I'm going to beat it off so bad you'll be spendin' the rest of the year lookin' out for a new ass."

Abie had the effect of making everyone back off and move their stuff away from where he was, but that day I was stuck in my corner with nowhere to go. Although I quickly shut my case, it was too late. His eyes had picked up my mother's neat rows and he moved over, opened the case, and began fiddling with my things with his fingers.

"Jesus Christ, kid! What's all this crap you got here?"

"Stuff I need," I said defencively.

"Stuff he needs!" he said to the locker room. "Holy hell! His case is like a chemist shop!" He then began one of the monologues that I would get to know so well: "We've got one guy with no chest, another with no ass, and you with a chemical set! I mean, what is this?" He'd found, of all things, a bottle of antihistamine that my mother had put in for emergencies. Once, while playing a small tournament in Queenstown, a swarm of bees had flown over the court, two of them stinging me as they passed. From then on, in my mother's mind, bees were one of the many risks that I would have to guard against while playing tennis tournaments.

"It's antihistamine," I said.

"Anti-friggin'-histamine," said Abie. "What's that for?"

"Bee stings," I said, embarrassed and feeling stupid.

"Bee stings! That's too much all together. Now I've heard everything! You're comin' in to net without your antihistamine, and as you go to knock off a volley a bee stings your ass! You'd be dead for sure!" He gave a huge snort of laughter and walked about the room picking up players' rackets, pinging them together, shaking his head, and saying, "What a balls-up! This isn't a change room! This is a mental home!"

Written down, his language doesn't look that good, but in actual fact he has a candid sort of way with obscenities that seems to take the edge off them. "They're the only adjectives I know!" he once said to me while we waited to play a doubles match in Cologne. He'd asked me what an adjective was and where you used it. He often used the times we waited to play doubles to ask me about certain things. "You see, Forbsey," he would say, "you had an education. I had crap! Ask me about hammerin' and weldin' and I'll tell you. But I had to find out for myself what that guy Columbus discovered and who people like Hamlet were!"

Abie had been to an engineering trade school in one of the rougher suburbs of Johannesburg where he learnt more about street fighting and self-defence than actual fitting and turning. What it was that caused him to develop a fascination for tennis even *he* is vague about, but the fact remains that for years he climbed the fences around the Ellis Park with a friend called Mailer Schneider, and sneaked onto the back courts.

"There was another guy I used to play with ended up in

jail," he once told me. "He had a good serve, but when they put him inside his game fell apart. It's no good havin' a big serve if all you're servin' is time"—and he gave a snort of laughter at his own little joke, one that he himself had not heard before.

Maybe it was the stoical way I had reacted to his jibes that day that caused him to take an interest in me. Or perhaps it was my small-town vulnerability. Or the jazz that we both liked. As it turned out we both won our matches, and afterwards he came up and asked me to practise with him. Later on, in the locker room, he asked me how I was getting home.

"They said I have to take a number-thirteen bus," I replied.

"A man doesn't want to go walkin' about this part of town alone, catchin' busses" he said. Ellis Park has always been iffy where neighbourhood is concerned, so he took me back to my hotel in a van marked SEGAL'S FASHIONS, instructing me what to do in case I ever got mugged. ("Keep a bit of sand in your pocket, kid, an' if they jump you, you throw it in their eyes and run like hell.") Abie's family had immigrated to South Africa from one of those (to me) shadowy Eastern European countries and had established themselves in the garment industry, which is another whole story in itself. For Abie, the garment industry was a minefield of calamities waiting to happen.

"It's a war out there, Forbsey," he used to say. "I figure that if a man can survive the garment industry without going broke, it shouldn't be too tough winning Wimbledon!" But afterwards we found out that winning Wimbledon was even tougher than not going broke in the garment industry.

Now, after knowing him for nearly a lifetime, I can safely say that there is not one single thing about Abie that is orthodox, formal, or rehearsed. He is a true seat-of-the-pants man, a shooter from the hip, the great improvisor. Everything that he does is spur of the moment and governed only by an instinctive fearlessness, a uniquely inventive streak, and—beneath his tough exterior—a compassionate and generous heart.

Inexplicably, but inexorably, I found myself being drawn along with him.

DIARY NOTES, LONDON (UNDATED, BUT ABOUT 1960)

It's Wednesday, second week of Wimbledon, and Abie and I are out of the tournament. Lost in the quarters of the doubles to Torben Ulrich and Laci Legenstein, of all *people! A makeshift, motley, unlikely team! The Wimbledon programme even says that Legenstein is "stateless." Everybody else comes from somewhere, but not Legenstein. I hoped this might make him feel depressed, but he sure didn't play like a stateless person.*

Abie had said we would walk it. "We'll murder them, Forbsey," he said. "Listen. Who knows even which planet this Ulrich will be playing on? With any kind of luck he'll be on Mars. And how good can Legenstein be? I mean, you tell me? How's a little guy like that gonna return our serves?"

When I told him that the size of one's opponents is not always a good way of working out how good they are, Abie said "bullshit!" So I asked him, "How about Rosewall?" and he said, "How many Rosewalls can there be?" and we left it at that.

We ended up playing the last match on court one. Windy, damp, greasy, heavy, and in fading light. I was then at a point in my career where I needed spectacles to correct a slight astigmatism in my right eye. I hated wearing them, however, and my dread of poor light had grown to be almost a phobia. From the very first game we were in trouble, and our opponents were flitting about in the dark like bats. Ulrich *was* from another planet, one where they must have had practise courts. At two sets to love down, Abie and I changed sides to receive service and nearly got back into the match, but. . . .

Afterwards, in the locker room, Abie threw his rackets into his bag and sat staring at his feet.

"A fuck-up, Forbsey," he said. "I know a fuck-up when I see one, and I'll tell you one thing for certain. That was a fuck-up."

I was about to take refuge in the showers, where you can cry without being seen, when Ulrich came and sat on the bench beside me, putting his arm on my shoulders. "You should try not to feel too bad, Gordon," he said in his deliberate way. "You know, Laci played, I must say, very well, and, you see, I played, well, I suppose you could say, not really so badly." He seemed genuinely sorry.

"It was so dark out there, Torben," I couldn't help saying.

He said, "Sometimes, Gordon, darkness is a good thing. But then, at other times, you know, it is *not* a good thing."

DIARY NOTES, LONDON, continued

Now it's Thursday night and we're in Brighton. We didn't mean to come to Brighton. I had arranged a tennis practise court at Hurlingham and Abe had arranged tickets to a world championship boxing match, but we've ended up in Brighton.

"We're not playing any more friggin' tennis," Abie said to

me at about four o'clock, when I told him about the practise
court. "We're going to this boxing match between Cassius
Clay and this British guy. Old Dennis gave me ringside tick-
ets." Abie has this selection of millionaire friends that I can't
keep track of.

"Why didn't you tell me this morning?" I wanted to know.

"I didn't know this morning," he said.

So I cancelled the court and off we went to the boxing, all
dressed up, Abie leading the way—tube at Marble Arch,
change somewhere, change somewhere else, and in this new
train, which, said Abie, should get us there at any minute,
were these two girls with canvas bags on their laps, sitting on
the seats across from us—tall, blonde, could be sisters.

"What you got in the bags?" Abie immediately wanted to
know.

"Our things," they said.

"Oh, your things," said Abie. "Maybe that's our problem,
Forbsey, we don't carry enough things with us. And where are
you going with your things?"

"To Brighton," they said.

"And what happens in Brighton?" asked Abie.

"My auntie lives there."

"Her auntie lives in Brighton," he told me. "And what's
your auntie like?"

"She's a nice person."

"Her auntie's a nice person, Forbsey," he told me, and just
as I began to wonder where the conversation was going to end
up, the girl with the auntie in Brighton asked, "And where are
you two going?"

"To a boxing match at Wembley," said Abie.

"Then why are you on this train?" she asked. "Wembley's that way," and she pointed towards the back of the train. "This way is the way to Waterloo."

"You hear that, Forbsey?" said Abie. "We're on our way to Waterloo!"

I knew then that we were in danger of being caught up in one of Abie's tangents, and when he'd asked, "And what usually happens in Brighton?" the tangent became a virtual certainty.

"There's a lot to do in Brighton!" said the girl.

So now we're in this small hotel in Brighton and I really don't care. It can't be as bad as yesterday. One minute I'm losing to a stateless tennis player called Legenstein and a man from Mars on court one, and the next minute I'm walking barefoot on smooth pebbles with a girl called Sarah. She's actually a very nice girl, too, with blue eyes and these unusually long legs.

"It was the legs that worried me for a while," Abie had said to me. "With them sittin' down in the train like that a man couldn't really see too well. But I said to myself, 'What the hell? how many times can you lose in two days?' And I'll tell you something else for nothing. Her auntie's not that bad either!"

And so a story unfolded itself in the notes. When I shed a few tears in the showers after that doubles match at Wimbledon, I had lost more than just the match. A small part of my confidence had gone too—slipped away like a clod of earth slips into the water from the bank of a stream. I needed a strong arm about my shoulders then, a voice to say that everything would be just fine. Instead, Abie and I went to a boxing match and ended up in Brighton. . . .

DIARY NOTES, JONANNESBURG, 1992

Abie and I played tennis today at noon in the hot sun at the Wanderers Club. Just as I was leading 5-3 and 40-15 in the first set, he suddenly stopped playing and threw himself down on the bench beside the court.

"What exactly do you suppose I think I'm doing out here, Forbsey?" he wanted to know, with the sweat pouring off his nose. "Here I am, sixty years old, tryin' to handle these three women all at the same time, and still tryin' to serve and volley in this heat."

"Which three women?" I asked him. It's not easy to keep track of Abie's activities now that he's a bachelor.

"The Witch, the Chimney, and Rumpelstiltskin," he said, then lapsed into a gloomy reverie, catching the drops of sweat in the palm of his hand.

The first two I knew about—a sexy blonde who kept him on the hop by sometimes disappearing unexpectedly when he most wanted her to be around, and an old friend who cheerfully stood in when all else failed, and who smoked virtually nonstop. ("You'd be great if the telephones caved in," he told her. "A man could throw a blanket over you and send up smoke signals.") But Rumpelstiltskin had me stumped.

"Who's Rumpelstiltskin?" I asked.

"The bird in the tower who let down her hair, idiot," he said.

"You mean Rapunzel!" I said.

"So who is Rumpelstiltskin?" he wanted to know.

"He's the guy who can spin straw into gold."

He thought about this for a while. "So maybe we should try to get his phone number, hey, Forbsey?" he said.

Gold! The eternal question. I now know that Abie and I were not the only tennis players who, when their careers were drawing to a close, would have dearly loved to have the phone number of Rumpelstiltskin. Aged about thirty, with still no sign of money in tennis, I made the following rather reflective entry in my diary:

"The trouble with being a tennis player is that you get used to the good life. Travel the world, stay in good hotels, eat good food, meet wealthy people. But beware! You are not a part of their world, just a borrower of it. Money! So easy to see, so hard to get. But what is there to do . . .?"

Answer came there none. And because we yearned so long for the comfort and security of wealth; because the rich people we encountered seemed so eager to meet us; because their wealth seemed so very near; because they seemed to enjoy our company so much, we stayed close to them, listened eagerly to the things they said, ate the elegant meals they seemed so eager to buy for us, thus living, for a while at least, in hope.

MIXING WITH

THE MONGOLS

Amongst some papers that Richard Evans had sent me after Jean died were letters I'd written to her when she lived in Texas. Richard is a writer whom Jean sometimes used as a sort of sounding board for her various projects, and she would often send him things that amused her.

"Dearly Beloved," I'd begun as usual, and after a bit of small talk I'd continued:

"Nothing much has changed. Autumn is mild and lovely, I still have dreams, and the other day Abie took a big bite out of one of Sol Kerzner's candles. You remember how, when he arrives at anyone's house, the first thing he does is prowl about looking for something to eat. Well, Sol knows this and puts food out for him—nuts, chocolate, dried fruit, crisps, almost anything will do, and when Abie arrives he wanders about the house eating things and hurling insults.

"Sol, by the way, is a business mongol (by Abie's definition).

He (Abie) used to go jogging every morning at Manny Simchowitz's house in Houghton with some cronies who are very
high-powered businessmen. Once when I asked him where he'd
been, he said that he'd been out running with the business
mongols. He was looking for the word 'moguls,' but by the
time he found it, it was too late. To everyone's delight they've
stayed 'mongols' ever since.

"Sol Kerzner is one of the chief mongols. He knows
exactly what to do next all the time, and never seems to question the location of his rose garden! I don't even think he specially wanted to become a mongol. It just came to him as a
sort of a by-product of all the things he likes to do. That, and
money. (Imagine money as a by-product! How's that for a rose
garden?)

"But back to Sol's candle. They'd gone skiing, and Sol had
hired this villa, and having just arrived he'd had no time to put
food out for Abie, who arrived from Johannesburg about an
hour after Sol. Abie dropped his bags in the huge living room
and immediately began looking for something to eat, but the
only things he could see that looked even vaguely edible were
these two exotic, fruitlike objects on the mantelpiece. So he
picked one up and took a great bite out of it, and it turned out
to be a candle made to look like an apple.

"'Look, Sol!' said Jeffrey Rubenstein excitedly, 'Abie's eating the furniture!'

"Jeffrey is one of the gang and also a mongol. He, too, is used
to Abie by now. They all agree that he is bit of a menace. . . .
(Abie, not Jeffrey, although Jeffrey himself is not as pure as the
driven snow. . . .)"

✳ ✳ ✴ ✴

Abie turned sixty not long ago. On his sixtieth birthday, his daughter, Nancy, organised a party for him at Sun City, the stunning resort in the African bush, built by his great friend, hotel magnate Sol Kerzner. One of the good things about the party was that it took place on the right day. For almost his whole life he had celebrated his birthday on the wrong day, until, finally, his error was pointed out to him by the Spanish immigration authorities.

This had happened during Abie's "Spanish Period," brought on by his lifelong friendship with Lew and Jenny Hoad, who lived at their tennis ranch in Fuengirola, in combination with a covert and smoldering liaison he'd had with a beautiful, dark, bachelor girl who lived in an apartment overlooking the Orange Square in Marbella. For a while all the fire of Spain flowed through his veins. He wore white cotton suits and the occasional straw hat, smelt of garlic, drank dusty red wine, bought a Spanish language course, and obtained a Residencia permit that, amongst other things, stated that he had been born on 22 October.

On one of his arrivals at Malaga, the Spanish found that his passport said he'd been born on 23 October, and they demanded to know, via a proper birth certificate, exactly when he had been born. The birth certificate, when finally unearthed, revealed that in fact he'd been born on 24 October.

"The way they questioned me you'd think I was Al Capone," he said to me. "Who was my father? Who was my mother, where did I live, what was my business?

"'You tell *me*,' I said to them. 'All my life I've been trying to find out what I do, myself!'

"What difference can a few days make, anyway?" (he said to me). "You think those Spanish assholes know exactly what day they were born? No way! They're lucky to know what day it is today!"

Finally, after endless discussions, Abie had said: "Well, my mother says I was born on the 24th, and she was there at the time!" Somehow this, above all else, got through to them.

But by the time he turned sixty everything had been sorted out, so that he was able with confidence to attend the party that his daughter, Nancy, had arranged for him. All Abie's cronies came to his party. People like Sol, Ruby, Hilly, Jeffrey, two Mannys, Robbie, Monty, Donny, Johnnie, and two Tonys—Bloom the miller and Behrmann the mad lawyer.

Most of the cronies are business mongols and the party was a huge success, because everyone had the chance to roast Abie for his manifold sins and wickedness over the past sixty years. Tony Bloom, as usual, took the opportunity to remind everyone of the soap incident. Abie and I used to play tennis with Tony while he ran Premier Milling (as a sideline, said Abie), one of the country's largest corporations, so he'd become known as "The Miller."

What had happened was that one day at the last minute Abie told me that it was The Miller's birthday, so I hurriedly passed on to him a piece of soap that someone had given me for my birthday. It was a very expensive piece of soap, on a rope, in a box—not the kind of soap that you normally use, more the kind that you pass on. I'd been careful to remove the card attached to the box by the person who had given it to me. But that person hadn't removed the card put into the box by the person who had given it to him.

The Miller, stupidly, decided to use the soap instead of passing it on. After his first shower Abie said he smelt like Christmas, but when he took the soap out of the box for his next shower, stuck to the bottom of it was a card that said "To dear Hymie, with best wishes from your friend Stanley."

DIARY NOTES, 1980

Abie says that The Miller phoned him up to say that he felt unclean.

"It's because you're makin' too much money," Abie tells him.

"Wrong," says The Miller, "it's because I'm washing myself with a piece of soap belonging to someone called Hymie."

"Which Hymie could that be?" Abie wants to know.

"Does it matter?" asks The Miller. "The card said he got it in 1977. So the soap is three years old!"

"That's terrific," says Abie. "Forbsey says that 1977 was a good year for soap!"

It took me a long time to live that one down. To this day The Miller harasses me with requests for soap of a good vintage. Or, should I say, suddage. But Abie says it's all part of the game.

DIARY NOTES, 2 DEC., 1992

We are at the opening of the Lost City, a modern, billion-

rand, thousand-year-old civilisation that has taken Sol Kerzner a full two and a half years to create. He, meanwhile, is a bit put out because it took so long—perhaps because he was hoping to break the six-day record that Old Mike set when He created earth and all that is on it.

Last night, at the great banquet, when Sol got up to give his address, Abie nudged me and said: "Look at him! I mean, look at him! Does he look that different to the rest of us? What do you think goes on in that head of his that is so different from what goes on in our heads?"

"I don't know, Abie," I whispered back, and although we thought about it all through the banquet, by the time we got to the dessert we still didn't know.

That evening Abie gave me one of his graphic descriptions of the time that Sol had located the site for the Sun City complex in what had then been nothing but wild mountains and African bush.

"Here we are, flying over these mountains in a helicopter, Forbsey. You think this Africa is a big place? Wait till you fly over it in a helicopter. They got mountains there they haven't even used yet. Big mountains, little mountains, you name it. 'What exactly are we lookin' for, Sol?' I keep askin' him, because it's getting hotter than hell. I mean, it's not like a man can see that much difference between one mountain and the next. 'Why don't you just choose one so we can go down and have a Coke?' I ask him.

"'Shut up, Abie,' is all he says to me.

"Suddenly he says to the pilot, 'Let's go down right here.

Right there, next to that clump of bushes,' so down we go, and the next thing you know we're standing in the middle of nowhere next to this clump of bushes. Sol walks up and down for a bit, takes a look around, figures out where the sun is, smells the wind, then he digs his heel into the ground.

"'This is where it's going to be,' he finally says, 'right here.'

"'You mean you're going to build a hotel right next to these bushes?' I ask him.

"'Right,' he says.

"'And why exactly right here?' I ask him. 'Why not on that mountain, over there?' and I show him another mountain.

"'Because it's got the wrong slope,' he says. 'This is the right slope.'

"Can you believe that, Forbsey? Suddenly I realise why I haven't been doin' too well lately. Everything's been on the wrong slope!

"'And where are the tennis courts going to be?' I ask him.

"'Abie,' he says, 'why don't you sit in the shade for a bit and give me a break! Here I am spending a hundred mil or more and all you can think about is tennis courts!'"

Sol's version, of course, will be somewhat different, but Abie did manage to capture some of the imagination and courage of the moment.

Now, a decade or so later, Sun City stands in its African valley, secure and permanent in its fields of bougainvillaea and palms, its forests and waterways. There is a book to be written about Sol and his Cities, about the effort and inspiration that he has put into them, the money that he has made, and the fun that he has provided for so many people.

And Abie did get his tennis courts. They overlook the Gary Player golf course and the little lake where, in the evenings, elephants come down to drink.

And so, inevitably, came the day when Abie tried his hand at golf. He'd been intrigued by the game ever since the time that Harold Henning, one of the South African golf stars of our era, had helped him and me out-hustle some of the Australian tennis-playing hustlers on the putting greens at Hurlingham (related in *A Handful of Summers*). But as was the case with many things, Abie at first misjudged the complications of the game.

"Listen, Forbsey," he used to say to me, "I mean, how hard can it be? You tell me! There's this little white ball, sitting there, looking at you. You even stick it up on a peg. It's not like you have to chase after it or anything, so you're not exhausted when you get to it. There's no hurry! You've got plenty of time. And look at the size of the fairway! A man would have to be a cripple to miss a thing that size!"

As it turned out, of course, the more Abie got to know the game, the more he modified this line of thinking. I, on the other hand, had spent quite a lot of time playing golf. For a while in the sixties I had actually got down to a ten handicap, but it was at best an uneasy ten. For me golf has always been a treacherous game. Unlike in tennis, I could never really visualise exactly what was going on when the club hit the ball, and only now and then did I achieve the more or less perfect "click"—when the ball lifted like an arrow, climbed, peaked, and fell to the green, stopping almost in its own pitch mark. At such times, it is true, there was a certain brief ecstasy, but this was more than cancelled out by the unnerving rattle of the shank that often seemed to follow.

One day Abie announced that he was "ready for me." At first I thought he meant at tennis, but then I saw him walking towards the caddie shop. There was the usual advice about bringing my ass along, and the information that he had just acquired a new set of left-handed clubs with which he intended to beat it off. We sat in one of his golf carts and set off for the first tee of the Sun City course. The resulting game moved me to write a complete set of notes, as follows:

DIARY NOTES, SUN CITY, 1982

On the first tee, Abe had to have a few swings to loosen up. Then he teed the ball up and took out a one-iron. His stance was lopsided—this huge serving arm on the left side completely overpowering the tossing-up-the-ball-arm on the other. When he finally let fly, the crunch factor was still very much in evidence. For the first fifty yards or so the ball seemed to consider a hook; then suddenly it reared up into an evil slice, which disappeared relentlessly into darkest Africa. I expected a remark of some sort, but instead Abie just stepped back and peered at the head of his club. "Friggin' things are all the same," he said. Then, after a moment, he went on. "This Sol," he said, "has lost his mind. Again. He's busy making a deal with the Pope," and before I could reply, he walked off into the bushveld to find his ball.

I made my shot and followed, pondering Abie's remark. Had Sol, I wondered, persuaded the Pope to play in the million-dollar Golf Classic Pro-Am? A distinguished four-ball crossed my mind: Nicklaus and Player versus Ballesteros and the Pope. The Latins take on all comers with Old Pete coaching the Latins. A five-ball in actual fact, complete with miracles. With Sol anything was possible.

After some activity in the semi-rough I arrived on the green for about four. Abie was still "somewhere in Africa." Suddenly a ball lifted from the bush, fell on the green, and made its way towards the pin, limping a little from a cut in its side. A little later Abie arrived. He surveyed the green.

"How about that?" he said.

"Are you sure that that is the same ball you started out with?" I asked. At ten rand a hole, you need to know these things.

"Listen, Forbsey," said Abe, "when you go out to where I was you need a tracker. You find a ball out there, any ball, and it's like Stanley findin' Livingstone." He gestured towards his ball and said, "So I've called him Livingstone."

"That's great," I said. "And how many shots has it taken you to get Livingstone to the green?"

"Three," he said.

It was going to be a difficult game. Abie starts out by hitting a new Dunlop 65 into virgin bush, and ends up on the green in three shots with a strange golf ball called Livingstone. As it was, we both ended up with fives, for fortunately Livingstone veered off line when Abie putted.

Walking towards the next tee, I said to Abie, "What was that you said about Sol and the Pope?" but he was deep in thought.

On his next tee shot, Livingstone kept very low and made

a noise like a partridge, but ended up on the edge of the fairway.

"I've improved," said Abie comfortably. "I've seen Ballesteros make a shot like that except his shots don't whistle."

We walked up the fairway, and Abie found Livingstone lying serenely on a perfect patch of grass. "You wouldn't think, Forbsey," he said, contemplating his lie, "that a little white ball, just lyin' there, could be so hard to hit. Did I ever tell you about the first game I ever played?"

He paused while we made our shots.

"It was in Bermuda, in '62," he went on, "when I first met Heather." *(His wife Heather was Bermudan.)* "They had this great country club there and the pro gets excited when he finds out I play tennis and he says to me that he'll play golf with me if I play tennis with him."

"'I need left-handed sticks,' I tell him, so we borrow a set from one of the members.

"'You have played before?' asks the pro, when we're on the tee.

"'Sure, I've played before,' I tell him.

"'Well it's your honour,' the pro says to me.

"'My honour,' I think to myself. 'Terrific.' So I tee up and take a swing, and the next thing I know, the pro falls over, and my ball's twenty yards behind us, lyin' on the grass."

I knew enough about Abie's stories not to interrupt him. He chipped Livingstone to the edge of the green, then went on.

"You won't believe what had happened. I hit the ball with the very end of the club and it went off like a rocket and hit the pro on the knee. He's rubbing his knee like crazy, and it's comin' up like a balloon."

"'You have a very unusual swing,' he says to me, rubbin' away.

"I tee up again, and this time I really get hold of the ball, an' I think to myself: 'I don't know where that's gone, but wherever it is, it's a friggin' long way from here.'

"So the pro says, 'I think you've got a problem with the copse.'

"'The copse?' I ask him.

"'Your ball's gone in there,' he says, and he points to this little forest down on the left.

"'You mean I'm in the friggin' trees! What a win! I thought you meant cops with guns!' The copse! I mean, Forbsey, can you believe that?"

While we were driving to the third tee, Abie thought of Sol.

"A chain of Vaticans," he said suddenly. "I wouldn't be surprised if that's what Sol's talkin' to the Pope about. A chain of Vaticans. Maybe he'll let us stick slot machines into those boxes where the priests sit."

"Confessionals," I suggested.

"Right," he said. "And in the men's rooms. I'll ask him for the franchise for the men's rooms. So people can stick in a few coins while they're takin' a pee. We'll make a fortune."

I thought that he'd forgotten about the Bermudan affair, but as we walked after our drives, he began again:

"So I go into this copse, Forbsey, an' it's quiet and shady. By a miracle, I find my ball lyin' on some moss like nothing's happened. I look around and there's just the three of us there."

"The three of you?"

"Me, the ball, an' this mushroom. Also these two trees blockin' my view. All I can see is this tiny patch of green between the trunks. So I figure that if I can hit a really low, hard shot, I can at least get out of the friggin' copse. I take an iron and really lay into the ball, and it disappears, and the head of the club disappears. All I've got left in my hand is the handle. So there I am, standin' in a copse, with a mushroom and a golf club handle. And where do you think the ball finishes up? Four feet from the pin. The pro gets really excited, till he finds out about the club. So we go back into the copse to find the club head, and where do you think it is? Stuck in the very top of the trees.

"'Don't worry about it,' I tell the pro. 'I climb trees all the time.'

"'Don't climb the tree,' he says to me. 'Please don't climb the tree!'"

But Abie had climbed the tree. The branch had broken and he'd fallen down. ("Big deal, Forbsey. I fell on the moss.") The club head had fallen down with him. They'd eventually quit after five holes, but the experience had badly shaken the pro and put Abie off golf until Sol built Sun City.

On the eighth hole, Abie despatched Livingstone back into Africa with a colossal hook, and on the ninth we both hit new balls into the lake.

"Let's leave it to the pros, Forbsey," said Abie. "Let's have a cup of tea." And as we sat down in the shade of the clubhouse verandah, Abie said that he'd thought of a way to figure out what kind of deal Sol was doing with the Pope.

"He's got this Monseigneur comin' out next week for talks,

and he wants me to play tennis with him, so I'll ask him. Maybe he'll tell me. Who knows? Maybe we'll end up with a few shares in the Catholic Church. How bad can that be? At least a man has got God on his side. Which has got to be a lot better than some of those big lardies with their Rolls-Royces!"

7

L E T   T H E R E

B E   L I G H T

It was towards the end of my tennis career that I became more aware of Abie's business mongols. At the tennis parties at Mandy Moross's house I would eye the luxury cars in the driveway, notice the airs of assurance, and overhear courtside remarks that alluded to such things as rights issues, takeovers, hard assets, gilts, and share options—a language of money that Abie and I did not understand and that was not intended for our ears.

As usual, Abie summed things up: "All I know, Forbsey," he said, "is that there seems to be a shitload of money about, and we haven't got it!"

It was on a Saturday afternoon at Maxie Segal's house that the vision of a different kind of rose garden first came to me. Maxie was no relation to Abie—one of several wealthy Segals whom Abie knew but who were not family. ("Just my luck, Forbsey! I came from the wrong tree.") The members of Maxie's school also had an intriguing combination of odd-looking backhands, big houses, and expensive cars. THE MAXIE SEGAL TENNIS AND FINANCIAL CLUB, it was called. Only singles was played. There was a large concrete mushroom in the lawn beside the court at Maxie's house, and if anyone lost a set to love, he had to sit on the mushroom for the duration of the following set; it was said he'd been "given a mushroom." House rules concerning the mushroom were rigid and explicit:

1. The mushroom was normally covered with a square of black silk.
2. If any player was down 5-0, the silk was removed, and the player had to bow to the mushroom to acknowledge that it was now ready for him.
3. The sixth game was then played. When set point was reached, the player holding the set point had to do ten press-ups to indicate that he had not yet had enough exercise. Only then was he able to try to win the point.

Never once did either Abie or I have to sit on the mushroom.

That particular Saturday afternoon I arrived late. A set was in progress, so I sat on the mushroom anyway and watched the tennis. The garden was particularly lovely. It was midsummer, they'd mowed the lawns, the trees were leafy in their pools of shade, the court was immaculate, and behind the court, by the side of the swimming pool, lay stretched out a girl or two, tanned, lazy, relaxed. Gardeners clipped at the lawns and hedges.

Suddenly, with an almost painful longing, I wanted a place

of my own. I wanted a garden with trees, a court, and a pool, a little thatched summerhouse and a shady verandah. A mushroom, even. The vision that afternoon was clear enough. The way to get it was not nearly so easy to define.

DIARY NOTES, HAMBURG, 1963

After losing the match I took a car back to the hotel, feeling pretty low. At the front desk there was a telex from Abie:

"BETTER GET YR ASS BACK HERE SOON. I GOT YOU A JOB SELLING LIGHTS. NOT GREAT PAY BUT GOOD COMMISSIONS IF YOU GET OFF YR ASS.

"YRS, ABE."

I had to smile. Asses had always been essential in the world according to Abie, and mine, it seemed, would still play a big role in a new career. I read his telex in the temporary luxury of my hotel room and in spite of everything, I felt better. Somehow his telex was a sign—a signal that would finally end this restless quest for a place in tennis that by then I knew in my heart of hearts would never be found. I played another tournament or two, and then packed my bags and headed home.

And so I became a lighting salesman. Abie had a friend called Harry Bass who was a partner in a company called Fluorescent Lighting Corporation (FLC), and Abie and Harry met at the airport by chance and discussed and decided my future in about sixty seconds, as Harry was just leaving and Abie was just arriving. Between them, they came to the snap decision that I would make a good lighting salesman—the sum total of research put into my career guidance programme!

When I finally reported for work one Monday morning, I found a small desk allocated to me in the sales office. On it was a page-a-day diary, a catalogue, a price list, and a panic button. The panic button consisted of a small white box with a red push button on top. When you pressed the button it made a sound like a fire-alarm bell ringing.

"Abie said that you sometimes panic," said Harry Bass to me, "so I got you this." He gave the button an experimental push. "You see! Abie says you like something to happen if things begin to go wrong." I was able to laugh at that, but I think that he sensed how woebegone I really was, how lost I felt, how long and hard the road ahead appeared, how bleak the little office seemed.

Harry, like Abie, was a seat-of-the-pants sort of man. His own desk, I was to discover, also contained a selection of various novelty items, which he sometimes fiddled with while he pondered: an aerosol can of "Bullshit Repellent" that got sprayed in the air when certain customers came to see him, a pen with a naked lady floating upside down in it, a small coffin with a hole in its lid and a sign inviting you to insert a finger, a piece of gold-bearing quartz, a foot candle, etc. Light, I was to discover, was in those days measured in units called "foot-candles," and Harry had found a wax candle made in the shape of a foot and put it on his desk. "You'll have to learn about foot-candles," he said to me. "Come to think of it, you'll have to learn about a whole lot of things. A whole lot of things," he repeated, deep in thought, and he tipped the floating lady upside down so that the glitter in the liquid rose up round her, then settled down again as she stood on her head.

✳ ✳ ✳ ✳

Even now, memories of those days return with a clarity that stops me in my tracks. At first the weeks and months welded themselves into an endless monotony of alien things. Strange people, strange products, strange terminology. Gone were the passing shots and forehand volleys. I now had lumen outputs, isolux diagrams, glare factors. I sat in traffic jams and waited, caught busses and waited, got lost in the industrial suburbs, arrived late for appointments and waited—and prayed for each day to end. My diary became full of times and dates and prices, and cryptic notes to jog my memory. Occasionally I would record a given event. One entry described the very first sales call I ever made.

DIARY NOTES, AUGUST 1964

Fordsburg, 7.15. Desolation. A winter wind blowing dust and plastic bags along the sidewalk. And cold! My God! The new, grey flannel pants do nothing. Nobody here except me and the wind.

"Be early, you hear!" the guy said. "I got my crews to get out. And have your price ready. I don't want a thousand words! Just have a good price ready so you don't waste my time!" So here I am, early, wearing a tennis pullover and my light Simpson's jacket. (I must get some clothes.) I open my catalogue in the wind and practise what I have to say. Then my nose starts running so I reach in my jacket pocket for a Kleenex, and out comes my player's badge from Hamburg, and an old lunch voucher.

FORBES. G.—PLAYER.

I am still staring at the badge when a bashed-up pickup truck pulls up and the foreman gets out.

"Oh, Jesus, it's you! Listen, it's this friggin' truck that doesn't start, man, it's always handing me grief, you hear, but that's just too bad because I can't talk to you right now, I got to get these crews moving."

"But Mr. Buddy, you said come early. I came early. I've been here since quarter past and I. . . ."

"Listen, Mr.—er—what's your name again?"

"Forbes. Gordon Forbes."

"Listen, Mr. Gordon-Forbes, so you waited a little while, so what can I say. Phone me tomorrow, you hear, what's your price anyway?"

"Fourteen twenty-five including lamps, delivery off the shelf, I've got all the details right here. . . ."

"You guys make me laugh, listen, don't bother to phone, I can get the stuff from the wholesalers all day long, twelve ninety-five, no favours, no big deal, delivered, complete with guarantees, everything, three bags full, so what am I standing here for, you tell me?"

"But Mr. Buddy, please, just give me a break. . . ."

"Don't come with your breaks, Mr. Gordon-Forbes, come with a good price, come with twelve ninety-four, if you can't, don't waste my time, don't waste your time, you hear me?"

Some sales call. How can I sell things to people like that?

After he'd disappeared through the door, I remember, I turned and walked back to the tram stop, still holding my catalogue against my chest to stop the wind. The tram took about thirty minutes to arrive, and finally dropped me at the downtown terminus. There was a little coffee shop where they sold hot toast. I found a corner table and there, looking out onto the windy street, I found that there was nothing I could do to stop tears coming into my eyes.

I don't suppose I'll ever really know how close I came that day to catching a bus back to our rented flat and phoning Harry Bass to say that I was going to try the circuit for one more year. One more year! The temptation at that moment was overwhelming. But then I ran through my mind the schedules of another year of tennis—the windy South African coastal circuit, the early European tournaments, Cannes, Monte Carlo, Naples, Florence, Rome, etc. The slow clay, the travel, the arrivals, the baggage, the waiting around, the first rounds against eager nineteen-year-olds with big serves and topspin passing shots. The nagging financial worries. I'd been that road before. I knew those milestones and signposts off by heart, and none of them pointed to a rose garden.

Somewhere I must have found the strength to hang on. Perhaps it was the fear of quitting—the tennis player's instinctive dread of being labelled a quitter; worse still, the fear of admitting to myself that I had quit.

All I know is that eventually that day I picked up my catalogue and walked south along Eloff Street until I reached the FLC premises in New Center. When I got there I sat down at the desk they'd given me, looked at my list of customers, and began phoning them up.

In the sanctuary of that little café with the buttered toast and the encouraging heater on the wall, I learned important lessons. The value of patience. The comfort of respite. A cup of tea. The taste of a Coca-Cola. A browse in the university bookshop. That there would be good days and there would be bad days, and you had to take them as they came. It was just as it had been in tennis, only then it had not been so clear or inevitable to me.

Sometimes I would yearn almost painfully for some other kind of life. At that time, Jean was completing her English honours degree, and she had rented a small flat in the university district of Johannesburg. My most favourite escape was to drop in for tea:

Suddenly I would glimpse a world of literature and music, with the intellectual types that always gathered around my sister—Beinhardt, with his brutal architecture; Radloff, picking out chords on the piano and throwing sardonic remarks over his shoulder; Lou Dryden with her poems; Phillipa Gavin, pale face, bookish body, the red slash of lipstick suggesting a sort of minor rebellion against anything establishment. Jeremy Lubbock with his music, Lakovsky, the Lees, Jenny, Jacques Sellschop, Jane Frazer. I can see them to this day. Jean would pour tea and gently stoke the flames of their discussions— liberalism, music, freedom, literature! F. R. Leavis's *New Bearings in English Poetry* is still on my shelf with Jean's own underlinings:

"In 'The Tower' Mr Yeats achieves <u>a kind of ripeness in disillusion</u>"; or "the <u>shifty, cloudy unseizableness</u> of the imagery"; "the seekers of <u>passionate art</u> and <u>higher reality</u>"; or perhaps O'Shaughnessy's lovely lines—

> We are the music makers,
> And we are the dreamers of dreams. . . .

—and her scribblings in the margin: . . ."the drought, the dark night which is an essential stage in the progress of the Christian mystic." It was Jean, of course, who taught me to love words.

> Who is the third who walks always beside you?
> When I count there are only you and I together.

Sometimes when I left I would walk across the road onto the university campus, see slender girls sitting on the steps with their hair tied back, and I would feel an heroic sort of self-pity, I suppose, at having missed out on this seemingly untroubled world of learning, debates about cosmology, Mozart, the new maths, the oddness of T. S. Eliot's imagery. Did the poet intend ambiguity? God, how intriguing it all sounded! And how I yearned to know! To be a part of it!

Then I'd walk back to my sales desk, sit down, look at the phone, and contemplate my customer lists, suspecting in my heart of hearts that I would never relish business enough to become a mongol. . . .

As part of my urge to escape I began writing in my spare time—tennis and travel articles, mainly, but also a huge, immature novel that was to include every injustice and passion ever to come out of the Beloved Country. Jeannie's literature began encroaching. Only the other day I came upon an old copy of *Anna Karenina* that she must have given me about then, and

93

I found a passage I'd underlined dramatically in black ink:

". . . the older he grew the more often the thought struck him that what he lacked was the vital force, of what is called heart, of the impulse which drives a man to choose one of the innumerable paths of life and to care for that one only."

And all this simply because I had had to stop playing tennis and go to work—do what others did all their lives! I smile, now, but then it wasn't easy. Simply that before I had been one of a special few, and now I was one of millions.

Success, when it first came along, approached with such stealth that I hardly noticed it. I began by realising that there was a fascination about the art of illumination. Light, the architects told me, was the sculptor of the night! I found the world of business populated by just as many characters as that of tennis. The lofty architects, the relentless engineers, the pompous buyers, the thrifty contractors. Each had his world, his habits, tricks, likes, and dislikes—and of course, his ego! My God, did I learn to massage egos. Lacking technical knowledge initially, I developed a sort of naive, please-help-me-out approach, the patient underdog, humble, determined to serve, to learn.

DIARY NOTES, 1964

Lost the order again at ——. I swear the buyer there just loves to see my face fall. He calls everybody "chum" or "chappie."

"Sorry, Chum, no go. Had to give it to Philips. Better tell your chappies to sharpen their pencils."

"Come on, please, Mr. . . .," I say, playing his game. "You know how badly I needed that order. I'm nowhere near my

target. . . ."

"Sorry, Chum. Not this time. Oh, and by the way, that sample floodlight you sent out to the mine. Dead. Burnt out. Water got in. Send your chappie out to take it away. Quality, Chum, quality. Very important. Pass the word on to your chappies."

"Do you know that you are a 'chappie'?" I asked Harry Bass.

"You've been calling on old Harry," he said. *"Never mind, it's nearly Christmas. Take him a good bottle of Scotch. That'll do the trick. He's too mean to buy a decent bottle for himself."*

They were a dry lot, those buyers. Sometimes I would be allowed to drag them out to lunch, and if things got desperate I would try to liven them up by telling tennis stories.

"Once, in Italy," I would babble, "Abe Segal thought that his matches were over for the day so he ate a huge lunch of bean soup, pasta, and about three Coca-Colas, only to be called to play men's doubles against two people called Warren Woodcock and Beppe Merlo. At about three-all in the second set he was suddenly seized by the most violent attacks of wind. Each time he stretched for a volley or went up for a smash there were these devastating echoes, and running back for lobs was a motor scooter with no tailpipe. The small Italian audience forgot about the tennis and began applauding Abie's sound effects. Finally Woodcock walked up to the umpire, tapped the chair with his racket, and said, 'Mr. Umpire, we can't play with all this wind. There must be a rule that says he can't do that.'

"'Oh, yeah, sure there is, Woody,' said Abie, underlining his words with another sturdy blast. 'It says that if a player can fart more than fifteen times in one game he gets a win by default!'"

I would finish my stories and hope for a good reponse, and sometimes I would be lucky. Slowly orders began to come my way. I began to learn my new trade, and to experience the unexpected pleasure of feeling wanted, and receiving nice commission cheques.

Abie's chance meeting with Harry Bass began a period of my life that lasted for more than twenty years. After about three years of working for Harry, his business was sold. The new owners were a dreary lot, so I joined forces with two other members of the sales staff whom I had gotten to know and like, and together we began our own business.

DIARY NOTES, 1967

When I told Abie that I had quit my job and started my own business, he said, "Well, it's about time!"

Some mornings I wake up in a cold sweat. Gavin is nine, his new sister is six months old, and we've just bought this new house.

"But is it the right time?" I asked Abie.

"It's exactly the right time, Forbsey," he said. "Now you have to get off your ass and make friggin' sure it works, don't you? So don't come to me with all this crap about the wrong time!"

Slowly, we began to succeed. I kept very few notes about

those days. Looking back, they remain in my mind more as a flavour than as a memory. The years merged into a period of total absorption. We worked with a passion, sometimes even mindlessly, like bees collecting honey. But even in our most mundane tasks there was the pulse of success. A lifting of the heart.

There came a day, many years later, when we found ourselves in possession of a large business employing well over one thousand people. There was money in the bank. Our trucks came and went. Our products were everywhere. And inevitably, there came along the large corporation that wanted to buy what we had created.

DIARY NOTES, 1986

I leave the office that has been my life for all these years. Get into my car, thinking of the faces of the people on the stairs. The old man at the gate salutes me as he always does. I drive down the road for the last time, away from the place that has done so much for me. A destination reached, and now, this new journey. To freedom! That which I have always wanted, say I to myself. But where is the elation? Why these feelings of regret? When do you discover that elusive place that will at last enable you to say: "Yes! Yes! This is where I want to be!"

HANDFULS OF

SUMMER

What happened to tennis during all those years when I was busy selling lights? What happened to the friends I had made, the tournaments I had come to love? I tried to keep playing, of course, stealing hours here and there, slipping down to the courts at Ellis Park at midday to feel the sun on my face and hit a few balls. I even played the odd tournament.

DIARY NOTES, PORT ELIZABETH

How many times have I woken up in this city and not listened to the wind! You know it's blowing great guns when you open your eyes in the morning, and the palms outside the hotel are bent over with their fronds rattling like sabres. Today is a gale. Yesterday was a gale. Tomorrow will be a gale. We're weary of gales. The players come off the courts leaning over like the trees with their hair all pointed inland. . . .

Today my tog bag disappeared before our doubles match.

Luckily Abie had two pairs of shoes and two shirts, so I could borrow from him. The shirt was a very large sort of shirt, and what with the shoes being size fifteen, when I served against the wind I had to tack up to net like a sailboat. Also, my shoes got there before I did, which did not escape Abie's notice.

"I'm waitin' at net," he said afterwards. "I hear the serve, a ball and some shoes arrive, but no Forbsey. Finally I realise what's actually happening behind me. His shoes are comin' in to net, and his body's goin' backwards with his shirt! Now that's what I call a friggin' wind! You go up for a smash on court three and you come down on court five!"

In 1964, aged thirty-two, Abie beat me in the final of the South African Open to win it for the first time. The decade from 1964 to 1974 proved to be golden years for South African tennis. It was then that Owen and Jenny Williams conceived of the idea of corporate sponsorships, which transformed the SA Open into one of the world's finest tournaments. The world's best players appeared on the twin centre courts at Ellis Park, and the gaunt old stadium, newly painted and softened with flags and flowers, echoed with the voices of high society and the artistry of such players as Santana, Emerson, Laver, Rosewall, Connors, Stolle, Drysdale, Okker, and Ashe. The women were no less distinguished: Margaret Smith, Maria Bueno, Evonne Goolagong, Billie Jean King. Our own Sandra Reynolds and Rene Schuurman. Jean. Heather Segal, Virginia Wade, Ann Jones. At Ellis Park on those April afternoons, tennis came as close as I have ever known to a sort of sublime and simple perfection.

But again, I am going too fast. Other things happened in the late sixties while I was busy selling lights. Important things—you could even say heroic things—which were to set the stage for the money-laden glamour of the tennis world as it is today.

In the game of cricket, there were two kinds of participants—the Gentlemen and the Players. The Gentlemen were true amateurs, and the Players were those who received financial reward. The terms alone speak volumes. There was something a little iffy about getting paid for playing sport. A little low brow. It was—well, it was not quite cricket!

Until the late sixties, tennis was very much the same. The Gentlemen were those who played the amateur circuit, the Players those who turned professional. If they wanted to earn money from the game to which they'd given their lives, the great players of the day would no longer be welcome at the scenes of their finest sporting achievements—stadiums like Roland Garros, Wimbledon, Forest Hills, or the Foro Italica of Rome—where they had become legends, where they had played their hearts out, and where the tournaments alone had profited from their efforts.

They would have to set aside their amateur status and turn professional, joining as rookies the small group of other former champions who toured the world, playing pro matches in venues ranging from Madison Square Garden to makeshift arenas in Des Moines, Iowa, Queenstown, South Africa, or Alice Springs, Australia. Never again (it then seemed) would they be welcomed back to the great tournaments to which they had contributed so much.

Who will ever know what magical tennis was played at those obscure venues? Try to talk to the participants about those tours and they are guarded, reluctant, as though the memories are their own and whatever they say can never properly describe those evenings on the road. It must be true that some of the best tennis ever played went to waste, watched by only handfuls of people while the old amateur system slowly died.

In 1993, at the glittering ATP Tour World Championships in Frankfurt's marvellous Festhalle, surrounded by the opulence of the maroon-and-green "Champion's Club," I sat at one of the tables with Fred and Pat Stolle, Cliff Drysdale, Charlie Pasarell, and Tony Trabert. We contemplated the surrounding luxury with rueful smiles, and I asked Tony to talk about his early days on Jack Kramer's pro tour. For once he seemed willing to remember.

"We were lepers," he said, "not accepted in any of the proper tennis clubs, the country clubs, the stadiums—we had to play our matches on cricket fields, ice rinks, town halls, anywhere that would seat people . . . on a canvas court that we carried with us, and that got laid when we arrived. . . . Vic Braden, then Hugh Stewart, drove the truck and laid the court . . . any old surface would do, ice was the best, nice and smooth . . . the court was very fast . . . it had these seams on the lines that we used to aim at . . . that was the best way to hold service—you tried to hit the seams . . . no tie-breakers, just long sets. . . ." A pause while he reflected.

"Five matches per week for fourteen months, a thousand dollars a match, the winner took ten percent more than the loser, and the promotor took forty percent. . . . We took out

Lloyds insurance against injury . . . but you weren't allowed to get injured. You had to play. Fayetteville, Oklahoma City, Tulsa . . . we'd finish at one A.M., drive our station wagon until four A.M., check into a motel, sleep till noon, then drive to the next town, lay the court, hit a few balls to test it out, check into the next motel, rest for an hour, eat, then play again. . . . Segoo [Pancho Segura] was the best driver . . . he could see in the dark, never got tired, we'd take turns sleeping on the backseat. Eat, play, drive, sleep, eat, play. That was our world."

"I never remember not trying for any match," Tony went on, having paused after that spate of words. "There were people who had paid to see us play, you see, and we had to show them. . . . It was something that had to be done—a kind of duty. We were a little team against the whole world. . . . I remember once, for instance, Pancho [Gonzales] used to play Spalding, and he'd made an arrangement to meet people and sign autographs at a sports store one morning at eleven, and he couldn't make it, so I stood in for him (although I played Wilson) and signed his name and talked about how good Spalding was. . . ."

Although I pressed him, Tony was understated about the tennis they played. Gorgo and Hoadie were the toughest, but they were all tough. "Jack [Kramer] could beat any of us over a set, and Sedge, Segoo, even Hartwig . . . they could all play. . . ."

Again the little silence. Again the flight of images, the fleeting sadness, the sense of waste. How many people had actually seen Tony play? How many knew just how good he was, what a great competitor he had been?

By the midsixties, the trickle of players turning pro had turned into a stream. Lamar Hunt's World Championship Tennis was created, and Dave Dixon recruited the Handsome Eight, headed up by Newcombe, Roche, Drysdale, and Buchholz. Pierre Barthes, Roger Taylor, and Dennis Ralston. Niki Pilic.

In 1968 the final remnants of the amateur world were swept aside by the announcement that Wimbledon, that most hallowed of amateur sanctuaries, was open for competition by all comers. A new era of tennis was at hand.

Cliff Drysdale was one of the pioneers of the campaign for open tennis. Sometimes my sister would accompany him on tour and while away the hours by keeping notes. Amongst the papers sent to me by Richard Evans was a manuscript filled with stories of her life on tour with Cliff. Reading them, it occurred to me that the young players of today might like to know about the players who made possible the lives they lead. No-one wrote of them better than she—the comradeship, the humour, the conversations lie on the pages like living things.

> *One of the most admired players among the players is Rosewall. He is quiet, self-disciplined (two beers only), ageless (thirty-seven), and a source of wonder to every other player.*
>
> *One evening at dinner, Jeff Boroviak remarked to Roy Emerson and Fred Stolle, out of the blue, that Ken Rosewall was exactly like Bach, pronouncing it "Bark," the American way. Jeff is a scholar of music with this rare tennis talent (or vice versa—I can*

never decide!). He is very profound and serious, with long, unruly black hair and an introspective smile, and he recently stunned himself and everyone else by reaching the final in Cologne.

"Who's Bark?" Emmo wanted to know—perhaps a little alarmed that there might just be another Rosewall lurking about somewhere.

"He's a man who lived not far from here about two hundred years ago, and composed music," said Jeff, patiently.

"Ah, Music!" said Emmo, relieved. "You mean like Rark?"

"Rark?" said Jeff, blankly.

"Maninoff," said Emmo. "You know, Rach-mani-noff!" He looked pleased with himself for this amazing piece of knowledge.

"No, he's different," said Jeff. "Rosewall's like Bark," and he launched into a complicated explanation of Bach—variety within a tight scale, flowing movement, perfection, precision, repetition of a part within the whole.

"Who does Fred play like?" Emmo wanted to know.

"Elvis Presley," murmured Brian Fairlie, but Jeff was too far gone in his analogy to hear them.

"Seeing Rosewall for the first time is like hearing Bark for the first time," he said. "It's impossible to really appreciate everything he's doing. There's a continuum. Perfect form. Flow and balance."

*"Like Bark?" said Emmo helpfully. "Did he have
any other names?"*

"Johann Sebastian," said Jeff absently.

*"Johann Sebastian Rosewall," mused Emmo.
"Listen, Jeffrey. Last night you talked about bloody
watercress for an hour. Tonight we got Jo-hann going
for us."*

*"Do you know what a cross is?" asked Jeff, still not
hearing and suddenly coming in from a new angle.
His audience stared blankly, forks poised in midair.*

"A cross?" repeated Fred.

"Yes, yes, a cross. A Christian symbol. . . ."

*"You mean a cross like this?" said Emmo, holding
his knife and fork up in graphic demonstration.*

*"Exactly," approved Jeff. "You have to think of
Bach's music, and thus Rosewall's tennis, in the form
of a cross. . . ."*

*"Hear that, Fred?" said Emmo. "That's been our
problem. We should have been playing like this. . . ."—
still holding the knife and fork aloft.*

Ken Rosewall frequently appears in Jean's notes—the
ultimate seer, holding a place all his own in the eyes of his
colleagues.

*"Kenny served an ace today," remarked Rod Laver
reflectively, "I nearly walked off the court. Said to
myself, I can't stand for that. Can't have Kenny
thinking he can serve aces. Not part of his game.*

Might start something."

"Blinky hell!" agreed Andre Gimeno in his picturesque English.

He had just arrived.

"How did you get here, Andre?" asked Cliff.

"I fly Vancouver to heaven-knows-where to heaven-knows-where to Frankfurt to here," said Andre.

Concerning Torben Ulrich, whom she adored:

. . . And then there's always Torben, rising like a phoenix with his warm, luminous eyes and his permanent awareness of the bounties of life. Today Roy Barth, who has been partnering Torben a lot in doubles, appeared at dinner, wide-eyed.

"Do you know what happened today?" he asked.

"Do you know what Torben did? We had to play Reissen and Okker. Every time we play them, we try very hard and lose. Today, they were announcing the players over the mike before the match, and after they announced Torben, he ran over and took the mike and made noises like a trumpet playing. Then the match began, and he didn't seem to be trying at all. We were getting slaughtered, so I asked him what was happening.

"You know, Roy," he said, "every time we play Reissen and Okker, we try very hard and lose. So this time, you see, I thought that if perhaps we did not to

try, we might win!"

In Australia, the old man giving out the balls became confused and got it into his head that Torben was Roy and Roy was Torben. Instead of trying to correct him, Torben became interested in this change of identity.

"You know," he said, "it will be a quite new experience to be Roy for a week. There would be surprises. My service would change, and I would never know what I was having for breakfast."

The enigmatic Arthur Ashe appears quietly amongst the cast of characters. Despite his campaign against apartheid, some of his best friends were amongst the South African players.

We find ourselves having breakfast at nine A.M. in the hotel in Barcelona. Arthur Ashe has detached himself with a book, and this arouses comment.

"Don't bother to talk to us, Arthur!"

"You just sit there and read your book."

Arthur disentangles himself with a grin. "Okay, Charlie, order me some cornflakes." Charlie Pasarell is the only one present who speaks Spanish. He has a lengthy discussion with the waiter.

"They don't serve cornflakes," he says.

"But those are cornflakes," says Arthur, pointing to a large packet on Rod Laver's table.

"Those are my own, private cornflakes," says Laver. "I bought them myself at the supermarket."

"Rodney," says Cliff sternly, "give Arthur some of your cornflakes!"

Rod looks taken aback. "There are none left," he says, peering into the packet. "I've finished them. Arthur can have the packet."

"Thank you very much," says Arthur.

"You'll need it at the supermarket to explain what you want," says Rod. "That is, unless Charlie's with you!"

Sitting in the Festhalle the other day I tried to imagine, say, Andre Agassi buying his own cornflakes at the supermarket and then offering the empty packet to, say, Boris Becker, but I was unsuccessful.

Meanwhile, here is Jean's account of a poker game played on tour:

After dinner there is nothing to do.

"We have game of poker," says Ismail el Shafei, of Egypt. "I take all the money in one hour."

There is a thoughtful silence.

"I don't mind we have game poker for one hour," says Niki Pilic.

"We'll play till ten," says Cliff.

"Yes, ten," they agree.

"We—ar—have to establish the—ar—rules before we—ar—begin," says Bob Carmichael.

"And the stakes," murmurs Brian Fairlie of New Zealand.

"What means 'establish'?" asks Niki. "We play poker. Why need for establish? Poker is poker."

A long wrangle ensues. Everyone seems to have different rules.

"In Egypt we play straight beats full house," says Ismail.

"Egypt!" says Pilic, lifting his nose. "You mean in your street in Cairo you play this way!"

"Ismail," says Cliff, "how many times do I have to tell you that Niki was once a professional poker player?"

"For once in life Cliff is right," says Niki.

At last the game gets under way. A tense hand develops.

Bob Carmichael inches up his last card. "Yippee!" he says.

"What means 'yippee'?" asks Niki. "This is not way to play poker!"

"It means I'm in for ten, and another twenty," says Carmichael.

"I see you," says Niki. "Not smart, but see you anyway." (aside) "When Carmichael goes 'yippee,' smart players don't see!"

Slowly Bob takes out a queen and lays it down. Then he lays down a three of clubs. Then two more queens, and finally, very slowly, yet another queen.

"In Yugoslavia," says Niki dispassionately, "man can get bullet for showing cards like that!"

"I'll—ar—remember that," says Carmichael,

raking in the pot. "Wouldn't like to—ar—get bullet."

Jean was especially fond of the English tennis writers, and simultaneously exasperated and amused by the American ones for their quirkish reporting:

> *July 1972. Stan Smith has just won Wimbledon, and what do you think one of the headlines here in Texas said:*
>
> SMITH NIPS WIMBY TITLE IN NET SET!
>
> *This must be the only place in the world that could reduce Wimbledon to the size of a mere "Wimby." Next thing you know we'll have "Forry" for Forest Hills, "Roly" for Roland Garros; maybe "Kenty" for the Kentucky Derby, and (could it be possible) "Ollie" for the Olympic Games!*
>
> *Wimby is no fun if you can't go out and buy all the English papers and read what writers like Rex Bellamy and John Parsons and Frank Keating and Richard Evans have to say. Here (in Texas) the reports are very dull. Some of the writers obviously don't know much about tennis and make curious blunders. For instance, they confuse the words "volley" and "rally" and you end up with some very odd images:*
>
> *"Both players played from the baseline and one volley lasted for several minutes!" Must have been a very deep, Texan volley!*

Although it's not part of Jean's writing on the early pro tours,

I can't resist including her description of a Texas cattle sale:

> *Texans love a show. Somewhere behind their practical facade lies a flair for the dramatic. Last week we were invited to a cattle sale in Kerrville. This was the real thing, Stetsons, pointed boots, big cigars, pancakes, cattle talk. The auction began while cows pawed and bellowed and children climbed up and down the railings.*
>
> *After surveying the scene for a while, Cliff disappeared thoughtfully and came back wearing his own Stetson. Then the auction began—unsuspecting cattle, floods of gibberish, and suddenly the bidding logjammed at six thousand dollars. The auctioneer mopped his brow.*
>
> *"Gennelmen!" he said reprovingly, "thishyere femayal is the best cow Ah ever did put up on sayal, why, Gahddemn, she's won more shows than. . . . Jim, hey, Jim, would you step up hayere and tell the folks what you sayad yesterday about thishyere cow!"*
>
> *Jim stood up undaunted. "Ah'd like to make a statement," he said. "I sayad it yesterday, and Ah'll say it agin today—this femayal is the best animal in her class in the entire State of Texas!"*
>
> *The bidding leapt up to ten thousand dollars. The cow was unmoved. . . .*

Somewhere towards the end of the manuscript Jean

mentioned Cliff's involvement with what she then called the Players Association—interesting in light of what it has now evolved into: the mighty, all-powerful organisation called the ATP Tour. The mention moved me to unearth some notes I'd made on one of the first meetings ever held by the Players Association in London.

DIARY NOTES, LONDON, 1968

Money is flooding into tennis. Thus saith Drysdale. To cope with the flood the players are forming something called the ATP—a sort of glorified committee, by the players, for the players, which, they say, will enable them to speak with one voice.

"One voice!" says Abe Segal scornfully. "Not only do those idiots all speak with different voices, they speak mainly crap, and they speak it in different languages! 'One voice'! Hah!" He can't stand it. The thought of all that money about is bad enough—but tennis players in committees drives him crazy. "And what does ATP stand for?" he wants to know scathingly.

"The Association of Tennis Professionals," says Drysdale.

"Just as well they've shortened it," mutters Abie. "Not too many of them can spell 'association.'"

Some time later I noted the following:

Drysdale says that they're going to hold a meeting. John Newcombe is the new president, Marty Reissen is secretary, Arthur Ashe is treasurer, and Charlie Pasarell's portfolio is unclear—a sort of general factotum and controller of things uncontrollable. What is more, Arthur is to propose a motion banning us (South Africa) from the Davis Cup (at least). Claude Lister says that Cliff and I had better be there to speak up in defence. "Nice easy job," says Cliff.

The meeting was duly held.

Charlie's done a good job. A lot of players attended the meeting. The committee sat at a table at the end of the large room. For a while, as Abie predicted, everyone talked at the same time. Then Newcombe hammered on the table and the uproar died down to mutterings and an Australian voice that said, "Hargh bloody tarme!"

"The secretary will read the agenda," said Newcombe, and Reissen solemnly complied.

"Any comments?" asked Newcombe.

"Short bloody agenda," murmured the Australian voice.

"Will the treasurer please read the financial report?" said Newcombe. By then each player was supposed to have paid his fifty-dollar dues.

Arthur Ashe got to his feet. "Not a lot to report," he said "Everyone's paid up except Zuleta. The money's right here," and he slapped a bulge in his trouser pocket. This visible evidence of the continued existence of their cash seemed to please most of the players, but Newcombe frowned at this unorthodox method of reporting.

"Come on, Zu," said Newcombe, "pay up!"

Zuleta, who had ducked into a doorway at this turn of events, put his head back round the frame.

"I geeve it you at Forest Heels," he said, suspecting, no doubt, that this new ATP might not survive until then.

"Ah, what? This is bloody ridiculous," came the Australian voice.

Newcombe, studying the agenda, ignored it. "Any progress on the club tie, Charlie?"

Pasarell, who had been waiting for this moment, stood up and opened his raincoat to reveal a huge, psychedelic necktie that he'd bought that morning on the King's Road. There was a great roar of laughter, and Newcombe rapped for silence.

"Ah, this is bloody ridiculous," said the Australian voice.

"Davo!" said Newcombe. "Kindly address your remarks through the chair!"

"Through you, Mr. Chairman," said Davo, "it's still bloody ridiculous."

Newcombe, determined to keep order, demanded silence in such a savage voice that the uproar died away. Then Ashe put his case in his usual calm, unhurried way, and Drysdale, with equal eloquence, defended the South African Tennis Union as being one that promoted equality, and asked to be allowed to remain in the competition. Ingo Buding, of Germany, citing many other instances of discrimination in sport, supported Drysdale. The debate continued for some time until Ashe proposed that the matter be put to the vote.

"And I propose," said Buding, "that we vote to see whether we put Arthur's resolution to the vote."

"Vote to vote," said someone, catching on.

"Through you, Mr. Chairman," said Davo firmly, "that's bloody ridiculous. I propose we vote to see whether we vote

on Ingo's resolution to see whether we vote on Arthur's resolution."

"Vote to vote to vote," said the voice.

In spite of Davo's tongue-in-cheek proposal, Ingo's resolution was finally adopted, and the voting went against Arthur.

"Bloody marvellous!" said Davo. "We take a vote and decide not to vote so we needn't have voted in the first place!"

Gradually, at first, the Association of Tennis Professionals gained stature and power. In 1988 it completed a restructuring programme that made it into what is arguably the most powerful body in tennis. Modelling itself on the PGA in golf, it added a "Tour" to the name, thus "ATP Tour," and chose for its logo the now famous "stick man"—a tennis player frozen in a classic service motion. Under the leadership of the calm and elegant Mark Miles, and the energetic Larry Scott, the ATP Tour now governs professional tennis players, and together with members selected from the tournament directors, it also controls and arranges the entire schedule of international tournaments, with the exception of the so-called Grand Slam events—the great traditional tournaments at Roland Garros, Wimbledon, Flushing Meadows, and Flinders Park, which are still the domain of the International Tennis Federation.

Yes, the ATP has come a long way since that long-ago meeting in London that John Newcombe struggled so manfully to control.

"For a start," says Abie, "these days the treasurer doesn't keep all the money in his trouser pocket!"

THE PILGRIM'S
PROGRESS

And Abie? What did he do when, as they say, the flames of youth began to die down? What passage did he take to find the right door? He did not give up tennis as suddenly as I had. He played on for several years, teaming up with Bob Howe, and once or twice with Lew Hoad, who had always been one of his closest friends. I know that at one time he had an offer from Jack Kramer to turn pro but refused it, preferring to remain in the garment business. When his father died in about 1969, Abie sold his shares in the family business and launched out on his own. The sum of money that he got as a result of the sale seemed to me to be a huge one.

"Don't you think you should save it?" I suggested. "You know, old age, and all that crap." With Abie you have to be very laid-back when suggesting a cautious approach.

"Sure, I'm going to save it!" he said. "What a question"— but of course he didn't, really. For a start, he flew round the world twice, first in one direction then in the other, to "find out exactly what was happening out there," as he put it, but in truth, just as a sort of a double war whoop to celebrate his freedom. When he returned he brought with him mountains of clothing samples and the usual tales of adventure, like the time when he'd lost his hotel:

On his second round-the-world journey he'd stopped off at Hong Kong and Singapore, and arrived in Tokyo exhausted, checking into a hotel and collapsing on the bed until he felt sufficiently revived to look for an English movie. Then he asked a taxi driver to take him to one and spent a few hours in a happy daze, watching one of his beloved westerns. When he came out of the movie he found that he had not only forgotten the name of the hotel that he'd checked into, but also had no idea at all where it was. So he began asking people in the street.

"And do you think any of those little guys could speak English, Forbsey?" he asked me later, when telling the story. "Not one! I could easily have been on Mars! 'I'm lost!' I tell them. 'Hotel-ly he gone!'

"'Aoww zoyy sushi mici tuukoghi hoh,' they tell me." (Abie fancies himself at mimicking eastern languages.)

"'Velly tired. Nowhere to sleepy,' I say, putting my hands like this, to show them.

"'Ausoh sukosakii mitsubishi soh,' they answer. So you tell me. What's a man supposed to do next?"

He'd begun walking a series of rectangular beats, each covering an area of about seven city blocks, and after about five hours he miraculously recognised a landmark that he'd seen from the taxi on the way to the hotel. After that he finally found his hotel, and, going up to his room, he subsided on his bed. But he'd learned a lesson about travel in the East.

"If you ever go there, Forbsey," he said, "make sure you remember exactly where your hotel is, so you don't have to ask anybody anything in the street!"

Abie also found out that tennis wear could be bought very cheaply in some of the eastern countries.

"Listen, Forbsey," he said to me one day after he had returned, "you won't believe what those little guys in Taiwan can do. Look at this!" He began throwing sample tennis shirts and shorts on the sofa beside me.

It was a Saturday morning and we were in his Bryanston house. Outside the sun was shining, the pool was sparkling, and Heather, his island wife, was sunning herself in the smallest of swimsuits.

"How much do you think these things cost?" Abie was going on. "One dollar each, that's how much. Everything these people sell seems to cost one dollar. That means they will land here at two dollars, maximum, and I can sell them all day long for six, so how bad a deal can that be? I'm going to give these things a bit of a punt!"

When the first shipment landed he found that the large sizes were small, the mediums fitted petite women, and the smalls were only useful to children.

"So I'll sell them to the kiddy shops," he said. "You see, Forbsey, what you got to know is that an extra, extra large Taiwanese is about as big as a medium-sized kid. Once you've got that straight, you've got it made!"

He gave me two sample shirts to play-test for him, and

apart from the fact that they became very long and thin when they got damp, they behaved well. After the first wash, however, I had to report to Abie that the sleeves had come off one of them.

"So now you've got a running vest and a pair of knee guards," he said.

After a fair amount of trial and error, the Lew Hoad range of sportswear by Abe Segal was launched. As an emblem they contrived a small and elegant version of the peace sign, and Abie made a verbal deal with Lew, the details of which they both instantly forgot.

DIARY NOTES, JOHANNESBURG, 1966

One of the business mongols that Abie and I sometimes play tennis with gave us a hot tip on the stock exchange last Saturday, so Abe phoned up "his broker" (suddenly he has this "broker"!) and made an investment. For a week nothing happened, and Abie began to get restless and to wonder whether "that asshole actually knows what he's talking about." The next week the shares went down a rand each, so Abie impulsively sold them, then phoned the mongol and told him what he'd done. That afternoon at Ellis Park Abie was complaining about his deal in the locker room, where Lew Hoad was changing for a match against Butch Buchholz.

"So what do you think the idiot says to me!" Abie asks. "'Your understanding of the words "long term" is different than that of most normal people,' is what he says to me, in this big lardy accent of his. 'So how long is "long term" for normal people?' I ask him. 'It all depends,' he says to me, 'but

one thing for sure is it's longer than five days!' Meanwhile the moral of the story is 'Don't ever buy shares on the stock exchange. And if you do, don't ever listen to any of these big deals.'"

"How much did you lose, Big Abie?" growls Lew. Lew has a way of growling questions, using very few words.

"Two thousand friggin' rand is how much I lost!" Abie answers.

"Only two thousand rand!" echoes Lew. "That's a very good deal!"—which goes to show what tennis players expect of business deals.

"So you think you're a normal person, Abie?" asks Fred Stolle, who has been listening.

"Sure, I'm normal," says Abie.

"What do you think, Emmo?" asks Fred.

"I am normal, you are normal, he is normal," intones Emmo, pointing at Lew. "I learned that at school. Abie is abnormal. Never been normal in his life. Wouldn't be Abie if he was. Be someone else that was a normal person."

But whether or not he is normal, Abie has never quite managed to escape from the garment industry. He now makes handsome car coats, race- and rally-wear jackets, and track suits for corporate promotions. And a lot of his time is spent at Sun City, the beautiful resort that Sol Kerzner founded in the heart of the African bush. Walk down to the courts in the late afternoon with the heat of the day still hanging heavy under the mighty highveld thunderclouds. The courts lie surrounded by fever trees, a clubhouse of thatch, and on the lawns walk guinea fowl and cranes.

Sometimes you will see Abie there, a craggy figure in a Nike cap and baggy shorts, working away at his groundstrokes. If he is giving someone a coaching lesson, which he sometimes does when the mood takes him, and if you stop for a while and listen, you will hear him give the instruction that has stood him in good stead for over forty years:

"Listen, Professor! Why don't you just forget about your feet, grip your racket, and look at the friggin' ball!"

For a very brief instruction, one can hardly do better.

A BRIDGE ON

THE SEINE

There came a Monday morning in my life when I awoke and there was no office to go to; no need for a suit and tie; no hurry. I was free to travel again, and it was tempting to retrace some of the journeys of my youth. One day, for instance, it was May, and I was in Paris again, and the boulevards were just as they always had been, with the tables laid out under the chestnut trees, the blossoms falling, and the Parisians strolling on the cobbled pavements.

DIARY NOTES, MAY 1991

This evening I get the taxi to drive down the Champs Elysées and drop me off on Place Clemençeau so that I can walk along the Avenue Winston Churchill and across the Alexander III Bridge. The setting sun is sending shafts of light through summer clouds, and as I reach the middle of the bridge, one of these shafts catches the gilded dome of

*Invalides, as it waits behind its jardins and its cannon.
The river views are caught for a moment like paintings in the
moving light and shade—upriver the Eiffel Tower, downriver
a curve of bridges as far as Tuilleries, and below, the river
water, in this light a blend of metals like mica, platinum,
silver; hints of gold. Boats and barges. A lantern on the river-
bank lights up. The evening gathers with a calm that catches
in the throat—the fleeting sadness that for me is always a part
of Paris.*

I have revisited this city off and on now for over thirty
years, and I am always surprised by the thrill of it. The sadness comes when I realise once again that I will never really be
a part of it. Sometimes I think that if I could have my next life
to specification, I might elect to be one of those handsome,
sophisticated, Parisian men who speak four or five languages,
have an apartment overlooking the Seine, a château in Aix,
belong to the Racing Club, are waved at in restaurants, know
the good wines, are friends with Jean-Paul Belmondo, and know
wise and illusive French women, somewhat mature, who wear
silks with leather and denim and leave hints of perfume in
their wake. In winter I would wear a cashmere coat and scarf,
carelessly, and go to concerts to hear Pierre Amoils play Brahms,
sometimes inviting one of the women, who, as it might turn
out, would also be a musician, probably a cellist. After the concert we might have a cognac at Antoine's.

On the evening when I walked over the bridge I was making for the Rue de Varenne, and the Restaurant d'Arpege, to
which, that afternoon at Roland Garros, Mark McCormack

had invited me, handing me its name and address written down on one of the cards he carries in his pocket. The appointed time was underlined, thus: "8.30.—Try to arrive."

The reason for this precision was that two nights previously he had verbally given me the address of a restaurant called La Gagouilly in Place Constantin, and I hadn't made it. The city, snobbish at the best of times, was impossible that evening. To begin with there was a Metro strike and the taxi drivers were all behaving as though they had just been deified. The one who had eventually picked me up grunted at my instructions and drove off into the traffic, blowing his horn and consulting a battered guidebook on his lap. Finally he pulled up with a muttered "merde!"

"Ça n'existe pas la Constantin dans une place," he said.

Constantin, it seemed, did not exist in Paris in the form of a "Place." The address was not precise. I should disembark and get my facts straight. ("Imbecile that I was" muttered under his breath.)

"What other 'Constantins' do you have?" I had asked, desperate not to lose him. *"Autre Constantins! Autre Constantins!"*— only to get driven back by an avalanche of French that swept me out of the cab and onto the sidewalk. To stay sane I retaliated uselessly with a broadside of Anglo-Saxon oaths, but his cab drove away, leaving me in chaos—heavy traffic, no taxis, no Metro, and a vocabulary of only about twenty French words, most of them aligned to ordering food or scoring in tennis. It's no good calling out "forty-fifteen!" if what you really want is a restaurant in the Fourteenth Arrondissement. So I walked back to the hotel, ordered room service, and watched Patrick

McEnroe play Andre Agassi on the TV. Hence, today, confirmation from Mark in writing and a more orderly approach to the restaurant.

There *is* a Rue de Varenne in Paris, with the restaurant exactly where it's supposed to be, behind the kind of doors that as young tennis players we would sometimes peer through but never dare to enter. With Mark, though, one can relax. He knows restaurants and, what is more, restaurants know him! The frosty Parisian airs thaw at once and you are sheltered and secure in the McCormack aura. Little things happen with laid-back flourishes—napkins are snapped open, menus arrive, a platter of tiny, aromatic bites appears. Wine is not far behind (a simple little Chablis les Vaillons), and then, nicely settled down in a cloud of well-being, the real debate begins.

What to order? The turbot is good this year, and so is the *asperge*, and one should not overlook the duck . . . but then the maître d' arrives with such a bow-wave of goodwill and information that all private decisions seem silly.

"Ah, burt Meester McCormack, for you zair ees surmseeng ce soir you wheel enjoy, zees I promeese wiss all my 'eart!" Fingertips are kissed upwards and the whole effect is so compelling that the mere thought of not taking his advice is madness. And so, eventually:

> *langoustines roties aux artichokes coulis des*
> *poivrons doux,*
> *turbotin à la moutarde,*
> *mille-feuille chaud caramelise,*

café, et
a bowl of ice cream for Betsy McCormack.

Afterwards, at midnight I walk back over the bridge. A different city now, a million points of light, the famous tower floodlit, the water brilliant with reflections, the evening warm and still. There is no hurry. In this mood I have to stop, lean on the stone parapet, and simply allow my thoughts to wander back amongst the memories.

DIARY NOTES, MAY 1955

My first morning in Paris! Abie and I take a taxi to Roland Garros and finally arrive after a lot of noise, what with the taxi driver and Abie going full blast. The driver honks his horn, mutters to himself in French, and has to close one eye against the smoke from his Gauloise. Abie has been here before and is behaving like a guide, talking nonstop, while I'm looking at a map and trying to work out where we are.

"Would you say that this Napoleon must have hired a few architects in his time, Forbsey?" he goes on. "Every time he won a battle he had to build something so he could stick a flag on top. How about this great big friggin' arch, for a start?"

We're rumbling over the cobbles of the Place d'Étoile with the driver shaking his fist out the window at other drivers, who respond with finger signs. "And how about this Avenue Foch that we're drivin' along?" Abie is saying. "When we've made our first million this's where we're gonna get a place. You won't believe the birds that walk along this street—an' what's more they've got movies and this American bar just down the road."

Our first million! A place on Avenue Foch. There is infinite promise in Abie's words. After all, we're young, and we're driving through Paris, we can touch it. Anything is possible. The city has a sparkle to it that takes your breath away—what with the sun out and all the trees along the avenues in blossom. Abe says they're probably oaks.

"Oaks don't blossom," I mention.

"So they're something else," he says. "Once you've seen one tree you've seen them all." But he's wrong. The trees in Paris are different than other trees.

The stadium is a bit of a disappointment. Grey concrete with gravel walks and courts like burnt caramel. Outside the "referees' office" the draw sheets for the tournament are pinned up, written out in round French handwriting. "G Forbes (Afrique de Sud)"—playing against a French player I've never heard of. I feel the usual bubbles in my stomach.

"Don't get too excited," says Abie. "This is clay, remember. These French assholes were born on clay. Even guys you've never heard of can keep you out there all day."

When they made the mixed doubles draw I entered at the last minute with a blonde girl called Darlene Hard whom I met as we stood at the desk, looking at the draw sheets.

Darlene and I won the mixed doubles that year, which in retrospect was not so surprising, as she was to develop into one of the great women doubles players of all time. Nonetheless, it was a major title, and in addition I'd reached the quarter-finals of the double messieurs with Russell Seymour. (Abie and I had not yet teamed up.) It didn't seem so hard to win major titles. I was on the South African Davis Cup team and life lay ahead, full of excitement and promise.

Abie had been right about the "French assholes" being born on clay. My opening match had alarmed me enough to make me scribble a somewhat frantic account of it on the flyleaves of the book I was reading at the time.

DIARY NOTES, ROLAND GARROS (FIRST DAY)

There I was, first round, court nine (in the jardin*), playing against a French player I'd never heard of, with a bald patch on his head, a bandage on his knee, and a tame-looking first service. When I asked about him in the locker room the attendant had shrugged and said, "Second catégorie!" waggling his open hand palm downwards and breaking a little wind with his lips the way the French do. Yet every time I came to net I had to lunge to survive. I'm used to lunging, but the score became 7-all, first set, and I was dying and getting nowhere!*

At 8-all, just as I got ready to serve and hurl myself netwards yet again, my unknown opponent suddenly held up his hand, walked up to the net, and pointed to his knee.

"I forfeit," he said pleasantly, "the knee is too unhealthy."

"You forfeit?" I asked, not believing my luck.

"Oui, forfeit!" he said, moving on to tell the umpire.

"Vous forfeit? Vous scratch? That's it? Finis?" I was so euphoric that even my French improved.

"You ween, Forbay," he said, still pleasantly. "You make

too many vollee. I have run thees way, that way, thees way . . ."
and he indicated all the ways he had to run and then pointed
at his knee, which looked to me in exactly the same condi-
tion as when we started.

"Terreeble!" I said, hurrying off the court. "You must see a
doctor—Il Doctore, which turned out to be Italian, as we'd
just played in Rome.

At the gate, Abie was waiting for me. He still had to play
his match against another French player who was ranked
above the one I'd just beaten.

"Beaten, my ass!" he said. "You have to be the luckiest
space cadet I've ever seen in my life!"

"Come on, Abie!" I replied, suddenly developing this
tremendous confidence. "The guy knew he had no chance!"

"You were hangin' by a friggin' thread, Forbsey!"

"When do you play your match?"

"Fourth match on court six. I think I'm just going to give
every ball a big crunch. These French guys mustn't think they
can mess with me. Fuck you, Forbsey!" He couldn't stand the
fact that I was off the hook. As we walked to the locker room
he said: "Who knows? Maybe my guy will turn up for the
match with a broken arm!"

On the way to watch Abie's match that day, Trevor Fancutt
(my friend and Davis Cup teammate) and I had come across
Art Larsen playing against Jean-Claude Molinari. Molinari was
by no means unheard of, and by the look of the churned-up
court and the state of the players, it was quite a major match.
Larsen, it seemed, was going through an experimental phase. It

would never have occurred to him that he might lose to Molinari, so he was trying out a game consisting of short angle chips to the backhand followed by long topspins to the forehand. In addition, he was playing a lot of the points with his chin tucked down to one side and the collar of his shirt clamped between his teeth.

"Why do you suppose he does that?" I asked Trevor.

"I suppose he just likes to bite his shirt," Trevor had replied, sensibly.

Every player had stories to tell about Larsen, especially Abie. He used to say that they should make Lacoste warm-up straight jackets especially for him.

Later on that afternoon, in the players' restaurant, I found Larsen playing poker, drinking a beer, and smoking a cigarette, so I asked him why he bit his shirt collar when he played. All he did was look puzzled.

"Who'd want to do a crazy thing like that?" he said, distracted by the meagre poker hand that Mervyn Rose had just dealt him.

The players' restaurant in those days was down a narrow stairway that led to a dungeonlike room with wood and iron chairs and tables, and an ancient bar with a coffee machine and piles of French loaves that got sliced in half and made into *"sandwich jambon, ou fromage,"* which, with Orangina, was standard prematch fare. Lunch was *steak-frites* or *omelette aux fines herbes*, and although we weren't too mad about the *fines herbes* it was almost impossible to get them removed. *Fines herbes* was what it said on the menu, and *fines herbes* was what you got. As there was no ventilation, the air in the place got thicker and thicker as the tournament progressed, so that by the second week you could virtually have a snack just by breathing. But no-one ever complained.

DIARY NOTES, 1993

How they have changed Roland Garros since we played here! It's become seriously splendid—but by some miracle manages to remain Roland Garros, with its concrete and its creepers and the patches of rich, red clay that are the courts. I have just been taken on a grand tour by Patrice Clerc (the tournament director), with Brian Tobin (head of the International Tennis Federation), his wife, Carmen, and Chris Gorringe (CEO of the All England Club, Wimbledon).

They've built a whole new show court complex, which is linked to the main stadium by a wide boulevard that runs between the rows of new clay courts. Around the new centre court is a veritable universe of facilities all supported by things Gastronomique, Alcoolique, and Historique. Patrice leads us through numberless restaurants and bars on the way to the players' facilities—clinics and training rooms, hair dressing and skin care, steam rooms, saunas, massage. The players' lounge is marvellous, a hundred games, videos, music, a counter with every kind of food, a fully equipped hospital, and a nursery for those with babies—equipped even for those who might just have babies on the spur of the moment.

After passing many bars Brian began to look longingly at the draught beer that was being tapped into long, frosty glasses. After all, it was hot and he is an Australian, and you

can't lead an Australian past too many glasses of draught beer
without giving him one! Finally, in the modern media center
with its hospitality lounge, we were all rewarded.

"That's more like it!" said Brian.

Mark McCormack has what he calls a "tent" in the botanical gardens across the road from the Stade. He has these tents at many of the world's great sporting events, but this one takes first prize. The other corporate sponsors have entertainment marquees inside the grounds of the Stade, but not McCormack. Somehow he has persuaded the French Authorities to let him use the lofty, hundred-year-old greenhouses of the Jardin Fleuriste Municipal to entertain his clients. You enter via a grand portal and make your way past waterways with tropical fish and varieties of palms and other flora until you get to the magical tent—luxury personified, with champagne and gourmet alimentation, and still more flora, and a carpet the exact colour of the clay on the centre court. The clients are as exotic as the plants—tennis players like Jim Courier or Martina Navratilova may wander in and nibble at the snacks, mingling with film stars and opera singers, the president of this, the sultan of that, or Herr Doctor Professor of some other important thing.

Strangely enough, the reserved way in which Mark behaves might even make you wonder whether it is, in fact, his tent. Rather, the proprietary air of the people who work for him might make you believe that it is their tent. Cino Marchese, for instance, or Eric Drossart, or Gavin Forbes, my son. Certainly when Bob Kain or Ian Todd is there it could easily be his tent—

but of course it isn't. It may take you some time to realize that in fact the whole thing, lock, stock, and barrel, belongs to Mark.

At this particular moment he is trying to find somewhere to open his mail. He gets so much mail that a few days' supply is often too heavy for one secretary to carry, so it has to arrive *en convoi.* Today the mail is housed in two Adidas tog bags, and he wanders about clutching his attaché case until he finds a wastepaper bin and a suitable, out-of-the-way sort of spot. Then he fetches the bags, settles down on a wicker settee, puts the bags at his feet, and creates a five-way filing system, if you count the waste bin as one of the files. File one is his pocket, which gets only the biggest, most amusing, or most secret deals; file two is his briefcase, already bulging with other deals; file three is a pile on the potted plant beside him; and file four is another pile at his feet. File five, the bin, receives the greatest volume of papers, but only after they have been scanned with eyes that never waver.

One of Mark's greatest attributes is his ability to set up "office" anywhere at all. Of course, he has formal offices all over the world, but he seems happiest when he's camping out. His powers of concentration are staggering and can apparently be turned on and off like a tap. He doesn't even seem to mind interruptions—like today, when I approach with a certain diffidence and he looks up and his face beaks into the sort of smile that speaks volumes; an "everything is O.K." sort of look that means you should sit down for a chat, although he also has another "don't bother me now" sort of look that means he would like to be left alone.

"Gordon! How've you been? Wait! I have something for you." He leafs through the papers in his briefcase and immediately pulls out a magazine article that I asked him for in a brief telephone conversation several months before. Not only has he remembered that I am coming, remembered our conversation, remembered to put the article into his briefcase, and remembered exactly where it was amongst his other papers— but he's also remembered what it's all about, and that at this moment he should give it to me! And the most sobering thing of all was that for a few moments I can no longer remember what it is I asked for, so that I had to look intelligent while I tried to read the heading upside down.

His remarkable memory and attention to detail have an unusual effect upon all people closely associated with him— that of making them feel that a) they have forgotten something, or b) they are about to forget something, or c) there is something they should know that they don't know, and any minute now it's going to arise.

But there is more to Mark than this. Volumes have been written about the one-time golfer who pioneered an entire industry now known as sports management; about the business called IMG (the International Management Group), an intricate, worldwide network that he runs from a filing system kept in his pocket; about McCormack, the author of books, the consummate speaker; about the life of travel, the love of sport and those who play the game; about the lifelong preoccupation with efficiency and the proper use of time. About his dislike of carelessness and his love of things associated with words like *brevity, quality, practicality, merit.*

For me, Mark is two separate people—one of them a man who knows the value of good friends, who likes philosophising over a glass of good wine, and who delights like other men in simple things—a funny joke, a Sunday lunch, a perfect passing shot, or the way a long putt curls in at the very last moment. The other Mark lives in a world entirely his own. No-one knows what thoughts and inclinations occupy that world, or what it is, when he gets there, that he thinks about or yearns for. All that we know is that he enters and leaves his other world quietly and without apparent effort, like someone moving in and out of a private and familiar room. Sometimes you would like to enter this other world with him—he might even like to take you—but that is not the way of things. You can't enter worlds that others have invented. A glimpse through an open door, a murmured phrase or two, is all that you might get. But to enter such a world you must find one of your own— and if you are able to, then you, too, will enter it alone, unable to take others with you. Only singular men possess these private worlds.

After a cup of coffee and a brief discussion about the game of tennis that we ought to play on Wednesday, I leave the tent and walk back to the Stade, and whom should I bump into but Torben Ulrich. He embraces me for a moment and I hear the familiar voice and see in my mind again the round-arm, swinging service, the profound poses, the deft volleys. There are dozens of things I want to ask him. How is his game? Does he still hang a tennis ball from the ceiling above his bed and look at it before he goes to sleep? Can he still sit on a grass court and levitate? And what about music? Whom should I be listening to? Does he still play the clarinet? As we talk I see, as if it were only yesterday, Torben walking on the court at Wimbledon to play a very young and eager Tony Roche; Tony getting ready to spin his racket, saying, "Would you like to call Mr. Ulrich?" And Torben saying, "You know, Tony, they say that you have a very beautiful service. I would like very much to see it, so why don't you serve first?"—and really meaning what he says!

In our world, you see, Torben was the ultimate seer—a true man of mystery. Everything he ever did, from hitting forehand volleys to catching planes at midnight, was unpredictable and somewhat enigmatic.

DIARY NOTES, 1956

Tonight at The Blue Note I sit next to Torben listening to the Bud Powell Trio. Kenny Clarke on drums and a French bass player. The place is dimlit and thick with smoke, and people listen carefully and murmur to each other over shoulders. The woman at the table next to me has an intense and naked face; a thick rope of dark hair pulled back; smoky breath; a coarse black shirt, carelessly open at the chest. (Wide shoulders, olive skin leading to a valley of slight movement.) An artist, for sure—and for a moment one is knocked silly by this hint of nakedness and the dark music. Torben listens in a semitrance, and sometimes writes in a notebook. He's unaware of anything except the plunging bass and the block chords that Bud Powell is playing:

I should care, I should go around weeping,
I should care, I should go without sleeping.

(Sometimes Torben whispers the chords, with his lips just moving the fine hairs of his beard.)

Strangely enough, I sleep well,
Except for a dream or two.
But, then, I count sheep well. . . .

(The tune unfolds like dark, silk cloth:)

Funny how sheep, will rock you to sleep. . . .

(resolves itself,)

Maybe I won't find someone,
As lovely as you.
I should care—and I do.

(and ends.)

"What do you write, Torben?" I ask him, conscious of the clang of reality that my question brings, and when he doesn't reply, I think he hasn't heard me. But he looks up at last and says:

"Some things, you know, some sounds, like these, cannot be written. Rather, perhaps, you could say that you should, well, listen only, and write of other things. This, you see, is life, and when you try to write of life it moves away, it moves away, to some other place."

Torben Ulrich, like McCormack, is a singular man.

ON CARAMEL-COLOURED

C O U R T S

Roland Garros! European clay! This velvet brickdust with its reddish hues (apricot, ochre, rust), forever changing with the dampness of the surface. Fundamental, organic, forgiving. A return to nature—to the very soul of tennis.

I have been reading a book called *A Brief History of Time* by the famous physicist Stephen Hawking. It deals with the quest for the unification of physics—a sort of Grand Theory of Everything (McCormack's also searching for it) that will link together all the forces in the universe. Abie says he sure hopes they find it soon, otherwise how will we manage?

Anyway, Werner Heisenberg's Uncertainty Principle is a key issue in this quest. Apparently, you can't measure the exact velocity and position of a particle at the same time. You have to solve the problem (that is, if you want to know exactly where a particle is) by predicting all the places it might be, then deciding which of them it's most likely to be in most of the time.

And that's the best you can do!

When I used to play someone like Manuel Santana on clay, and I came to net, say, on his forehand side, and he hit a passing shot, I, too, was not able to predict exactly where the ball (which reduced in size to about a particle anyway) would be at any given time. Had I known about the Uncertainty Principle then, I would have been able to predict all the places where the ball might be, decide which of these was the most likely one, and then lunge in that direction.

It follows that if you are a net-rusher, and you wish to play on clay, you should swot up on your Uncertainty Principle. This may avoid the kind of conversation that I once had with Martin Mulligan after he had beaten me 7-5 in the fifth in Hilversum.

"You really do rush the net on every point," he'd said as we shook hands.

"Yes, I suppose I do," I admitted.

"You really like to come to net on clay, do you?" he asked.

"Not very much," I said. "But staying back is even worse."

DIARY NOTES, PARIS, 1992

The special pass that Philipe Chatrier has arranged for me has upon it my photograph and the words NON JOUEUR, which in the logic of France is a very particular title: "Nonplayer"! A bit unkind, perhaps, but nonetheless the title written on the passes of those very close to the players themselves—parents, coaches, family, etc.—and best described in Anglo-Saxon terms as one who is (or was) "very nearly a player," which in my case is perhaps closer to the truth than I would like to admit!

Whatever the logic, the pass allowed me virtually to roam about the Stade at will—and the freedom it afforded was sheer luxury. There is nothing as devastating as facing the cold-eyed guards at the Porte Susan Lenglen without a ticket to get inside. Or standing waiting outside the competitors' enclosure that at one time was one's own private place. But as a NON JOUEUR I was able to pass unchallenged through even the very exclusive gate opposite McCormack's tent, to find myself inside the area of the Stade reserved for the corporate elite and their luxury marquees.

The ultramodern number-one court stadium now stands where the two shady garden courts used to be—where I played against the unknown Frenchman with the sore knee all those years ago. You skirt the circular structure and pass a row of promotional stands and booths before reaching the mall that gives access to the outside courts. Glance at any of them and you find matches in various stages of progress, names from computer lists suddenly materialising into flesh and blood— Oncins versus Karbacher, Reneberg versus Prpic, Volkov versus Vajda, Gustafsson versus Krajicek—each one of them intense, personal little dramas generating their own force fields of emotion.

On court eleven I come across Niki Pilic, watching doubles. Niki is one of those older players who has hardly changed at all. Some of the older players have tended to go somewhat to seed (a few seem already even to have been harvested), but not Niki. He still has the cool, noble air that somehow enabled him to look down on all opponents, even the few who were taller than he was. And he still discards all the small words of the English language as being quite unnecessary. Now he is watching a German player called Michael Stich, whom at that time I had only just heard of, and I sit down on the stand next to him.

"Hello, Niki," I say.

"Forty-thirty he make stupid double fault," he grumbles, as though the years for which we haven't seen each other have melted away to nothing. "Look, what he does," Pilic is saying, "now he talk to linesman. It's not linesman who serve double, it's Stich!" He frowns briefly then brightens up.

"How are you, Forbey?" he asks. "And how is backhand? Still puff powder, like always?" In a flash all the old images are reestablished.

"Same as it was at Forest Hills, Niki," I say. We had a mammoth match there in the 1962 U.S. Open, and I scraped through in five sets.

"Lucky, Forbey. Lucky match for you."

We are both silent for a moment, remembering. The world of the tennis player—a moment in time suddenly recalled—relived, reappraised, a common language, once learned, never forgotten.

Amongst other things Niki is now a high-powered coach, advising the German Davis Cup team with his mixture of discipline, wisdom, and disdain. ("They still young. Have lot to learn. Take life too easy. Rather have bath bubbles and massage than practise make volley.") Now we watch Michael Stich—before, mind you, he has reached the semis of the French, won Wimbledon, and become a superstar; while he is still a young hopeful, fluid and loose-limbed, awash with talent, but only one of at least a hundred others jockeying for position.

"Look, look!" cries Niki, "he hits ball going in back fence! Leave long balls, I say him hundred times. He still takes. Bad habit. Not way win matches."

"Shouldn't be that much of a problem," I say carelessly. I used to be a very good leaver of balls that were going out—in fact, now that I think back, it was about the only thing that I did as well as the players of today.

"It problem," Pilic is saying. "He should have rank higher. In Sweden last week he serve for match. Thirty-all he volley ball hitting back fence, then match ball they call him footfault. Still young. Must learn. But I explain him: 'To learn this way cost money. You don't care about money, you go ahead, take long balls.' "

Which settles that question.

"How do you say 'Stich'?" I ask him idly.

"Schteeccch," he says, sounding like the top coming off a bottle of soda water.

"It's actually easier to say 'Stich' the English way," I say, off guard, "you know, like in knitting. When you drop a stitch."

"But Stitch not name of this player," says Niki ruthlessly. "Anyway, easier for German people say 'Schteeccch' than learn knitting."

So much for Pilic—for the time being, anyway. With him you never know. He may easily crop up in this book again, especially if I come upon him in conversation with, say, someone like Cliff Drysdale—if you can call the exchanges that take place between them "conversations." Often they just pass each other on the way from somewhere to somewhere like crusty old warships, trading salvos of insults that bounce harmlessly off the armour plates of their egos without doing the slightest bit of damage. Just the other day, for example, Fred Stolle and Cliff, on their way to make their daily television commentary, happened to pass Pilic on his way to dispense another installment of wisdom to the German Davis Cup team.

It may have been Pilic who started things by suggesting that Fred and Cliff, also playing together in the veterans' invitation doubles, must by now be so old and useless that it was surprising that they could even get from locker room to court, let alone "play match when get there," finishing off by advising them both to "sell racket, buy rocking chair."

Cliff and Fred replied by having a little conversation between themselves.

Cliff: "Pilic used to play for some communist country, didn't he?"

Fred: "But in those days they only had two players, and neither of them could play worth a heap a—you know that stuff you're always talking while the young guys are trying to play tennis?"

Cliff: "We both talk that all the time, Fred, but Pilic's game isn't worth a heap of it anyway."

Pilic: "If my game heap like this, your game heap like that"—using his hands to demonstrate the extent of the heaps before walking off contemptuously to find his team.

In the notebook I kept in my pocket that week I find these brief images of Roland Garros:

In the foyer of the Tribune International, Richard Evans is chuckling about the remarks of the new young Russian sensation, Andrei Medvedev. At seventeen he is remarkably mature and bright, with this impish sense of humour. Asked by the press what his game plan for a given match was, he replies thus:

"I decide to lose first set to find out what *his* game plan is!"

Often his answers seem quite off the cuff, but carry signs of remarkable perception. Having beaten Kevin Curren, almost twice his age and ranked much higher than he, he says that he had nothing to lose.

"All I have to do is play tennis against another guy playing tennis! I look at the ball. When I look at the ball I don't see face of opponent, so I don't see Curren."

He is tall, and growing steadily taller. "Look at-a the feet!" says Cino Marchese, his agent. "Special shoes. You cannot-a buy bigger shoes. The next size after this is-a luggage!"

On court three, as I pass, Anke Huber, the latest German superwoman, is methodically bombarding with forehands and backhands a tiny, dark-haired girl, who frantically scurries about the court talking to herself, to the gods, to the umpire, and to her coach. She seems to be all energy and no mass, like a sort of miniature black hole. But Huber is too strong, too methodical, too determined.

Farther along, on the practise courts at the end of the little back-court mall, Jim Courier is rallying with Brad Stine. There are few things in sport as intriguing as watching at close range a master technician working on his game. From the courtside his skills are startling—new levels of power and accuracy, precision of movement, impacts of racket on ball like gunshots, and a concentration almost trancelike at times.

On the court next door, the Yugoslavian girl, Iva Majoli, practises with her brother while the whole family watches avidly. Back and forth goes the ball, an endless repetition of strokes like a musician practising scales. Is it not, one wonders, too mechanical? Where has all the artistry gone? But then one remembers Monica Seles and her machinelike precision and wonders whether, in this modern tennis, there is room any longer for such things as artistry. "Skills!" the experts say. "Practise skills. Play the court and not the player."

"Yes, but come and look at this girl play tennis!"

My son Gavin is standing beside me. He takes my arm and leads me to another practise court. "She's still young, Dad. But she could easily become another Graf. Easily! You won't believe how well she hits the ball!"

We have stopped to watch a tall, blonde girl of slender yet robust form. Long legs of an athlete, thick coil of fair hair tied back, and the ageless face of a woman. It takes only a minute or two to recognise a restless, almost scary talent of unlimited potential, and now, watching her, I have the same feeling that I remember when Harry Hopman first took me to watch a very young Rod Laver.

"Who is she?" I ask.

"Her name," replies Gavin, "is Mary Pierce. She's only seventeen."

From the food stalls on the parapet behind court eleven, odours of crêpes, waffles, coffee come drifting down amongst the players and spectators, mingling, it seems, with the calls of the umpire, with the flow of shots back and forth, with the very clay of the courts themselves. Again the word *edible* occurs to me, describing this tennis, these caramel-coloured courts, the spectators with their waffles and their *cornets de fraise!*

Next door, Italian Paolo Cane is playing doubles with Jimmy Arias against somebody and somebody. I like watching Cane because he seems constantly to seethe. As I glance across he is in the grip of some recent deed that he obviously considers to be an absolutely major fiasco, for he suddenly has a full-blown Italian fit. His face goes maniacal, as though an intense pressure has suddenly built up inside him and there is no single act that he can think of that will relieve it. He looks heaven-wards, earthwards, takes a mighty breath, and then emits a long and massive bellow during the course of which his face is directed through 180 degrees until he is bellowing upwards at the very gods themselves. It is so violent that even Arias stag-gers back. But the paroxysm vanishes as quickly as it came, like a dust devil blowing across the court, and having exorcised the evil, Cane plays on quite happily.

On the centre court, an uneasy Steffi Graf is playing Arantxa Sanchez-Vicario. They have become almost set pieces, these matches between the top-ranked players, instantly recog-nisable. The regal, willowy form of Graf, the long legs made even longer today by a small, plain, wraparound skirt. Such easy movement, such supple power! Such flanks! My God! One look at her and you see at once the ultimate combination of femininity and athletic perfection.

And Sanchez-Vicario, stocky, cheerful, happily absorbed in

her world of forehands and backhands, tucking the spare ball into a little holder behind her back and ever glancing up to where her family is watching. "How'm I doing, how'm I doing?" ask the Spanish eyes. Modern players need off-court inspiration far more than we did. Then, you just kept your head down and talked to yourself!

So we settle down on the *court central* to watch Jim Courier play Andre Agassi in the *"demi-final des simples messieurs."* The court is packed and the air charged with expectations. Our seats are in the special boxes reserved for friends of players competing on the centre court. The boxes are positioned side by side and across the aisle from one another in the very front of the players' enclosure. I'm in the Courier box, at the end of the little row that forms his support team. Across the aisle from me is the Agassi contingent.

The reason that I am able to sit at so elevated a point of vantage is that Gavin Forbes now works in the McCormack organisation and is Courier's friend and manager. Sitting next to Gavin are Brad Stine and Jose Higueras, Courier's coaches. It is a sunny day. Higueras, as usual, is dressed in tennis gear, as though he is about to play a match himself, and he has on his face the inscrutable expression that he always uses for watching Courier's matches.

Gavin's eyes are alight with excitement. "Mentally," he says to me out of the side of his mouth, "Jim is too strong. He knows he can win. And that, I think, is the bottom line in this match." In this modern, constantly shifting tennis world, the "bottom line" of almost anything is a very rare commodity.

"In every match," adds Brad Stine, also out of the side of his mouth. He has picked up on mental strength and bottom lines. At moments like these the sense of tension and intrigue is so strong that everyone behaves in a conspiratorial way, jotting things down, whispering cryptic thoughts sideways into loyal ears, or making mysterious hand signs to invisible people located somewhere else.

But Higueras remains aloof. Higueras, the practical one, the technician. He frowns slightly, looks at his feet, his mouth moving as he chews away at whatever it is he chews, his thoughts his own. Having been a top-ten player himself, he knows exactly the tenuous nature of high-level matches like these. He is unquestionably the leader of the team and has about him a sort of detachment that contains just the right measures of confidence, athleticism, coolness, wisdom, technique, toughness, and severity that are necessary, amongst other things, to counter the psychological effects of rival coaches. Tennis matches these days are not only the on-court encounters of player versus player. On the sidelines there are also the subtle undercurrents, the whispered perceptions, the covert mental battles of coach versus coach.

Just behind us somewhere, avoiding the limelight, quiet and watchful in his private world, is Father Joe Dispensa.* He is Courier's adviser and confidant—a round little man who was once a psychologist, before deciding to devote his life to the God that he loves. There is something a little mysterious about

---

* Not long after this event Father Joe died, and the news was received by all with the greatest sadness.

Father Joe—some force that moves between him and Courier that only the two of them share. They talk quietly before Jim's matches, but neither will tell what they say.

Sports psychologists or "mental coaches," as they are called, have become popular amongst some of the top players these days. They certainly seem to know everything, these would-be oracles—have absolutely mastered the subliminal, are experts on such things as positive thinking and inner fortitude. The fact that very few of them have ever played a match, have ever known the pressures, the subtle mental agonies, the ever-rising tensions, does not seem to faze them. They always have a glib answer, and there are always people ready to listen.

Father Joe doesn't fit this description at all. There is a calmness about him that suggests other things—spiritual strength, unspoken confidence, something to do with God, perhaps, although he never talks of God. Stealing a look at his serene face, though, one feels that he has firm control of the divine side of things. If the Lord is to intervene in this semifinal—and one wonders secretly whether He ever really gets involved in semifinals—one has the feeling that Jim's case will have been well presented.

Across the aisle from me the Agassi team presents a quite different—but nonetheless formidable—picture. Nick Bollettieri sets the scene in his luminous warm-ups, midnight blue glasses, a burnished tan, a street-smart awareness, a shrewdness that leaks into his every word and gesture. Nick, too, acts like he knows everything, but then you forgive and accept him because he really knows the game—has seen it all, has served his time.

Gathered around him is Agassi's array of specialist coaches. Most of them seem to have names like Phil or Gil, and they are no less inscrutable than the Maestro himself. The strength coach is a fiercely muscular man, while the technical coach shifts in his seat, either sitting on his hands or cupping them around his mouth and shouting, "Waytogo! Andre, letsdoitnow!" very quickly, as though in this way his words will follow a straight and private path between him and his player.

Collectively the team is impressive in a somewhat eerie sort of way. A kind of sporting Mafioso comes to mind, adding yet another vital force to the electricity that seems to charge the air.

The players have been hitting up streams of perfectly struck clay-court strokes, and now they are ready to begin. The crowd breaks into applause and one hears snatches of the random phrases that float about before such matches:

"Courier hits the ball too heavy . . . both sides. . . ."

"Andre's going to make him play the short angles. . . ."

"The first set's the whole match . . . Jim has to start good. . . ."

"This will be the fourth time they've played in the French. . . ."

This last is, of course, true. Of the first three encounters, Courier has won two, including his memorable win in the final last year. And so again it will be a conflict in two realms—the visible battle on the court and the intriguing, invisible mental undertow.

Sometimes in conflicts like these, a mental command of the match by one of the players is established in the very early stages.

I remember in 1978 sitting high in the concrete bleachers of Roland Garros at the beginning of the final between Bjorn Borg and Guillermo Vilas. Here were two of the best clay-court players of all time, similar in technique and approach, pitted against one another in the final of the French Championships, unquestionably the world's greatest clay-court event. Even now I remember the dramatic moment as the players appeared, the tangible weight of pride, reputation, competition—the feeling that an unstoppable force was about to meet an immovable object.

The court surface was immaculate. Its damp, creamy clay was brushed to such perfection that each footprint left by the players as they warmed up was etched into the surface. By the time they were ready to begin the first point, the centre of the court on both sides had the familiar scuff marks of the warm-up. I've forgotten who it was that served first, but it really doesn't matter. On the first point the ball crossed the net over fifty times and eventually it was Vilas who faltered, hitting one of his heavy forehands with too much topspin so that it dragged itself into the net. When Vilas finally lost the first game, it seemed only the beginning. The crowd sighed and settled down, preparing themselves for a mammoth battle.

But there came a slight change in the attitude of Vilas—a thoughtful sort of pause, a fractional adjustment, perhaps, in the lift of his head; and when you looked down at the court surface, you could literally see the path of the match, graphically marked out in the clay. On Borg's side the slide marks of his feet were contained in an area behind the baseline more or less between the doubles tramlines. On Vilas's side, the marks were spread out to cover the entire court, some of the wider ones almost touching the courtside boxes.

The match lasted for several hours, and Borg won 6-1, 6-1, 6-3. But you had the feeling that Vilas was merely going through the motions. In his mind the championships were lost to him, gone forever with the inner realisations made in that very first point.

In most matches, though, the struggle for supremacy is by no means settled early on. Rather, they become balanced on a knife edge, the physical skills stretched to the limit by ever-present mental tensions that envelop the entire match with an invisible force as tangible as a cut of stretched silk.

Such were the musings going through my head that day at Roland Garros when Jim Courier took the balls to serve the first point to Andre Agassi. Although Courier won by the apparently overwhelming score of 6-3, 6-2, 6-2, if you had asked him about it afterwards he would have told you that it had been a very close match. The long game at 3-all in the first set, the little cross-court angle to end it that had hung for an instant on the tape of the net, the 2-0 lead that Agassi had in the second, a point here, a line call there, all the little things that could so easily have made a difference. The sly mischief of tennis!

When the match is over we all walk back towards McCormack's tent, talking about Courier's tennis. Gavin and Brad are openly elated, and even Higueras smiles. I walk beside Father Joe, and we are carried slowly by the crowd out of the players' enclosure, past the tribunes, down the steps at court three, past the *maison de la presse*, the boutique Roland Garros, and the cafés under the trees near the Place des Mousquetaires; past the Pierre Barthes booth and the tent village with its extravagant marquees—Cinzano, Lacoste, Perrier, Peugot, etc., where the wealthy people have champagne and caviar and talk of the matches:

"Leconte can ween against Korda? Maybe, maybe, burt zey are bose a leetle craz*ee, oui?*" and foreheads are tapped while more champagne is accepted with a "yes, O.K., but jurst a lee-tle." It is all very cool and polished.

Father Joe is skeptical about this opulent world. "You know, Gordon, I don't really like all this," he says, the wave of his hand indicating everything—the pompous officials in the president's box, the godlike young players, the endless talk of money, deals, contracts made, contracts broken, the hype, the hurry, the constant jostling for a place in the sun, the constant feeding of insatiable egos.

"It's not a world I really like to live in," Father Joe is saying. "None of it is real. I tell this to Jim. He should not be fooled by all these things. Being good at tennis, being rich, doesn't mean that you've changed, become a better person. It means only that you are good at tennis. And if being good at tennis makes you into a big shot, then there is no sense to it. I don't like this world," he says again, "but I put up with it. I'm not going to do anything to end it. I put up with it because I know that there is a so much better place waiting for me"—another gesture, this time vaguely upwards.

Before this, we have talked about the role he plays.

"But what do you tell your players?" I ask. What I really want to know is what he tells Jim, but I feel that asking too directly might be an intrusion. At first he is silent. It is obviously too wide a subject.

"I tell them that if they wish me to work with them they have to follow one part of my advice exactly," he says at last. "They have to behave properly. I cannot work with people who can't control their feelings. One shouldn't misbehave in sport. It is not proper. And besides, it gives too much away. It tells your opponent what you are feeling. You have to be serene, composed. 'Own the court,' I tell them, 'it is your court. But only to play tennis on!' Owning a court for a while does not mean you own the world!"

We pass through the exit of the Stade on the way back to McCormack's tent, and the gatemen eye us with suspicion, this thin man and his roly-poly companion with their NON JOUEUR badges. Little do they know that—for the moment, anyway—we have achieved a superior tranquillity!

THE CAFÉS OF

PLACE PIGALLE

DIARY NOTES, PARIS, 1956

Sure enough, last night the wall above my bed began to fall over. I've had no problems with walls for quite a while now, so in a way it had to happen. ("And with French walls, a man can never be too sure," said Abie.) I had to use my left arm and shoulder to push the wall back into place, and in doing so felt a distant twinge of pain. This morning we had a practise court at the Racing Club de France, and everything was fine until I practised some serves. Then I found that I had injured a muscle in my left arm, and couldn't toss the ball up to serve.

Abie was disgusted. "Jesus Christ, Forbsey," he said. "You're the only guy in the world who could pull a muscle in his throwin'-up-ball arm!"

Abie used to think that "The French," as he called them,

were all mad. (They in turn retaliated by thinking the same about him.) A lot of the little things they did worried him. Even the way they looked at him sometimes made him edgy. I have so many memories of Abie and his skirmishes with France that it is hard to choose the best example. One day, however, I remember, he had a specific complaint.

"Anyone," he said to me, "who sticks all those small letters into one word can't be too normal."

"Vowels," I ventured.

"Right, vowels," he said. "Take that place we had to catch the train to, that place near the courts. . . ."

"Porte d'Auteuil," I ventured again.

"Right, Auteuil," he said. "A man can pull a muscle in his tongue just asking for a ticket."

Auteuil is one exit before St. Cloud, another Porte that Abie had a running battle with.

"Sangcloo!" he used to say with disgust. "That's French for you, Forbsey. Their words never actually end. Like this other Pont they got goin'. This de Sevres. You start out great and then it just kind of peters out and leaves you nowhere!"

By the time we arrived in Paris Abie and I had played in Rome and Barcelona, so that a few Italian and Spanish words had become lodged in our heads. These Abie simply added to his sketchy French vocabulary, unleashing the resulting verbal conglomerate on any unsuspecting Frenchman who crossed his path. His broad philosophy was that while in Europe, any language that wasn't English would do, so that some of his utterances were nothing short of spectacular.

That afternoon he had nearly been late for our doubles

match, bursting into the locker room at the eleventh hour, tearing off his clothes and pulling on his tennis gear all at the same time.

"I'm on this Left Bank," he told me with his head through his shirt, "and I've got these three things happening—I'm hungry, I've got to have a haircut, and I've got to get to the courts at three for our match. So I sit down at this little café and I ask them for a chicken sandwich and where I can find a coiffeur, and they bring me a glass of wine.

"So I think maybe the wine comes with the sandwich (who knows with these French?), so what the hell, it's only a small glass and I drink it, and then I see the guy at the next table gettin' my sandwich and he's goin' crazy because he's expectin' wine. So you think all that's so easy to sort out?

"So finally I get the sandwich and then I ask the waiter how long it will take me to get to Sangcloo and he brings me more wine. In this France a man can go for a haircut and end up smashed in a different part of town!"

After all that we had gone out to play Merlo\Woodcock on court *deux*. By coincidence we had played them several times that year. I had always felt that a doubles combination consisting of Beppe Merlo and Warren Woodcock was "passing strange," and as usual, Abie clarified the matter.

"It has to be a complete fuck-up," he said as we made our way to the court. "The two worst friggin' serves in the history of tennis. Woodcock hits himself on the head and Merlo tosses the ball up like he's suddenly gone queer! They have to play together because no-one else will play with them!"

The match was like a coconut shy. We were able to have a

free tee-off on every serve. Abie's forehand got going in the second set and virtually bowled them over. After the match Woodcock told us in an injured tone that Merlo had told him (Woodcock) not to come to net behind his service.

"Better you-a serve and we both run-a back-a-wards!" he'd advised.

"I would rather come to net behind my serve than come to net behind your serve, Beppe," Woodcock had replied.

"What a friggin' choice!" cried Abie. "Imagine comin' to net behind serves like that! I'd rather stay in the garment industry!"

Finally they'd ended up playing us from the baseline, but that didn't work either.

"As a team," said Woodcock, "we're much better at poker."

For those who have inside them something of the muse, there is no city quite like Paris. Every new scene reflects some memory—a continuing déjà vu that never fails to quicken the imagination.

For instance, now, in 1992, I sit watching Leconte playing Korda on the centre court ("Henri! Henri! Henri!" chants the ecstatic French crowd) and straightaway I hear echoes from another time. This is the same court, after all, that Abe and I walked onto in 1962 to play the doubles final against Emerson and Santana. It's probably still the same clay! Some of it must be the same—they say that matter is indestructible. And these are the same stands, the same concrete balustrades, though now they have plastic chairs instead of the rough concrete benches that we'd had to sit on.

My reverie continues while down below they're having

spectacular clay-court rallies. ("Henri! Henri! Henri!") There used to be something about those concrete benches, I remember—not the actual benches themselves so much as the limbs of some of the girls who sat on them. Sleek female limbs on rough concrete benches—that was it!

Sometimes the men-about-town of the circuit such as Phillipe Washer, Nicola Pietrangeli, Budge Patty, or Beppe Merlo, who owned such things as sports cars and money clips holding crisp franc notes, would arrive escorting exotic town women all dressed to kill in Chanel suits, with glimpses of lace underwear and stockings, rampant Paris haircuts and portable clouds of perfume that followed them wherever they went. I would listen to the musical French murmurs while observing the silk-covered thighs appear even more fragile set off against the brutal texture of the concrete.

It was virtually impossible for us colonials to find that sort of woman in Paris. Even Abie had difficulty applying his customary tactics of surprise, shock, paralysis, and, finally, capitulation.

"It's all these friggin' vowels!" he used to complain. "A man has to do the best he can makin' signs and sendin' smoke signals!"

For me, talking to strange women in English was bad enough—to use smoke signals was unthinkable. I had to be content with trying to impress the women tennis players—not that there was anything wrong with them, just that they wore tennis gear and ordinary talcum powder and almost never moved about in private clouds of perfume and mysterious silken underclothes. Besides which, tennis romances were wholesome, sporting affairs, while the getups of the town girls hinted at something quite different, something that we could not define but that often made Trevor Fancutt and me want to do urgent and unusual things.

Sometimes, in the grip of these powerful urges, we would take the Metro to Place Pigalle and make cautious little forays into the twilight of its bars and cafés. In those days the seediness of Pigalle was gentle, the small streets dimly lit, the doorways emitting licentious smells and quick with the movements of women of the night. The coffee bars sold rich, creamy coffee at a few pennies a cup, and there were bookshops with improper literature where you could browse undisturbed, rivetted by pictures of unfamiliar anatomy. The Paris escapades of Henry Miller, banned everywhere else, fascinated us, providing the inspiration for the odd moments when we tried to emulate his lifestyle.

These moments took place in another bar we had found, and where we would often finally end up. There, after getting used to us, the girls were languidly friendly behind their sometimes alarming arrangements of makeup. On our first visit they nuzzled up as usual, their hands interfering with our persons, their smoky voices asking for drinks and trying to make deals.

"But we are poor tennis players!" we would say, à la Miller, and Trevor would use his well-known technique of pulling the linings out of his trouser pockets to prove their emptiness. When they got to know that we really were, in fact, poor tennis players, but nonetheless were playing at Roland Garros, they tended to become friendly and protective, trying to persuade the surly bartenders to give us free drinks, and sometimes even succeeding. We'd sit together and talk in Segalesque mixtures, and when real customers came in the girls would ask us what we thought, and wink when they left for the little rooms upstairs and again when they came back down.

"*Très ordinaire,*" they might say, "*très bourgeois!* Razzer we 'ave a young tennees playeur. Burt eef ze playeur 'ave no murnee, zen what murst we do?" and shrug like only French girls can shrug.

We would save up like mad for the odd special occasion, and once, on a slow night, we persuaded a girl called Colette (what else?) to return temporarily to the ranks of the amateur, which she did with the utmost cheerfulness, in the process giving us some telling instructions. Biological coaching, I remember, is what Trevor called it. "She improved our short game," he said with his careful smile.

In return for her hospitality we invited Colette to Roland Garros one afternoon to watch the tennis. To our alarm she accepted, and sat between Trevor and me on the concrete benches, and when we walked amongst the outside courts she walked between us, linking arms. In the light she was taller and thinner and whiter than we had expected her to be, and her eyes were made very big by the way she had done them up. But she watched the tennis quite happily, clapping her hands in slight mystification when the rallies ended, and smiling and chatting away. Somehow, though, we got the feeling that we were being looked at sideways. There was something about Colette's mystery and cloud of perfume that made us feel a bit furtive. Even the lunch we bought her was suspect, as though her thin, white hands, her red nails and lips, were not used to dealing with such lusty things as foot-long *sandwiches jambons.* ("Although, who knows?" said Trevor. "She ate it, didn't she?")

"Who was that girl, Gordie?" asked the South African girls when finally, to our great relief, Colette had left to "go back to work," and Trevor and I had collapsed and were mentally fanning ourselves.

The South African women players were like sisters to us. Sandra Reynolds and Renee Schuurman in particular—two of the incomparable women of tennis, graceful, gentle, female through and through, with tennis games designed by Pete on one of His on-days. Above all they had an innocence and charm that was irresistible. Colette had obviously amazed them.

"Who was she?" they persisted. "Where did you *find* her?"

"Just a sort of a girl," I replied lamely, adding something about her being the daughter of one of my mother's father's sister's children—desperately needing credibility but at the same time putting into it as much ancestral distance as I could, just in case.

Such thoughts continued to invade my head as I watched Leconte and Korda and listened the French fans becoming ever more fervent about their hero ("Henri! Henri! Henri!").

DIARY NOTES, PARIS, 1992

Finally the weather has returned Paris to us. I open the drapes of my window in the Hotel La Fayette Concorde, and there it is, fine and warm, bathed in misty sunlight after days of overcast weather. On the left is the hazy Arc, with the avenues going off into the city like the spokes of a wheel. On the right is the Bois. Immediately below, a great snarl-up of traffic, with the cars on the periphery moving like a river of ants.

In that sort of mood again, I take the Metro at Maillot, direction Château des Vincennes. Every station name brings back memories. Trocadero, La Muette, Ranelagh, Jasmin, on the way to Roland Garros; Courcelles, Monçeau on the way to Galleries Lafayette—names like old friends. Today I emerge at Place Clemençeau and walk over the bridge again to test it in the sunlight. In the gardens on the far side they're cutting the grass and spreading compost, and these smells, together with the diesel fumes and the thin sausages grilling in the sidewalk kiosk, are yet another small breath of Paris.

On the way back I disembark at George V and walk towards Étoile, for this is the part of Paris we used to know best. The Bistro Romain on the Champs Elysées, with its red awnings and potted conifers, still offers a plate du jour. *On the corner of the Rue Balzac is the place where Fancutt and I used to stand to observe another group of girls, trying to decide whether we ought to do something about them. Farther up, near Étoile, there is a whole warren of narrow streets where we used to live in small hotels. They'd have coatracks in the lobbies, these hotels, and little tables for the* café complete. *Rue des Acacias. Rue Tilsitt, Avenue Wagram, the Venus club\bar, Café d'Angel, le petit Marches, Hotel Regina, Elysées Star. Restaurant Vancouver. Shadows of the past flicker through the mind, all the carefree laughter, the youth, the lovely reaches of* *time that lay ahead.*

Every evening in these small streets we would gather on the sidewalks outside our hotels to discuss the important question of where and what to eat. It became a matter of prestige to know which bistros gave the best deals. Abie refused to become party to these events, muttering things about "peasants" and "showin' a bit of class" and taking Heather off to more extravagant places.

But then he had his "shippers," and we had to make do on "expenses"—in Paris about fifty dollars for the two weeks. So evening meals were grave financial considerations.

"How about," Trevor might say, "vegetable soup, a *steak-frites* with *petit pois*, fruit salad and a glass of *lait frais* for seventy francs? Is that or isn't that a deal?" (Seventy old francs—about a dollar.)

"At the Restaurant Sylvano you get the same for sixty-five and they put an egg on top of the steak," Vermaak might say. For Ian, a fried egg on top of a steak worked all kinds of physical wonders.

"But it's a thinner steak," Jean might add.

"A much thinner steak," Renee would confirm.

One evening Torsten Johannsen, the wily Swede, listened to this discussion with a twinkle in his eye, then finally said: "How about soup, a thick steak, peas and chips, fruit salad, and ice cream, bread and coffee, for fifty-five francs?"

"Where?!" we chorused.

"I dunno, but it's cheap!" he said, hugging his joke to himself.

Occasionally, though, we ended up at better restaurants.

DIARY NOTES

*Always this question of food! Today Abie and Budge Patty
had a discussion in the competitors' stand. Abie was hungry
and going on about sandwiches and meatballs. They were
watching Ramanathan Krishnan playing Boro Jovanovic, and
between points Patty argued that there actually were other
foods in Paris besides hamburgers and meatballs. Eventually,
to prove his point, he'd taken us to this restaurant, where,
when we got there, he muttered something to the headwaiter
and was given a table. Patty speaks French.*

*After the waiter explained everything, Abie, wanting the
plate du jour, caused the first stir by ordering the pas de deux.
Then, when it didn't immediately arrive, he accosted the
waiter and said: "Hey, Camerera! Per favore! Before uno hom-
bre dies! That is, if it's not too molto trouble! Subito la man-
giare. Chop-a chop!"*

*"You must excuse my friend here," said Patty wearily. "He
speaks only Italian."*

*To keep Abie quiet they brought a few small, pielike
objects, which he put in his mouth and swallowed. "What's
happening, Budge?" he asked. "Why are they givin' us these
samples?"*

And then the question of Don Candy, who had a habit of
simply inventing people whenever he needed them.
Sometimes, on the outside courts, you would find him talking
to an empty chair where a linesman should have been, then
turning to the umpire and saying, "This man is blind! You
must remove him!" or some such remark, which of course led

to all kinds of conversations, one of them recounted in *A Handful of Summers*.

Sometimes Don would arrive at the restaurant of the evening apparently alone, but having with him a mysterious, invisible companion whom he would talk to, ushering him through the door and even pulling out a chair for him.

"Nice little spot," he would say to the chair. *"Très simple.* Now. What are you going to have? The *poule au pot du chef*? Good thinking. I'll stick with the *steak-frites.* Better for the legs. The legs, do you see?"

We would all quiet down to listen to Candy talking to his invisible friend—usually either his private eye, Sam Shovel, or someone he called "Harvey" after the character in the James Stewart film.

"There I was," he might say, "sitting in my private office, putting some private drops in my private eye, and giving some private notes to my private secretary, Effie. Suddenly a tall blonde passed my window. I knew she was tall because my room's on the second floor. Suddenly my first case came up. I drank it. . . . Your steak all right? Too raw, is it? Can't cook, the French. No idea. Not a clue. . . ." He had a limitless range.

On one occasion he arrived alone. There were no free tables, so the waitress showed him to a free seat at a small table opposite a dapper little Frenchman who was drinking wine and eating oysters through a hole in his large beard. We all watched transfixed. It was really only a matter of time. After regarding the man gravely for a little while, Don gathered himself together in the very chatty way he had.

"Candy," he said, tapping himself on the chest. "Australienne.

Joueur. Tennees. Stade Roland Garros." He played a backhand in the air.

The Frenchman looked up briefly with a very small nod.

"Championatts de France," said Candy, comfortably, playing a few more shots, one of them a drop volley.

Another small nod.

"Good forehand!" went on Donald cheerfully, demonstrating. "*Très bien*. Bad backhand. Safest to lob on that side. *Lob*, vous comprendre?" Another demonstration. "*Une très* high lob." His eyes would follow the lob up to the ceiling and back, then he'd turn to his companion again. "Just missed. How are the oysters? *Très bien*, are they?"

An even smaller nod. We would hold our breaths in delight. No-one was able to come up with more original utterances than Candy.

DIARY NOTES, ROLAND GARROS, 1984

Today, from the GreenSet courtside box, I watched what could possibly be some of the most magical clay-court tennis ever played. For two sets John McEnroe controlled his final against the great Ivan Lendl as though the match was a puppet show with McEnroe working the strings. Never could there be a mixture so elusive—deftness, touch, the use of spin; and of course the quick, dangerous power. While under McEnroe's spell Lendl was helpless. He could do nothing. But the potion weakened with time, and ever so slowly Lendl was allowed to enter the match. His rhythm returned, his big groundshots got going.

Finally I was to hear an example of McEnroe's on-court

dialogues with linespeople and umpires. McEnroe, up at net, made a sharp, angled volley that left a mark very close to the sideline.

The linesman, who had his nose virtually touching the court (heaven knows why they have to get down so very low), gave a great cry of out!!! and threw his arm so far out to the side that he nearly fell off his chair.

McEnroe stopped with the sort of faraway, long-suffering, intensely weary, almost trancelike look of pain that he some-times gets. He looked up at the sky, into the distance, down at his shoes, back up at the sky. Then he walked up to the net with his racket pointed at the linesman and said to the umpire: "What did he say?"

"He called 'out,'" said the umpire, shifting in his seat.

"Why did he call out?"

"The ball was out."

"Are you sure it was out?"

"Yes," said the umpire, although you could see that he was starting to have doubts.

"Ask him to look at the mark?"

The umpire said something to the linesman, who sullenly replied.

"He says there are many marks."

"Tell him that for people with eyes, there is only one mark."

McEnroe walked over and made a circle round the mark, then pointed his racket back at the linesman and the finger of his other hand at the umpire. "The mark is on the line!"

"Please continue."

"This is a big point. You agree this is a big point?"

The umpire nodded.

"Then you must look at the mark. On big points you look at the mark."

"There are many marks."

The outburst that had been simmering just below the surface, finally, inevitably, erupted. The crowd whistled and hissed. And at some point, in McEnroe's mind, the incident was suddenly over.

He started to play again, all passion and intensity, and I realised that it was not just that one particular call that he was protesting, not that single mark so close to the line. It was an eternity of other close calls that lay in the past, and that he knew would recur in the future—incidents that he felt were there to frustrate his plans and his genius. Every now and then the frustration emerges. In someone as highly strung as John McEnroe, it simply cannot be contained. The blood suddenly boils, and there is nothing to be done about it.

After the tumult of the Stade, we walk over to Mark McCormack's tent in the Jardin Municipale to drink a cup of dark coffee or one of the nutty-brown French lagers. Inside the tent there is a lot going on. Cino Marchese is talking on two phones at once and still managing to dictate a fax. Gavin and Bill Ryan are in discussion with the parents of a top junior player. Patrick Proissy is talking to Henri Leconte. Jim Courier and Pete Sampras drop in, casual and relaxed, and seemingly unaware that they, in fact, are the cause of all this activity.

At one of the corner tables, Andy Mill, Olympic skier and husband of the legendary Chris Evert, is tying trout flies. His passion is now fly fishing—from steelhead trout in the streams of Montana to the big tarpon that live in the sunlit shallows off the Florida Keys. I tell him of fishing in the mountain streams of South Africa, and I am rewarded with a little hatch of bronze nymphs and the mysterious flies into which they apparently mutate. Andy is an expert!

Meanwhile, Cino Marchese is still going full blast on his two phones. The scraps of conversation that drift over to where we sit allow us a glimpse into this strange world:

"You can't get the player, you talk to the coach! You can't get the coach, you talk to girlfriend of the coach! Or maybe the brother! But for sure you talk-a to someone!"

"This Greek is-a mad. He must pay!"

"For one patch for one day this player want fifteen thousand dollars? You tell him he first reach semifinals. Then we talk again!"

"No! No! Not-a the mother! The boy! The boy wins the matches! The mother eat-a the pasta. She *talk* like she win the matches!"

"You tell-a the Greek no money, no players!"

"He want fifteen thousand, they offer five thousand, we make-a deal at ten thousand. This is good idea for everybody!"

"Where are the shoes for this boy? You want he should play with the bare feet? If mother wants shoes also, she can have!"

"Ciao, Gorrdon! Today it is-a crazy! Easier to walk on the water than to handle family of tennis players!"

Later on, over a last glass of wine, Mark tells me that Sol

Kerzner is flying into Paris the next day for the men's semi-finals. Will I join them for lunch?—life on quite a different plane than the quiet afternoons in Johannesburg, with the white clouds towering above the jacarandas. . . .

DIARY NOTES, PARIS, 1986

Sol Kerzner arrived at McCormack's tent today to announce that he was going to the Paris air show to buy a plane.

"What kind of a plane?" Abie wanted to know.

"Never mind what kind of plane, Abie," Sol replied.

"Will it have a decent television and a video set?" asked Abie, and Sol, to silence him, said that it would. The kind of plane Sol buys is important to his friends, because he is very generous with his invitations, and they (the friends) want to be sure they will be comfortable. "I'm only tryin' to look after our interests," Abie said to me, and then instructed Sol to make sure that it was a big plane. "We may as well go first class," he said.

With Sol being Sol, the French authorities had arranged for him to have two top security passes and a black Citroen and military driver from the Air Ministry to take him to the show. The technician who was supposed to be accompanying Sol had cancelled at the last minute, and when the car arrived, the French, typically, were put out by the fact that there were two passes but only one passenger and no technician.

"You'd better come with me, Abie," muttered Sol. "You'll have to be the technical consultant. Only don't say a word. Don't open your mouth. Don't even breathe! Just shut up, because whatever you say will be wrong. All you have to do is

listen, and try to look like you know something about planes!"

"Listen! I know planes! What do you think? One of my best friends used to be a pilot."

They went in the back of the black Citroen, haggling with each other the way they always do:

"Don't tell me you know about planes. You know shit about planes!" "I know that I want seats that fold back all nice and comfortable and decent air-conditioning. . . ."

"Listen, who's paying for this thing, you or me. . . .?"

"Don't come with all that crap! If I had your money, and you were my friend, I'd buy a plane with seats that you could lie down in and a friggin' huge TV screen. . . ." Etc., etc.

I got separate, fragmented versions of the expedition from both Abie and Sol afterwards. They'd arrived at the air show to full VIP treatment, and had been shown a whole selection of executive jets. Abie had apparently done very well for a while before raising eyebrows by patting one of the engines and wanting to know how many "horses" it had.

"They develop thrust!" Sol had whispered fiercely.

After inspecting the narrow-bodied Learjet, Abie had bumped his head on the way out and had then walked under the plane, still rubbing his head, and kicked one of the tyres. "This one's too thin," he'd told Sol. "Get one that a man can stand up in. Otherwise we'll have to take a chiropractor with us everywhere we go."

Sol has reserved one of the wide-bodied jets. It's being specially done up inside, and Abie is going to get his big television. On the way home from the tennis we were again trying to work out where Sol gets all his money from.

On the evening after Jim Courier won the French Open for the second time he gave a celebratory dinner near the Étoile. I sat next to Father Joe, and we had a philosophical talk. Quite a number of beautiful women attended the dinner. Father Joe referred to them as "French architecture."

"I am allowed to admire architecture," he said, obviously sure of his ground.

So he and I sat and admired the architecture, and listened to the younger people talk, and I wondered what it was like to be twenty-one years old, handsome and strong and very rich. After the dinner I walked back to the hotel along the Avenue de la Grande Armée. It was a perfect summer night, with a half moon showing through the clouds—the last night in Paris, and I felt the same quick sadness that I had felt while standing on the bridge over the Seine.

13

D R I V I N G

R O D R I G O

One night in Paris in 1993 I received instructions from McCormack to be at the Racing Club de France at eight A.M. the next day, in my tennis gear. I was living in a flat in a little village called Buc, near Versailles. The flat belonged to the tennis-court company called GreenSet for which I served as consultant. My only means of transport was a very old Renault named Rodrigo, so called because he used to belong to our squeegee expert, Rodrigo de Lima. (Squeegeeing is a primitive science peculiar to the tennis-court surfacing industry, involving the tenuous application of a volatile green liquid to a nearly complete court surface with an almost prehistoric implement called a squeegee.)

Rodrigo (the car) had done over five hundred thousand kilometres and could at times be very difficult. Almost any knob or handle that you pulled or turned came off. Changing gears had to be done with a sort of stirring motion, so as to take the gearbox by surprise. To switch on the radio you twisted together two wires emerging from the dash. Pull the choke and it came out about a foot. Stop too suddenly and the seat lurched forwards. For anyone but a French squeegee expert, driving Rodrigo in Paris on the wrong side of the road while simultaneously mapreading and watching for French signs could be a very serious matter.

However, having coaxed Rodrigo onto the freeway that day and finding him in a docile mood, I decided to risk a little practise (tennis, not driving), using a technique developed and perfected by Mark McCormack, to save time. You practise in your head while travelling to the courts—all the usual things, watch the ball, get your racket back, make the stroke, come in to net, etc., nothing too difficult—except it all takes place in your head. Mark swears by it. He says he sometimes even wins tournaments this way, and once got to the quarters of the French Open where he lost to someone who, he admits, was simply the better player on the day. (In his head.)

I arrived at 8.01 and of course Mark was already there, with his daughter, Leslie, and Kwassie van de Merwe (a tennis specialist from Stellenbosch who subsequently died in a tragic accident while bicycling near his home). Somehow, I discovered, Mark and I had challenged Leslie and Kwassie, and as Kwassie was very good, and Mark very competitive, I knew that we were in for a difficult time.

Well, we won—but by a miracle, and not before there'd been a major debate about a volley I'd hit on set point that landed, Mark said, just *on* the sideline, and Kwassie said just *off* it. However, when we compared the mark left by the ball to other marks nearby, we found a difference in their shapes, very slight, but enough to persuade Mark that the point should be awarded to us and not them.

Afterwards I had to drive Rodrigo to Roland Garros and park him somewhere, which is also not so easy, so I had to practise driving in my head while I was taking a shower. The McCormack technique offers a whole new approach to life!

The two Rodrigos, I was to discover, were only a small part of the strange world of tennis-court construction. Although my involvement there was a limited one, it proved at times to be just as quirkish as the lighting business. ("And the garment industry," said Abie.)

It had all begun in 1969, on a sunny afternoon in Johannesburg while I was playing tennis on one of the then very modern, green hard courts that were rapidly to become the norm for South Africa. It was a good court, with a smooth, consistent surface, and we were having some nice tennis.

"Why doesn't someone build these courts in Europe?" asked one of the players. "Surely they would be better than those clay monstrosities they have, where the ball bounces badly and your socks turn red with dust?"

It proved to be a question in which destiny would take a hand. At Wimbledon that year a meeting was arranged, attended by Lee Frankel, Monty Wolpe, Brian Young, Adrian Harding, and me. Somewhat to my surprise, a few months later the tennis-court construction company called GreenSet France came into being. Lee Frankel was named the chief executive officer, and Adrian Harding agreed to act as his aide until things got started. Lee was an American living in Paris at the time, in charge of the marketing for a large U.S. sporting goods company.

"If we're going to build tennis courts in Europe," he had said, "we might as well start in France, because that is where I live."

His decision began what was to be, for all concerned, a long, bittersweet flirtation with the tennis players, the soils, the weather, the geology, the workmen, and the mores of the French nation.

For many years, busy with my lights, I was hardly involved. I would get vague reports of Frankel and Harding traipsing about the French hinterland in Wellington boots, trying to control such things as fussy French mayors, alcohol-ridden French workmen, muddy sites, and the various layers of earth, gravel, asphalt, and green acrylic toppings that were supposed to harden and turn into flawless tennis courts that carried ten-year guarantees, but that were inclined at first to crack, move, subside, peel off, bubble up, or cave in. The dreaded birdbath (a slight depression in a court that holds water) became a constant concern.

But Lee stuck to his guns. The more trouble the courts gave, the stronger he constructed them, until GreenSet sites became crowded with huge machines that dug, compacted, and flattened with such might that the courts they produced would last forever.

"GreenSet courts never fail!" became Lee's motto. He gave up relying on complicated engineering reports to prove the durablity of a court surface, and simply insisted that, before approving it, a fully loaded twenty-ton truck be driven across it in all directions without ill effect. The method is used to this day, and together with the science of squeegeeing by hand and Wellington boots, still imparts a comforting hands-on feel to the business.

In 1986, when our lighting business was finally sold and my work there had run its course, I was able to spend more time at GreenSet. The premises in Buc consisted of a factory, well-appointed offices, a small flat, and an indoor tennis court that was unique in that it had different kinds of surfaces on the two sides of the net—on one side a surface of definitive speed and bounce, on the other an experimental surface of whatever type was being developed at the time. In this way, the playing qualities of surface types could easily be compared.

Together with Lee, Monty Wolpe, and a young man called Graham Woolford, I spent many weeks working in France. We would share the flat, learning to go to the small French *super-marché* for our breakfast baguettes, and at night exploring the small restaurants in Versailles and the surrounding country. At the Blue Bistro, for example, the menu of the day might be:

> soup du jour;
> a peasant-style lamb stew with vegetables coarsely
> cut into the rich, auburn gravy;
> a wedge of *tarte des fruits* with *crème Anglais*;
> a bottle of young, red wine;
> and a cup of black coffee.

After a cold winter's day with the wind blowing sleet against the shutters, such fare tasted fit for kings!

A tennis court is as good only as the people who build it. While we had our own team of finishers, we would rely on local workmen from the area surrounding the site to assist with the heavier construction work. There are no workers in the world quite like those found in France. In the evenings we would sit in some little restaurant and Lee would talk of them while I made notes:

As soon as you arrive there you sense France—as when, arriving at the coast, you may smell the sea—a sort of innate Frenchness, the suggestion that here things are not quite the way they are in other parts of the world. You can't immediately put your finger on it. It is not so much that the immigration man studies your passport with that kind of look, or that the customs people seem about to open your suitcase and talk to each other in French about your things. Nothing, in fact, actually goes wrong. The airport is modern and well arranged. Granted, the parking garage is confusing, as the French often seem to have difficulty with exits. *Sorties*. The one leading out of the garage at Roissy airport is under repair and introduces a complication of loops that rectify themselves at the last minute and deposit you on a highway.

No sooner have you sighed with relief when there comes a major intersection that somehow symbolises the whole French philosophy. One side the sign says, emphatically, PARIS. The other side of it says AUTRE DIRECTIONS—and that, virtually, sums up the whole thing. It is these *other directions* that make the French a nation apart. If you actually take the route that says AUTRE DIRECTIONS (which I once did by accident), you soon come upon another sign that says TOUTES DIRECTIONS. AUTRE becomes TOUTES, and while you may wonder what has become of Paris, you have the feeling that it will reappear sooner or later. The French system has begun to infect you. In no other country in the world does such order and logic emerge from what seems to be a definitive version of the Uncertainty Principle!

Lee Frankel has lived in France almost all his life. Apart from the strange things he sometimes eats, the American side of him is still singularly un-French. Building tennis courts causes him to mix with all the elements of French society, from the sporting and political elite to the actual labourers who build the courts—builders, drivers, diggers, cutters, pavers, and that rarest of all specimens, the expert with the squeegee! Lee therefore knows a lot about the nature, the skills, and the drinking habits of the French workman.

"The main reason the French are the way they are," he says one day while we sit in the shade beside a half-built court, eating French bread and cheese, "is because as a nation, their bodies contain the world's highest alcohol content." Monty Wolpe agrees, but being Monty, he adds other things that have to do with the whole history of France—Napoleon, the Louis, the revolution, Robespierre, Voltaire. Even Charlotte Corday is mentioned. My theory acknowledges both the Frankel and the Wolpe hypotheses, but includes a more elusive ingredient that, after discussion, we decide should be called the "Croissant Syndrome." Then Lee leads his evidence on alcohol:

At seven in the morning, he says, what with the day that's gone before, and the day that lies ahead, they must have a *pousse-café*—literally, a push-coffee, a coffee laced with cognac or calvados—to help them start the day. This gets them through to about nine, when the next great need assails them, resulting in what in some provinces is called a "Chote-Bistou," in others, merely a "*canon*"—either another *pousse-café*, or else a mug or two of warm wine. (Winter weather amplifies the urges, necessitating another *canon* at eleven.)

By the time the lunch break comes along (with the *canons* virtually worn off), aperitifs are urgently needed, and each workman must buy a round in the interests of fair play. Then there is wine with lunch, and after that, more as a contingency really, and, as Lee mildly says, simply "so they can go out into the afternoon," they need at least one *digestif*.

The result is that afternoon work sessions in France have different mores than those of the mornings. ("A tennis court surface applied in the afternoon, for example," says Lee, "may give different bounces from a morning one.") The *matinée* duly comes to an end. At sunset, several beers are needed to stabilise things, and then, dinner (that most holy of events) must be properly attended by more aperitifs, wine, and finally the last *digestifs* and *infusions*. Late-night cognacs are not unheard of. It can thus readily be seen that at seven the next day a *pousse-café* is again a very real necessity. The cycle is really just a sort of self-generating form of chemical action and reaction, a sort of perpetual motion from which withdrawal is almost certain death.

DIARY NOTES, VERSAILLES, 1987

Tonight Lee recommended a new restaurant, and the directions given to Monty Wolpe and me by the concierge of our little hotel are very French in character:

"Out of the hotel door à droit, then down the Boulevard to the Place. Then, on the Place, deuxième à gauche along a short road that manifests itself into another petit Place. Premier à droit, but pay attention to ze leetle . . . etc., etc., . . . and, finally, a road of very small dimensions, which is the street of the restaurant, the porte of which is situated directly opposite the petit jet d'eau."

The result is that we never actually find it—rather that we come across it exactly where we half expect it to be, except that it is on the other side of the rue.

The table is booked in the name of M Volp. Monty keeps the French constantly on guard by the suspicious way in which he spells his name. Monty Wolpe, pronounced, simply, Wolpy. For the French it can become such things as Voolpay, Veuilpey, Vaulpaix, Veaulpaux. But tonight he is simply Volp. I am usually Forbess, but tonight, I am Forbay. Hence Forbay et Volp— an odd couple if ever there was one.

Somewhat unnerved by this new identity, we sit at our little table and talk about the Croissant Factor.

The French, of course (we muse), regard themselves as normal, and the rest of the world as odd. The dapper businessman in his bowtie who pauses at the little oyster shop outside the Gare St. Lazarre at 7.45 of a morning to thoughtfully consume nine oysters and a glass of wine on his way to work cannot but look sideways at the Englishman with his coffee and sticky buns. We dwell idly for a moment on the merits of buns and oysters, and agree that they are not at all of the same genre, concluding that a man arriving at work full of wine and oysters may well behave quite differently than one containing *coffee and buns.*

The next fact that follows is that, if one is what one eats, then the French must be different. For a start, they steer clear of fibre. Bran for them is a coarse substance sometimes fed to animals but harmful to humans. Monsieur Volp, increasingly of the opinion that health stems from diet, is a fibre fanatic. He refuses to enter any French territories without a plastic bag filled with a mixture of oats and bran, dried fruit, nuts, raisins, and other such roughage.

This very morning, when at breakfast at our small hotel he produced his bag of cereal, the Madame was very suspicious. The fact that in order to eat it we needed two bols and lait froid was by itself a major deviation from the norm. As it was, there were no bols, so we had to use the large French coffee cups, while the lait froid arrived piecemeal in a number of very small metal jugs. We were then watched from a safe distance as we filled the cups with Volp's mixture, added the milk, and proceeded actually to eat it.

"The reason," theorises Volp, "is that this stuff is probably illegal in France. That's because the sewerage system is simply not designed for it. If only half the French nation awoke on one given morning and each ate a bowl of my mixture, the resulting blockages could cause chaos. There could be manifestations. Maybe even riots. No, Forbay," he concluded, "the French are stuck with their starches—forever doomed to a life of constipation by their sewerage disposal systems!"

Over our small table, tasting the beaujolais nouveau and waiting for our plates du jour, we mull over the evidence at hand. We are confronted by a nation with:

- *a high alcohol content;*
- *a complicated history;*
- *a meagre sewerage system;*
- *a deficiency of fibre;*
- *a very high croissant count in its blood.*

"That could be it," concludes Volp. "Croissants may be the root cause. Take one man of, say, fifty, who every morning of his life has eaten two croissants and some black coffee, and put him beside another man who every morning has had a bowl of fresh fibre cereal and an apple, and you rest your case!"

Our theory is confirmed the very next day. Being in a hurry, Monsieur Volp has left his bag of cereal on the breakfast table. The following morning, when he asked about it, the Madame informs him with a certain aloof satisfaction that it is gone.

"Gone where?"

"I have sprinkled it on ze jardin," *she replies, and with great relief arranges before us the kind of breakfast that she understands—croissants and coffee with hot, foaming milk.*

In the early mornings Wolpe and I would jog in the *jardins* of the château. Lee, whose sport was golf, never accompanied us. Brian Young sometimes did, but he lagged behind and had to shout his remarks in order to join in our conversations. Wolpe was an architect by profession, and was constantly dumbstruck by the splendour of the château.

"How did they do it?" he would always ask.

"How did who do it?" would come from behind us.

"The Louis," Wolpe would call back.

"Plenty of cheap labour. Slaves and things," Brian would pant. He had an accounting background and didn't like mysteries.

"Look at the detail!" Wolpe would say, ignoring him. "The proportions! The scale of things! Look at that bronze dome! Just that alone is a masterpiece! Their architects must have been masters at domes."

"Good at domes, bad at plumbing," panted Brian. He had been amazed not only at one of the pedestals in Marie Antoinette's bedrooms, but also at the toilet arrangements in his own hotel room. ("The hot taps bark at one," he complained.)

"Modern builders seem to have grown out of domes," I remarked sadly. "They're better these days at concrete slabs. In a thousand years from now they'll walk about their archaeological excavations in Manhattan and say: "Those old guys were great at slabs.""

"Good at slabs, bad at domes," came faintly from behind, and Wolpe would frown at our levity.

DIARY NOTES, VERSAILLES, 1987

This evening Graham and I drove to the palace. We parked in open ground near the Orangerie, then jogged up the hundred steps, onto the water terrace in front of the château, and from there down the broad avenue they call the Green Carpet, towards the Grand Canal. It's huge—a scale so large that you can't perceive it, and magnificent beyond words. By the time we had circled the Grand Canal I was winded, and on the way

185

back called a halt at what turned out to be the King's Garden.
I stood with my hands on my knees, while Graham looked at
the garden. We were the only people there, and the great trees,
the perfect lawns with their borders of flowers, the stillness,
gave the place a quiet splendour that was quite out of this
world.

"One day I want to have a garden like this," said Graham
in a quiet voice. It seems a satisfactory "anywhere" to aim for.

Slowly, Lee and his team were able to expand the tennis-
court business. They say that every business has its own particular characteristics. Well, when it comes to building courts,
nothing could be truer. Few products seem so simple, yet are, in
fact, so subtly complex.

The base, or foundation, must last a lifetime without moving so much as a millimetre. The surface must have great dura-
bility and must provide a perfect and natural ball bounce and
good footing for the players. It must be hard but not too hard,
remain stable and colourfast in summer heat and (in Europe)
under winter snow, drain quickly after rain, not be slippery
when damp, be aesthetically attractive, not get too hot in summer, provide good visibility . . . even as I write I can hear Lee
telling of the solving of one problem and the emergence of
another! Our activities were almost never without incident—
such as, for example, the day of the new surface, the piece of
steak, the glass of wine, Herr Schultes, Rodrigo, and me. It happened thus:

To augment the GreenSet range of surfaces we'd needed a
good artificial-grass carpet, which, in combination with the

right kind of sand, would create a surface similar to natural grass (although never quite the same). One of the best sports carpets was made by a company called Mastersport, and we began negotiations with Mr. Horst Schultes, its CEO, to obtain his product. On one of his visits to Paris I arranged to have dinner with him to finalise our deal. As it happened I'd spent that afternoon absorbed in testing yet another new product, lost track of time, and suddenly realised that I was in danger of keeping Herr Schultes waiting. I leapt into action, pulling on a suit, taking my map of Paris, and setting off in Rodrigo, only to lose my way in one of the Paris suburbs.

By the time I got to the restaurant I was late and somewhat stressed out. Herr Schultes was a pleasant, serious man who at once forgave my lateness. We ordered our food and while we waited for it to arrive began our negotiations. By the time the main course came, we had just reached the crucial subject of price. I made an impassioned plea for a price that I secretly knew to be too low, he countered with a higher one, and, finally, I was ready to announce my final offer.

I had ordered steak with *frites* and salad, and before speaking took a mouthful of steak, only to find that it was much tougher than I had expected it to be.

"The last offer I can make, Herr Schultes," I began, then impatiently swallowed the steak to get rid of it. It refused to go down my throat, lodging itself in such a way that I could breathe but not utter a sound. Although, surprisingly, I was still alive, I felt a rising panic. Mr. Shultes waited expectantly. I decided to wash the steak down with wine, so took a mouthful and swallowed. Instead of moving the steak, there was a squelching noise in my ears and the wine deflected off the blockage and reappeared out of my nose, running back into the glass that in desparation I held up to catch it.

What Herr Schultes thought I cannot imagine. It certainly must have seemed unusual for someone at such a *moment critique* to take a mouthful of wine and then return it to his glass via his nose. I got up in a panic and made for the men's room, in the privacy of which I took a long, deep breath, held my nose, and exhaled sharply. The steak shot out of my mouth like a wad out of a shotgun, and the crisis was past. Feeling a complete fool I returned to the table, and with a weak smile said to Herr Schultes:

"You see what happens if the price becomes too high?" Then I explained what had happened and we laughed about it, and he hastily accepted my offer, alarmed, no doubt, at what I might do next if he refused!

But the evening was not yet over. Driving back in my weakened state, I finally escaped out of the maze of small streets and came to the landmark that I knew well—the great circle of the Porte de St. Cloud, from which the Avenue Edouard Vaillant ran straight to the Versailles motorway via a series of underpasses that during the day avoided the cross traffic. At midnight, though, there was no traffic, and Rodrigo and I were bucketing along, taking the underpasses at full gallop with the sense of relief that comes when it's all over and you're nearly home.

We took one underpass too many. Just before reaching the highway we veered right for the final underpass, only to find ourselves speeding into the biggest underground parking garage

in Paris—a maze of ramps and barriers, which, once negoti-
ated, we could never go back through. Seized by about the sixth
bout of panic that day, I drove around desperately seeking the
way out, and finally came to an exit sign that looked like this:

SORTIE

In 1991, at the Festhalle in Frankfurt, after years of devel-
opment, and months of play-testing by some of the ATP Tour
professionals, GreenSet unveiled a brand-new tennis court for
the ATP Tour World Championships. It was called GreenSet
Trophy, and, ironically, it was a strong blue—the colour most
suitable for TV viewers, when seen as a background to the yellow of the tennis balls. The new court's surface was firmly
cushioned and finely and evenly textured to provide what we
felt to be the most consistent and natural ball bounce yet
achieved on an indoor surface.

There is one thing that is consistently true of any tennis-
court surface. One can test and theorise until the cows come
home—the truth emerges only when a player walks on the
court and hits the ball. With the world's best players, it takes
only minutes to gain a first impression, and in nearly all cases,
the first impression is the definitive one.

On the first day of practise in the Festhalle, we watched

anxiously as the players walked on the court, scuffed at the surface with their shoes to get the feel of it, and began hitting up. After we had spent nearly the whole day observing the quality of the ball bounce and the movements of the players, and listening to their comments, we began to feel that we had hit the nail on the head. We had produced a surface upon which, as Ivan Lendl put it, "You can play any game you like"—meaning that our surface was fair to all styles of play. That night at dinner in the sumptuous ATP Tour hospitality suite, Lee Frankel and I ordered a special bottle of wine, and drank a toast to the new court.

QUEEN'S CLUB

D I A R Y

At length they all to merry London came,
To merry London. . . .
—Edmund Spenser

We lived in London for almost a year in 1990, and I was able to become a member of Queen's Club, some thirty-five years after first playing there in 1955. In those old days the order of things had been very simple. If you were "good" you played "Queens," and if you were "not good" you tried to qualify for Wimbledon at Roehampton. "Queens" was not big on "expenses," but because it was the only tournament held during the week before Wimbledon, all the players shrugged their shoulders and played there for nothing. Lunches and teas, however, were free, and they served excellent salmon mayonnaise. If you ate a good lunch and a big-enough tea at five, you could save a bit by having a smaller dinner.

They still serve excellent salmon, and at tea, some of the basic buns are the same as they were in 1955. (Not the actual buns, but more the shape or style of bun.) Like many old British clubs, Queen's has about it a sort of absolute inevitability, reminding me a little of the "anthropic principle" described in Stephen Hawking's *A Brief History of Time*. It could thus be defined as follows:

"We see the Queen's Club like it is because if it were not like it is, it wouldn't be the Queen's Club!"

And it seems somehow fitting that it needs something as profound as mathematics to actually "nail it down," as Abie would say.

After I became a member, I was invited to play league in the over-fifty-five national doubles. We had a very British team consisting of Palmer, Stokes, Wing, Field, Sellman, and Klima, all of them simultaneously distinguished and cagey. Doubles only was played. As it happened, we won the league (handsomely, we all agreed) and were awarded engraved glass beer mugs that were immediately filled and field-tested.

Brian Palmer, our captain, plays easy, elegant tennis, in spite of the great mechanical appliances that he wears on both knees beneath his long white pants—machines that lend him a sort of bionic mobility. The other day he pulled a muscle in one of his appliances. He was coming in to net and there was a great twang and he veered off course and caved in near the umpire's stand like a crashed biplane. One of the stay wires parted, so a pair of pliers and some wire had to be sent for to do temporary repairs.

It was a good year. At Easter we went to stay at my friend

Brian Thomas's house at Langton Long, Nr Blandford Forum, Dorset. Other spots in the area are called Piddle Hinton, Tarrant Monkton, Childe Okeford, Keynstone Mill, Lullworth Cove, etc., so that what with those names and the chilly showers that scurried in from the sea, we knew for sure that we were no longer in Africa. At the little country pubs you could have draught beer with brown bread and local cheeses. One of the pubs had a wooden bridge over a stream and specialised in pickles.

English summer. Blowing days, with the parks and squares in filtered sunlight and the last blossoms falling from the chestnut trees. In the small streets the flower sellers are out, housewives shop for gooseberries, and warm scents of lilac and privet come from the gardens.

On Palisser Road, though, they're boiling tar. About halfway between the Baron's Court Underground and the Queen's Club gates an antediluvian machine is puttering away, issuing clouds of oily smoke. It's sunny, and while they wait for the tar to boil the road-repair crew have removed their shirts to reveal a variety of torsos and tattoos and are making tea in a kettle nearly as old as the tar machine. A pothole in the road is cordonned off and there's chaos everywhere, with people trying to park and the players' cars being held up and club members on their way to lunch in billowing cottons, gingerly skirting the pothole and battling the smoke. But the tar machine mutters away to itself and the crew have about them the air of busy men—people with a cause.

Richard Evans and I, arriving by tube, are on foot and thus

free from the traffic jams. Nonetheless, conditions are perfect for Richard to vent the scathing wrath that he keeps in reserve for just such outrageous occasions.

"Typical!" he cries superbly. "Defies speech! That pothole has been there since Victoria reigned; there are fifty-two weeks in a year, and now this! During the tournament!" He waves a hand at the smoke and chaos, and as we pass the pothole he shakes a furious finger at it. "That," he says, "is why the pound is weak! That is why England is going broke! And who suffers? Not them!" (Indicating the crew with another wave of loathing.) "We suffer! England suffers!"—and at that moment I catch a glimpse of the sum of all of England's woes reflected in a pothole in Palisser Road and a motley crew of workmen simultaneously boiling tar and tea.

Richard Evans. Writer, bachelor, wanderer. The ultimate sports scholar, observing life without ever quite becoming involved in it, watching the passing parade with a slight upwards tilt of his head. As long ago as I can remember, where there was tennis being played, there was the ubiquitous Evans, making notes. A flat in London, a hideaway in a castle in the countryside of Spain. A place at Lew Hoad's tennis ranch near Fuengirola. But at heart a rover. Roots have tried to emerge, have sometimes even looked like gaining a precarious purchase in the ground beneath him. But they never have time. He moves on, you see. His roots are in his writing, his place to go the fields on which his beloved sporting heroes do their deeds.

As we approach the club gates, the smoke clears and we can actually smell the tournament before us—a warm, grassy smell, the kind of smell you get only if you keep mowing the same grass, playing the same games in the same place, for more than a hundred years. And as we enter the club I can see in my mind's eye the labyrinth of passages in the clubhouse; the old and battered woodwork; the medieval, lopsided racquets courts that you find every now and then when you're searching for covered court seven; the smell of bitter ale and furniture polish in the bar; the old man in the locker room who won't give you a towel until you hand over fifty p. There is nowhere in the world quite like the Queen's Club, W 14, and the best thing of all about it is that it will never change—it's far too late for that, now, even if. . . .

But at the moment the club is decked out in all its tournament finery. As we pass the big boards that show the draw, we glimpse the upper portion of Wally Masur's first service above the canvas of an outside court, and we hear a powerful British voice call, "Out!" and Wally's mild Australian protest. "Ah! What?" Nothing has changed. It's June, it's summer, and it's the season of grass-court tennis. What more could any net-rusher wish for?

The centre court at Queen's Club is one of the best match courts in the world. It is a nice centre court. The solid old clubhouse watches over it in a fatherly sort of way, and the spectators know their tennis. On the clubhouse terraces the older members sip their drinks and mutter things: "This new *Japanese* fellow, then," they might say. "*Looks* a pleasant enough sort. Didn't know they got so tall, actually. . . ." Or perhaps: "This chap Edberg! Still going strong, I see! Always good value, is Edberg." Or else: "A lot of *foreign* types about these days . . . odd names they've got . . . Pescosolido! I ask you! Was a time when most them were Australians, you know?" And so forth.

On the little parapet at the top of the steps to the locker rooms, Czeslaw "Spike" Spychala is at his post, in charge of allocating courts, balls, and towels. As I pass he fixes me with a stony stare, and although I haven't seen him for a year, he says, in greeting: "This, my friend, is a used ball. It is old. It cannot thus be used again!" He hands me for inspection a brand-new tennis ball that has upon it one single green patch—the result of one bounce upon a grass court.

"Someone must have hit one shot with it," I suggest.

"I tried to give it to one of *them*"—haughty gesture towards the players' enclosure—"but I was told it is a *used* ball, and it was given back to me."

Czeslaw is seventy-something, ageless, stoic, an ex-player, the stuff of which all civilisation is made. As I speak to him, Grant Connell, the Canadian star, pauses to collect balls for his match and casually picks up two or three of the large Stella Artois towels.

"Americans are very fond of towels," says Czeslaw, his eyes following Connell. He observes the actions of the modern young players with a mixture of fascination, wonder, and disapproval. "In *my* day, Forbes, we brought our *own* towels," he says. "Now there is more equipment. They [the players] need more *things*, otherwise, it seems, they cannot play, you see." His method of address, "Forbes," dates back to 1954, when, aged nineteen, I played in one of the small tournaments for which he was, even then, referee as well as player. "Now," he says, making a wry face, "I have no title. Mr. Bernstein asked me what I wished to be and I said 'Road Sweeper'! He did not object. . . ."

Clive Bernstein's office is farther along the little parapet. Clive is the unproclaimed doyen of tournament directors. Grey-headed now, he wanders about, unflappable, not saying much, taking everything with a pinch of salt, his shrewd eyes missing nothing.

"In this business, Gordon, you can't afford to," he says. "Chancy things, tennis tournaments. I have a feeling about Ferreira this week," he goes on. "I keep telling them"—indicating the television crews—"but they think I'm mad. Perhaps they're right. Never mind. I trust my feelings. Time will tell!"

"How is your service getting on?" I ask him.

Clive is a good player. His service action, however, incorporates a sort of small, pilot toss-up that takes place just before the real toss-up. After that it's all fairly standard, but he knows that the little toss-up always makes me laugh.

"Get away with you," he says. "I suppose you will be wanting tickets for your special friends. Well, I haven't got any."

But he usually has.

On the centre court below, Wayne Ferreira is at this moment playing Jason Stoltenberg. Today is one of those bright and breezy days when the ball flies off the grass, lightning fast.

I move on to the clubhouse balcony to watch the match and find myself wedged between a lofty Englishman and the archetypal English girl who has the look of a beautiful horse, blonde and willowy with an endless, slightly crooked nose.

When something amuses her she smiles by raising only the corners of her mouth. And when she pushes back the mane of fair hair, her fingers are very long and also somehow equestrian. Even her ankles are lean and racy. In my younger days I would have tried to do something about her—attract her attention, perhaps, by asking a Segalesque question like, "Where have you tied up your horse?" but now it is too late.

As one gets older such liaisons are best carried out only in the imagination.

The Englishman, meanwhile, seems to be having a bad day, because he scowls continuously. "Who is this Ferreira fellow?" he wants to know, but his manner is so elevated, and his striped shirt with its white collar so correct, that I don't feel like telling him.

Pat Cash versus Stefan Edberg, next match on. Cash, returning to top competition after various interruptions, now wears a Sioux-like ponytail, and has a pagan look about him, a little wild of eye. His game, too, is willful, and, as always, it sometimes seems to me to be improvised, made up as he goes along and held together by creative talent.

Edberg, as usual, is all elegance, but today it seems the long, harmonious strokes are without feeling—as though for the moment the word *game* has been mislaid and all that remains is mechanics, like a line of poetry recited over and over until the words lose their meaning.

At 6-5, 30-40, first set, Cash's hair ribbon comes undone and he has to retie it while Edberg waits. In our day we didn't have hair ribbons. Today, as Spike Spychala says, the players need a lot of things.

✳ ✳ ✳ ✳

On one of the back courts near the ice cream machine, I watch Christo van Rensburg playing a little-known Frenchman called Guillaume Raoux. Christo is a competent and popular player. He has very deft volleys—today referred to as "good hands"—and a good service motion, slightly flawed by a little spasm in the swing that makes the racket head stop with a bit of a clang somewhere behind him. Although Christo has made strenuous efforts to remove the kink, the best he has come up with so far is to have it move to other parts of his swing. He is a bit rueful about his service:

"For a while I tried to move it [the clang] right to the beginning of the swing," he once told me with an impish smile, "so that I could get it over before I even began. First have the spasm, and then serve! Maybe even leave it in the locker room!"

He has recently seen the movie *Dead Poet's Society* and he tells me that he has decided in the future to seize as many days as he can, because there are not that many left. "We must all seize them, Gordon!" he says with his impish smile. "Let's begin tomorrow!"

"A good idea!" I reply, and we agree that we will both try to seize tomorrow for a start, and see how we get on after that.

In the first semifinal the new Japanese superstar, Shuzo Matsuoka, is playing Stefan Edberg. He is superb in designer tennis gear with Lurex gym pants under his shorts. He also seems highly strung—full of small tensions that seem to lie just below the skin, causing his eyes suddenly to widen, the bridge of his nose to twitch, his eyebrows to leap upwards, his knees to bob. On his own service, Japanese grunts emerge, and on Edberg's service he moves back and forth in sudden samurai-like rushes, sometimes virtually disappearing into the hinterland behind the baseline before hurtling forwards to the net like a ninja.

In the stand behind the court, Tony Pickard sits alone, watching. Tony is Edberg's entire support system, a modest and sensible one in comparison to some of the other superstars' elaborate entourages. As Tony never shows the slightest emotion, it is impossible to tell what he thinks of this unexpected Japanese peril. And to everyone's surprise, the match becomes a very close one.

At 4-3 in the final set the crowd is absorbed and excited. Matsuoka holds on and suddenly finds himself with a break point on Edberg. Now a tremendous arrangement of twitches and jumps and some serious self-instruction in Japanese must ensue before he is ready to handle the point. Finally Edberg serves, misses with the first, and Matsuoka is able to hit a winner off the second for the break.

Pickard is granitelike in his implacability as Matsuoka prepares to serve for the match. He hitches up his outer trousers, then suddenly his tics go out of phase. His wiping, twitching, bouncing, and bobbing all take place in the wrong sequence and he finds himself down 15-40. But he claws his way back to deuce, has a private celebration, wins the deuce point to give himself match point, goes for a last short walk, serves, comes in to net with a roar, hits a winner, falls over, bows to Edberg, bows to the crowd, bows to the umpire, gives another bow or two for good measure, then collapses into his chair and buries his head in his towel. Edberg's face is calm but very serious.

Ferreira versus Brad Gilbert in the second semifinal: Ferreira wins but not before Gilbert has had his say. "Stonehead!" he frequently calls himself. Here is a true character—part seer, part showman, part clown, but with an amazingly good tennis brain. He knows exactly what to do to win it is simply a matter of getting his body to do it. For this match he wears wraparound amber glasses and has long discussions with himself: He serves; he misses with the first service; he tells himself to do better on the second; he serves again; it is another weak one, far too shallow, and he gets hopelessly passed by Ferreira.

"That's not a second serve!" he tells himself. "That's not even a third serve! That's about a ninth serve!"

At set point he double-faults. "Nooooooo!" he scolds himself, "no control whatsoever. Nothing left! Stupid prick! I serve so bad. How can I double-fault? My serve is out to lunch." Then suddenly, turning to the umpire: "Which restaurant do you think my serve is at?" And on another occasion, to a line judge who has called his service out: "You saw that out? I saw it good. We must be watching different matches. Could we check that out? I make this the men's semifinal. Gilbert versus Ferreira!"

But Gilbert is now over thirty years old. He has in his career won over four million dollars in prize money alone, and is far too well balanced not to take things with a pinch of salt.

Watching him, one has the feeling that underneath the crusty exterior he is enjoying himself. Perhaps Christo and I should get him to give us lessons on how to seize tomorrow.

Tonight at the French brasserie on the Brompton Road, I sit over *steak-frites* and beaujolais with Richard Evans. He is in one of his expansive moods, which means that all you really have to do is listen while he talks. Everything comes under discussion: mental strength, the vagaries of single women, the rise of cricket in Pakistan, McEnroe's touch, the elegance of David Gower's cover drive, marijuana versus alcohol. Thatcher versus Major; England's current woes again; single women again (Why were they so difficult? Why were the best ones always married?). He picks up his wine, sips at it, then peers reflectively at the colour. Did I know that the French have the lowest cholesterol levels in the world? And that they continually stuff themselves with duck pâté and red wine? And cheese. Kilograms of cheese. Now what do I make of that?

Afterwards I walk down Sloane Avenue reeling with information but not quite sure how to make use of it.

In the Queen's Club final, Wayne Ferreira brings to an end the winning streak of Matsuoka. A great victory with no apparent fuss. "I hope he turns out to be a really good player," says Clive Bernstein with a frown. "Only really good players win at Queen's." To prove his point he takes me round the lounges and shows me all the great stars who have won before.

On Monday morning, because it is that kind of day, and because London, more than any other, is a city in which memories linger on certain street corners, I walk at a leisurely pace from South Kensington through Knightsbridge towards Piccadilly. At Thurloe Place I am able to swing onto one of the red busses, which drops me off at Hyde Park Corner, so that it is easy then to wander through the small streets of Shepherd's Market and across Berkeley Square to where the two Bond Streets meet.

When as children we played Monopoly, the properties on Bond Street were always the best ones. "A good street for shops," my father used to say. As a young man he had served in the Royal Flying Corps and for a while had been stationed in London. He told us about the wonders of the Underground Railway, and that Piccadilly was the centre of the earth, and he'd still had a tweed jacket that he had bought on Bond Street in 1918, just before shipping back to the remote sheep farm in the Karroo that was to be our home.

So I turned left into Bond Street. I try never to visit London without buying something in Bond Street, usually something made of wool. Nowadays you have to search for exactly the right kind of shop, but if you look hard enough you will still find it. A lot of the shops have tended to veer towards designer gear, or have become so rarified that you pass them by. But in some the tradition of old London lives on.

Mappin and Webb. Perry and Bell. Kings of Sheffield. Waterford. Wedgwood. In the window of Holland and Sherry, slabs of rich Harris tweeds neatly piled up, cuts of pure Irish linen set amongst scarves and buttons, tartan knee rugs and cashmere shawls—a veritable harvest of pure fabrics waiting to be measured up. The sun is out today and the British women are wearing loose clothing with glimpses of fine, fragile English skin, pale, blue-veined, giving them a sort of intimacy, as though they are recently out of some upstairs bedroom.

In 1956 Abie and I had walked down Bond Street full of the joys of youth. Abie was in one of the deal-making moods that used to come upon him from time to time. "We got to figure a way of making a few bucks so we can buy a bit of all this stuff they got here," he would say, stopping in front of exclusive shop windows. On this particular day he lagged behind, and I turned back to find him staring into a small shop window with a notice that said:

SEA ISLAND ESTATES. LITTLE EXUMA!

YOUR OWN PRIVATE PIECE OF PARADISE!

$10.00 DOWN PAYMENT, $5.00 PER MONTH.

Beneath the notice was a marvellous picture of an island with beaches, umbrellas, and palm trees, divided up into lots with streets and shops. There was even a copper-skinned islander holding up a giant lobster. Never was there a bluer sea, never whiter sand.

Abie had about him the kind of look that made me nervous. He put his hand into his back pocket, pulled out his wad of cash, and contemplated it.

"Holy hell, Forbsey," he said, "do you realise that without too much of a problem we could end up with a few pieces of paradise?"

"Do we know where Little Exuma even is?" I asked, ever cautious.

"It's in the middle of one hell of a blue sea, for a start," he said, "and how far can it be from *Big* Exuma? I got this friend with a place in Big Exuma, and he always looks so relaxed he's nearly falling apart! Like that guy there with the lobster! So let's go in and find out."

So in we went, with me experiencing yet again that eerie, open-ended feeling I used to get when following Abie into the unknown. It was a minute shop, nearly all of which was taken up by a big relief model of the island, even more inviting-looking than the map in the window. There were even tiny figures relaxing on the beaches. Abie regarded the pinstripe-suited man behind the map.

"These pieces of paradise you got going," he said. "What can you tell us about them?"

"You'll be meaning the ones in the window," said the man. "You see, we also have offers on the Isle of Man and the Hebrides."

"We want our paradise without wind and snow," said Abie.

"Of course you do," said the man, beaming as though delighted that this much, at least, was settled. He then launched into a sales promotion of such enthusiasm that even if we hadn't wanted a piece of paradise, we would have been hard pressed to refuse. Finally Abie had to cut him short.

"Okay, you can relax," he said. "Don't lose yourself completely. We're going to buy anyway. What have you got left here?"

"Well there's been a big demand," said the man, sucking his teeth, "but we still have some prime sites left. Beachfront, of course, is the thing. And there are also these business lots on the top of the hill."

"Which ones do we want, Forbsey?" asked Abie.

"I can't afford any of them, Abie," I said, half disappointed and half relieved that my bankroll consisted of only a few notes.

"So you'll share one of mine," he said, really meaning it, and he proceeded to select two beachfront sites ("We'll take the ones with the palm trees and the umbrellas on them"), one business site, and one hotel site ("We'll need space for our buddies, Forbsey"), happily parting with about fifty pounds and signing a great screed of papers without really reading them.

"Shouldn't you actually read that stuff?" I asked him.

"Take me all day," he replied, "and then what could I tell you? I get these feelings about things. You got to have feelings about things, Forbsey. After that you win some, you lose some."

This one turned out to be one that he lost. Although he paid his installments for years after his purchase, there came a time when the accounts simply stopped coming. The next time he visited London he went straight to the shop on Regent Street, but the island had gone. The phone numbers had been disconnected and Abie's letters got returned marked ADDRESS UNKNOWN.

But Abie's feeling had remained so strong that he kept all the maps and deeds pertaining to his purchases, meaning one day to visit the island to finally see it for himself. And he did. I received the final installment of Abie's South Sea Bubble in his Bryanston home about ten years later. He and Heather had been on a visit to Bermuda, where Heather had a cottage. One of Heather's island friends owned an oceangoing yacht, and Abe had persuaded him to take a cruise to the Bahamas, where, he felt, there was still the faint possibility that he could find Little Exuma and lay claim to his properties. They sailed, and one afternoon the island hove into view. It was wild and jungle-clad, with a great mountain of rock rising out of the forest.

"Where are the umbrellas and the guys with the lobsters?" Abie wanted to know.

Close up to the shore they could actually make out the remains of a road network, with streetlight posts on the corners. While Abie ranted about "those thievin' English con artists," the captain of the yacht studied the maps that Abie had given him. Finally he looked up and interrupted Abie's raving.

"By my calculations," he said, "we're right over your beachfront properties! You could really only have used them at low tide, you know."

"Jesus Christ!" said Abie. "I would have been the only guy in the world with a lawn that didn't need an irrigation system!"

By now the story has been told and retold. Abie enjoys the uniqueness of the deal, and the fact that it fits in well with some of his other entrepreneurial activities.

"Just as well it turned out the way it did, Forbsey," he once said to me. "Cheaper than ownin' a place and having to maintain it."

But on another day in London, in another mood:

DIARY NOTES, 19 JUNE, 1992

It is two o'clock. I am standing in the exit doorway of a cinema in Jermyn Street. It is raining, a steady, grey rain, and there is death in London today. Death in the squalid cinema, death in the traffic, in the faces of the taxicab drivers, under the black umbrellas, in the Piccadilly subways with their wet litters of garbage, the brick facades with their TO LET signs. The afternoon lies stretched out—a mournful flatness that brings life down to the dead level of things.

When you are alone, beware of cities. Visit them only when your mood is high, when you have business to do, a purpose to guide you. Expect no welcome from a city. If you are lucky, you will have a place where you belong. Go back to it. There is no comfort here. This is a cold, grey city.

In the tearoom at Simpsons they still serve what used to be called "cream teas." White china cups with scones, Jersey cream, and raspberry jam. But even here there is a lingering worry that things will change, that soon the cups will be made of plastic. The march of progress! Well, let the young people deal with it. I will keep on searching for the old London that I knew. . . .

15

YOU CHANGE AT EARL'S
COURT

In 1954 the Cromwell Road, SW 5, was much quieter than it is today. It was lined with small hotels, simple but neat and well kept. One of these was grandly called The Hotel King Charles. You walked into a cosy living room with a fireplace, and a breakfast room that smelt as though it had harboured fresh bacon and toast for hundreds of years. There were encouraging English chambermaids in starched uniforms with white caps. Steep carpeted stairs led up to bedrooms with eiderdowns on iron beds. The higher up you went, the cheaper the rooms became.

When Gordon Talbot and I arrived that year, both aged nineteen, we stayed on the fifth floor, where our board was seventy-five p per day, bed and breakfast. Although it was after eleven by the time we arrived, they had kept our breakfast ready, and although we'd had a large breakfast on the boat train from Southampton, we ate the King Charles breakfast as well.

"We may as well," said Gordon Talbot. "You never know."

If you walked out of the hotel and turned right, you came to a lane blocked off with cast-iron bollards, called Kenway Road. If you turned down Kenway Road you found yourself in an English village with a willow tree on the corner of Redfield Lane, and a little farther on a pub called The King's Head, which offered Charrington ale and bass on draught. Another fifty yards or so and Kenway Road became uncertain of itself, allowing a narrow sliver of a lane to defect, call itself Hogarth Place, and then widen and become Hogarth Road. Here began the little English eating houses, Copper Kettles and Ma's Kitchens, etc., although one or two small Italian restaurants had somehow crept in and been allowed to stay. A hundred yards down Hogarth Road brought you to an underground station with a sandstone facade into which were cut the words:

GN PICCADILLY AND BROMPTON RAILWAY

although even then, it was better known as Earl's Court.

"Go to Piccadilly Circus," my father had once said, on a winter evening in front of the fire, when we were very young, "stand there, and you will be standing in the centre of the world!"

So that day, after our two breakfasts, we took the tube at Earl's Court and went to Piccadilly Circus. We stood there and contemplated it, and although it was not quite what I had expected, it was a very satisfactory centre of the world. Then we went to Golden Square to get two Fred Perry shirts, and then to Victoria to get the two rackets that Dunlop had promised us.

DIARY NOTES, LONDON, MARCH 1954

*The Maxplys are perfect, with the latest leather grips, and
head covers with our initials set into them. We also got new
shoes! Green Flash! A great bonus.*

*"If you qualify for Wimbledon," said Pat Hughes, the
Dunlop man, "you'll get another pair."*

*When we asked him the best way to get to Wimbledon,
he asked, "Physically or mentally?"—and laughed.*

"Physically," we replied.

*"You change at Earl's Court," he said, "and take the
District Line to Southfields."*

In 1992, I went back to Cromwell Road. It is tired now,
racked with traffic fumes and heavy vehicles. The Hotel King
Charles has gone, and the building where it used to be is
un–cared for, with dirty sidewalks. There is no longer a smell of
fresh English breakfast.

But Kenway Road remains—even the old iron bollards are
still there—and as you enter it, for a little while you still feel
just a whisper of old London. The pub, the willow, Redfield
I ann, ann a Huughith Plass, But Hogarth Road has turned traitor,
defected again and gone eastern. Gusts of curry emerge from
the shadowy doorways of restaurants—the New Asia, the
Matahari, the Al Sharaq, with eastern writings, Chinese,
Lebanese, Arabic. A mysterious-looking doorway under the
word BAALBEK. Gone the English kitchens, the milky-skinned
waitresses with the starched caps. Gone the London that we'd
known as a home from home.

The station facade, though, is still the same, with the same words cut into the sandstone. After all these years, there is still something compelling about the London underground. Even now, I emerge from wherever I am staying, hesitate upon the pavement, then more often than not make my way to the nearest tube station.

DIARY NOTES, LONDON, 1992

On the Wednesday after Queens, I go to Roehampton to watch the players trying to qualify for Wimbledon. The weather is fine and I've plenty of time, so I take the train at South Kensington and change at Earl's Court—the District Line, platform four. There is a train waiting, and above it, on the ancient signboard, a lighted arrow points: WIMBLEDON. *The train is old and stands there with open doors, panting and muttering to itself. I board and sit in the soft old seats. At last, with a sneeze, the doors close, and we canter off at a measured pace along tracks that are now so out of shape that the train lurches and sways.*

West Brompton, Fulham Broadway, Parsons Greens. Every station has its memories. At Putney Bridge I glimpse the great trees of the Hurlingham Club and the old mansion block where Abie and I once shared a flat.

DIARY NOTES, HURLINGHAM, 1956

It's early April with the trees just coming into leaf, and when the matches start at ten, the morning mists still hang in the hollows.

I stop to look at the gardens, but Abie is more concerned

with the way the umpires call his serves. They are very old and don't see too well. Abie calls them all "Professor," and I have to keep reminding him to behave properly. He likes to curl his serve into the court at the last minute, and today they called three good serves out almost before they had bounced. On the third one he couldn't stand it any longer. He walked up to the chair and gave it a shake, and looked up at the old umpire with his right eye twitching like a madman, and said:

"Hey, Professor, do you see what's happening here with this eye of mine? That's what happens when you keep callin' my serves out! I go crazy and they have to take me away!"

Later in the game it happened again and although I had warned him, he let rip with the mother of all four-letter words.

"For Pete's sake, Abe," I said fiercely, and he came up to me and said: "So what do you expect me to say? 'Alas! I have double-faulted!'?" I didn't know he knew the word alas.

The flat in the old mansion block that we had shared that year had a very big bedroom with twin beds fitted with castors, so mobile that even the smallest push sent them rolling across the polished wooden floor. I'd had a couple of nightmares in that flat, and the memories make me smile to myself even now, as the train creeps cautiously over the Putney Bridge.

Amongst other things, the wall fell over twice in about three weeks—the first cave-in taking place on the night before the opening day of Wimbledon. Sure enough, at about one A.M., down it started to come. As usual I leapt into action, kneeling up at the head of the bed and giving it a great shove to get it back in place. The shove not only rectified the wall, but also sent my bed careering across the floor towards the bedroom door.

Of course Abie awoke and uttered his usual expressions of surprise. Order was restored, and eventually peace once more reigned. Having had one nightmare, I would never have another on the same night. ("Christ, Forbsey, what a win!" said Abe when I first told him that.)

The next day though, to my chagrin, everyone had to hear about it.

"I wake up," said Abie, "and what do you think's happening? Forbsey's bed's pullin' out from next to mine like a train, and Forbsey's hangin' on the end like the guard. 'Jesus Christ, buddy,' I say to him, 'stick on the brakes!'"

I awoke when the bed hit the doorjamb, and there was nothing for it but to get off and push it back across the room like a fool.

For Abie, the incident was full of possibilties.

"Good thing the door stopped you," was one of his musings. "You could have ended up goin' straight on down the stairs and over Putney Bridge," and for a while he went on about me "travellin' to Wimbledon by bed." But all that happened a long time ago.

Now, in 1992, I leave the train at East Putney and begin walking along the Upper Richmond Road. Sometimes there are taxis. If not, you just keep going until eventually you get to Priory Lane, and then if you turn left you get to the Bank of England Club, Roehampton, where they've played the Wimbledon qualifying tournament since time began. To tennis players it is a sort of initiation ceremony, an entry fee into a club for those who have been through the mill of tennis. "I qualified in '63," you will hear someone say, and you know they have been out on the grass at Roehampton—have taken the strain and served their time.

Under the great plane trees the matches are in full swing. It is a deceptively simple scene—the mild English lawns, the sprinkling of spectators—parents and coaches, mainly. But the place crackles with a sort of latent tension. Here, if anywhere, is the closest thing to the tennis we knew of old. An honest struggle where victory means very little other than a place in the first round of the greatest and most elusive of all tennis championships.

For the players, there are plenty of distractions. The courts are laid out in threes with no physical dividers, so close together that the matches seem at times to overlap.

"It's the only place in the world," said Abie more than once, "where a man can start out playing one guy and end up beatin' someone else!" And he'd told me about the time he'd been playing there, and the woman on the court beside him ran for a very wide ball, and her desperate forearm recovery attempt passed him down the line just as his opponent's backhand passed him cross-court.

"It's bad enough to be passed once, Forbsey," he'd remarked, "but at Roehampton that day I got passed on both sides in the same point!"

On the first court I come to, Glenn Layendecker is playing, of all people, Guillaume Raoux. It is remarkable how these players crop up. In Paris, every time I arrived anywhere, a somewhat frantic Paolo Cane was screaming at the sky. In England it's been Raoux. Anyway, today he and Layendecker are locked in a final set, and the situation is very tense. Raoux is once more seething like a pressure cooker. To make matters worse, there is an epidemic of bad calls and the wind is gusting very strongly.

As I watch, a long point develops, a real backbreaker, with great gets and tight lobs and desperate lunges. Finally, Raoux gets a very bad bounce—not even a bounce, really; more of a roll—that he has no chance of reaching. He drops his racket on the grass, kicks at it, points, appeals to the sky above, screams at the wind in French, quite unable to think of enough ways to loathe everything that's happening at that precise moment.

On the very next point he comes to net behind a huge approach. Layendecker's only play is a high, defencive lob into the wind. Up the ball goes, and as it swirls and begins to descend, a small, leafy branch blows off one of the plane trees and swirls and descends with the ball. Raoux manages to hit the ball and not the branch, but his smash goes straight into the backstop. The branch settles gently at his feet. A curious calm descends. He picks up the branch on his racket and carries it to the umpire.

"Look what 'as 'appened! Ze weend. Ze tree!"

"Yes. Well. Sorry about that. Shouldn't have played the shot. Should have asked for a let! Too late now. Have to play on."

"O la la la la la la la la la *laaaah!*" The last *laaaah* nearly unseats the umpire, but his mind is made up. The point is history. Play should continue.

Layendecker, meanwhile, is having his own share of adversity. The women's match next door is in a tie-breaker, all the stops pulled out, everything at full stretch. One of the girls gets an easy volley, misses it, and lets out the most heartrending wail, which floats across to where Layendecker is tossing up the ball for a vital second serve. A double fault suddenly becomes inevitable.

"You wimp!" screams Layendecker at himself, then suddenly he stops and reconsiders.

"Shut up, Layendecker!" he cries, "you're doing your best! What more can you do?"

"How about a first service!" comes the scathing reply.

Poor Layendecker! It is a classic case of self two trying to stand up for itself against self one. W. Timothy Gallwey would have been ecstatic. His two selves locked in argument! What more could any self-proclaimed sports psychologist possibly wish for?

I feel a presence beside me and it's Jim McManus, one of the stalwarts of the ATP Tour.

"Makes you pleased you don't have to do it anymore," he says.

"Yes, it does."

"Here it's life or death. At Wimbledon it's only money!" We nod, each knowing what the other means. McManus, too, lived in the days of train tickets and lunch vouchers.

"A little lunch?" he suggests. "Maybe carbo-charge ourselves?" We walk towards the players' canteen, thinking of the piles of pasta that seem to be the modern path to instant energy.

"Carbo-charging may do us the world of good," I say.

"Get you in shape for the party tonight," he says, and goes on to remind me about the players' party at the Hard Rock Café to which my ATP Tour membership card will give me access.

"One of the few places that the players really relax," he explains. "It's very loud. Very loud. However loud I tell you it is, it's louder. All there is is sound. Nothing else—only sound."

DIARY NOTES, HYDE PARK CORNER, 19 JUNE 1992

Frances (my wife) and I present ourselves at the players' party. Outside the Hard Rock Café a great press of people waits. Only the joueurs *and* non joueurs *are allowed through. You don't really enter—you commit yourself to the deep like a burial at sea, offer yourself to the tide of bodies that closes about you and carries you along, out of control and into the blinding sheets of sound. McManus was right. I take hold of Franny's wrist and the current takes us, pressed against young bodies, chest to chest, thigh to thigh, gusts of silent laughter, fresh beer breaths, shouts like whispers, deeper and deeper into this vortex, behind me in my hand the wrist, ahead the noise and the bodies.*

We get carried along until Gavin materialises out of somewhere and steers us towards a sort of a bar, a little backwater, an eddy in the stream. Beside us are Bill Ryan of IMG and his wife, Caterina. I get a glimpse of Bob Kain, John Evert, Mark Miles, J. Wayne Richmond with his customary minor smile as though he's seen it all before. Weller Evans, for once unable to speak. Pasarell is screaming at V. J. Amritraj. Trays of bot-tled beer and hamburgers drift past, balanced somehow on hands emerging from the human tide. I see a hand reach for a beer and realise that it is my own. And once the hand is up, there is no room for it to get back down, so I tip the bottle and let it run into my mouth, which seems to be the system the players use.

And all the time these cosmic, all-embracing sheets of sound—great rackings of guitar chords crashing down like tim-ber falling, wailing fifths and sevenths amplified beyond mere sound to a vast, vibrating silence that shakes the room. You may shout, but you can't hear yourself. Up on the stage to the right John McEnroe is standing with the band, singing and playing a guitar—or rather, that is what he seems to be doing. You simply can't hear him. A boy with a great beard is playing a tenor saxophone, but he might as well be blowing on his thumb. The guitars and the drummers reign supreme.

On the floor, eager, happy, packed together are the young tennis stars, suddenly become ordinary teenagers. Wayne Ferreira is carrying too many beers, losing some, drinking oth-ers. Connoll, Luke Jensen, wildly modern, Saint David with tweed scarf and goatee. Pat Cash has taken over from McEnroe. Glimpses of Sampras, Courier, Ivanisevic, others, young millionaires with tennis in their blood and laughter in their souls, having fun, lost in this noisy escape so that for a long moment one envies them, wishes achingly to be young again if only for tonight, to be able to embrace all this and not get dizzy spells.

But we are not young, and again, McManus was right. It is

too much, the voice cracks, the ears reject the vibrations, and after less than an hour we are back on the pavement outside. It is one of those sublime London evenings, simultaneously cool and warm. We walk across Park Lane and along the park, murmuring to each other in the silence.

16

THE LOVELY
G R A S S

What is it about the Wimbledon Championships that make them the most distinguished of all tennis tournaments? This quiet green club with its few hundred members who always seem so friendly and laid-back. What has made it so special? One can make a list of reasons, but the true answer is not an easy one to write down. Rather, it is something that, when you arrive there, you feel in the air. One summer's day in 1956, when Jean and I entered the gates of Wimbledon for a practice game before the tournament, she suddenly gave her happy laugh, nudged me in the ribs, and said:

> "'Breathless we flung us on the windy hill,
> Laughed in the sun and kissed the lovely grass.'

Rupert Brooke. I looked it up specially for when we got here. Now let's you and I go to our court and fling us on the lovely grass!"

The All England Club lies in what must once have been a blowing English meadow. You can approach the club from the Southfields side down Wimbledon Park Road, or from the Wimbledon side down Church Road. The roads surrounding the club are winding and confusing, but one thing is certain. Whichever one you take, when you first see the centre court with its purple raiments and green ivy, you always get that same feeling.

DIARY NOTES, WIMBLEDON, 1964

Abie has done it again. "Everything happens to me," he sang in his bath this morning, and he was right. He had to play Clark Graebner in the second round, and because Graebner has one of the few serves in the game as terrifying as his own, Abie arrived at breakfast with a worried look. "If you were me, Forbsey, you'd have crapped yourself by now," he said.

The match went on for a long time, with all the usual crises. Abie kept blocking back the big serve and eventually found himself with a match point. He served, came to net, made a firm volley, and saw Graebner's passing shot go wide into the tramlines by at least a foot. It was all over and knowing Abie, all he wanted to do was shake hands and get off the court as fast as possible. There have been many accounts of what followed, but Abie's definitive version goes like this:

"I run up to the net with my hand out, so what do you think this Graebner does! He just stands there and says: 'Where are you going, Abie! Nobody's called out. The rules say that if nobody calls out, the game isn't over!'

"Suddenly I realise that he's right. He's lookin' at me and I'm lookin' at the umpire and he's lookin' at the lineswoman, and she's lookin' like this"—and with his head on one side and his eyes closed, Abie demonstrates.

"'She's either asleep or else she's dead,' I say to Graebner.

"'She sure hasn't called out,' he says.

"'Listen, Clark, you know that ball was out and I know it was out! Let's go and have a drink. Just because a lineswoman's died doesn't mean I haven't won the match!'

"'She's still supposed to call out,' Graebner persists.

"By now the crowd's starting to laugh and the umpire asks a ballboy to go up to the dead woman and prod her on the shoulder with his finger. Meanwhile I badly need someone to call out so I can get off the court. So I go up to the lineswoman to help the ballboy.

"'Hey, Madam!' I say to her. 'Hey, Madam!' and the ballboy gives her another nudge, and suddenly her eyes open. 'Hey, Madam, do you mind callin' out?' I ask her, and what do you think? 'Out!' she calls, and points with her arm.

"'There you are, Clark,' I say. 'She's called out! Now do you think we can go take a shower?'

"'Kind of a late call,' he's still grumbling as we shake hands.

"Meanwhile, as we walk off the court, all the press people want statements from me. Statements, they want!

"'What can I tell you?' I say to them. 'I always knew my game was boring, but I didn't think it was that bad! In Italy they fall asleep all the time, but never on match point!'"

Abie first visited Wimbledon in 1952 with a friend called Mailer Schneider. Their entries for the tournament had arrived too late for acceptance, and so it had not been possible for them to fling themselves upon the lovely grass. They'd decided to go watch the matches anyway, but when they'd gotten to the All England Club there were long lines of people waiting in the street.

"As far as the friggin' eye could see!" said Abie. "So I go up to a policeman, an' I ask him where the end of the line is.

"'Over the hill, sir,' he says.

"'Over the hill,' I say. 'That's terrific. And how long does it take for it to get back to our side of the hill?'

"'Could be a day or two, sir,' he says.

"'All we want to do is watch tennis,' I tell him. 'It's not like we're tryin' to have tea with the Queen!'"

Abie has always hated queues. For him, they are simply things that in one way or another have to be jumped. This queue, however, was at a complete standstill, so that even jumping it was no use. Other plans had to be made. Abie had long since perfected ways of climbing the fence surrounding Ellis Park, so that to him it seemed reasonable to apply the same methods to the fence surrounding the All England Club.

"You keep our place in the queue," he said to Mailer, "and I'll jump over and see what's going on inside."

He chose a likely looking spot adjacent to where court thirteen now lies, took a quick look round, then—scrambling up the concrete wall and over the strands of wire on top—he jumped down inside the hallowed grounds, rolling over with the impact of his fall.

"The first thing I see are these shiny boots," he would tell me later, "and as I look up I see another cop lookin' down at me!

"'Have you lost your way, my boy?' he says to me.

"'I'm tryin' to find the centre court,' I tell him.

"'Well it's over there,' he says. 'You can have a look at it while I escort you out. Best way in is to join the queue, sir. That's how other people do it, you know.'

"'Other people haven't travelled here from Capetown on a ship, peelin' potatoes,' I tell him. 'I'm only here for two days, you see. By the time the queue comes over the hill I have to be back with the potatoes.'

"'I'm sorry! There's nothing I can do about that,' he says. I really think he was sorry. One thing about those British cops, Forbsey. They were very polite when they caught you jumpin' over fences!"

I first met Mark McCormack when he was invited to South Africa to give an address at a prestigious business function, and I was asked to introduce him. While deciding what to say, I'd found myself struggling with superlatives, until eventually I solved the problem by describing the man and his achievements as simply as I could. Later I was to discover that Mark is addicted to simplicity and brevity. One of his greatest gifts is the ability to take a complicated subject and reduce it to its barest essentials.

After he had made his address that day, we sat and talked, and I was able to get my first real glimpse of this remarkable man. He had the clearest perceptions. He loved sport, was intrigued by top sportsmen, and above all loved the traditions and legends that grow as a sport evolves. Great sporting events and venues held for him a fascination—Augusta, St. Andrews, Pebble Beach, Roland Garros, Lords, Gleneagles. Of course we talked of Wimbledon, and when he asked me why I seldom returned to visit it, I explained that as an ex-player who had once virtually been given the run of the club, I found it painful to return as an ordinary spectator.

"But surely," he said, "they provide some facilities there for people such as you. A few tickets, perhaps, a place to go?"

"Not really," I said. "Only the actual Wimbledon ex-champions are provided for, and I never quite made it, you see. They're very kind—they try to help, but you always feel that you are on the outside, looking in. And at Wimbledon, of all places, that's hard to take."

"Well, your problem could be solved," he said instantly. "We have a tent there, and we sometimes have spare tickets. You're always welcome, you know!"

The McCormack marquee—cool, white, and beautifully appointed—has, over the years, become a haven for me. As in the Paris tent, famous people abound there, but because Mark is at heart an informal man, the atmosphere is friendly and relaxed. There was more to come, however.

In 1986 I received a letter from the All England Club inviting me to become a member of the "Last Eight Club." It was a club, the letter said, that any player who had reached the last eight of any event at Wimbledon was invited to join. There was to be a photo pass for members, a marquee for relaxation, catering and entertainment, certain centre-court tickets, and various other privileges. I read the invitation with growing excitement, and wondered whether McCormack had breathed a word in someone's ear. It was just the kind of thing that he would do—and by then the McCormack organisation had taken on the commercial marketing of the Wimbledon name.

DIARY NOTES, WIMBLEDON, 1986

At last we have our own tent at the All England Club!—not the biggest, or even the smartest tent, but a very nice tent, just the kind that you would like to sit in if you were an old tennis player who had once played at Wimbledon and lost in the semifinals. There is draught beer at a bar that is the right height to rest an elbow on; a counter with salmon salad and strawberries, and at teatime, scones with Devon cream. Helen Morrison stands guard with a proprietary eye. She has a dry and whimsical sense of humour that sometimes overflows into this merry laugh, a fine sense of tradition, and a very small Italian car called Luigi, who lately has been playing up.

"He's very stubborn in the mornings," she told me.

"We should introduce him to Rodrigo," I replied.

The Last Eight Club membership is situated in a court at nineteen, and for all the former players it has become a veritable home from home. The older players drop in all the time—people such as Tony Trabert, Rod Laver, Nicola Pietrangeli, Gardnar Mulloy, John and Angela Barrett, Fred Stolle, Frank Sedgman, Wilhelm Bungert, Rosewall, Newcombe, Luis Ayala, Bob Howe, etc. The list goes on and on, but for me it is impossible to think about the Last Eight Club without thinking of Lewis Hoad.

Lew died in July 1994, and with him died a part of all those who had played tennis in his time. He loved the Last Eight Club. Even though he had won Wimbledon twice (in 1956 and 1957), and was welcomed at the innermost sanctities of the All England Club as an honoured member, he always chose to base himself near the little bar. I can see him now, beer mug in hand, with one eye on the tennis and the other half closed against the smoke of a cigarette—on his face the quizzical, half-surprised frown he used to wear nearly all the time. He liked to have a friend beside him, but there did not have to be a conversation. In his later years he had a beat-up look, as though ravaged by a life that had somehow seemed to puzzle him, a life in which the most lovely rose garden always beckoned—but one to which he never really found the door. ("Shut up, Forbsey!" I can hear him growl.)

But a few more words must be said. Lew played as an amateur for only a few years, but while he played he was invincible—a quiet man who never spoke a word about himself, who never complained, who scorned cheating, who respected the game he loved and the people who tried their best to play it; who was able to play, without fuss or effort, the most harmonious, majestic, and creative tennis of all time. Ask any of the players of his era; they will all want to tell you, but become silent, searching for words.

"Lew Hoad," they might say. "What can we say about him?"—not being able in their minds properly to blend the true measures of gentleness and strength, modesty and pride, simplicity and genius, loyalty and honour.

In his tennis game were merged together infinite grace,

infinite strength, and infinite touch, and in his heart was infinite courage.

"Yes, but wait a moment . . . ," you might say, not quite trusting the weight of such words—and strangely, perhaps, no-one will try to convince you further. For the memory of Lew Hoad is, in a way, the private property of those who knew him well, and as such they tend to keep it for themselves. If Lew was your friend, you see, he was your friend for life.

DIARY NOTES, LAST EIGHT CLUB, 1992

The picture on TV at this moment is that of Jimmy Connors trying to hold his service against Mike Pernfors (of Sweden). Lew is sitting next to Abie, conversing in monosyllables and grumbling to himself about the inefficiency of Connors's service.

"Would you look at that!" he growls. "A bloody great swing, a bloody great grunt, and out pops a mouse!"

It's not that Lew does not admire the Connors game—just that he himself used to play so effortlessly and with so little fuss that anything showy worries him. He likes to see tennis uncluttered by mannerisms and quirks. Understatement, for Lew, was a religion. And above all, in his book, tennis players had to respect the game.

There is a lot of comment and opinion in the Last Eight Club—in general an open admiration for the speed, skill, and power of modern tennis. But older players long for the variety and finesse, the classic grace, that they remember. They think wistfully of the art of the game—the delicate inventions of players like, say, Ken Rosewall, Art Larsen, Manuel Santana, Nicola Pietrangeli. Changes of pace and spin, deftness, touch— the absolute grace and versatility of Rod Laver, the right stroke carefully selected for the right moment from a whole range of strokes.

Sitting beside Niki Pilic while watching a searing doubles match in which the sole intent seemed to be to hit as hard as possible, I asked him whether he thought that he and Boro Jovanovic (the doubles partner with whom he nearly won Wimbledon) could have lived with these modern teams.

"Of course, live with!" he replied superbly. "And not only live with! Also beat! Young player know nothing of dink and chip. Also hit low volley like man who cuts the trees!" (Lumberjacks, I supposed.) "Young player know only of hit cover off ball!"

The art of the game!

"You don't have time for art!" the young players will scold you if you mention it. "You go out there being arty and you find yourself straight back in the 'quallies'! And one thing is for sure—they don't teach art in the quallies!" They're probably right. The game has changed. And the question arises: Are the subtle skills gone forever? Will the Torben Ulrichs of our day never again live to serve a whispering slice into the wind that slides off the grass and finishes up in the water jug under the umpire's seat? Probably not, one decides. Even the water jugs have gone.

DIARY NOTES, LAST EIGHT CLUB, 1992

Joseph Stahl, once a joueur, *now a lawyer, slips a note into* my hand that says:

"You'll be hearing from my solicitors in the near future!"

Joseph is suing me on the grounds that I rendered him null and void in my previous book (A Handful of Summers). He feels aggrieved, and knows his case off by heart:

"On page one hundred sixty-six you state that you played someone called Roger Werksman in the first round of the Southampton [Long Island] tournament in 1962," he says, with all the relentlessness of a California lawyer in full cry.

"I have a right to remain silent," I say.

"You can remain anything you like, but you didn't play Werksman," he says. "You played me." He thumps himself on the chest as if to prove that he exists. "You played Werksman in the second round."

"What was the score?"

"Against me? Love and love!"

"Then that explains it!"

"It doesn't explain it! It's irrelevant! What is relevant is that you expunged me. Caused me to cease to be! You stole a part of my life. That's theft!"

"It was a very short match," I say. "Don't matches have to be more than a given length of time before they are deemed to have taken place?"

"I will now add a charge of contempt to my case of theft and grievous mental harm," he replies. "You will never know what it's like when a match you played is deemed to have disappeared and you cease to exist."

"Oh but I do!" I tell him. "I once played Rex Hartwig in the first round at Queens, and he beat me love and love in *about ten minutes. I ceased to exist for days after that! But I didn't sue Hartwig."*

Thus Joseph Stahl. Every year we argue about whether he exists, and if so, whether I need to compensate him for what he calls mental anguish. The Last Eight Club is full of such conjecture. You can hang your coat and umbrella there, then sally forth and watch the matches, although most of the members are by now too old to sally as well as they used to. ("We'll say that we shall be deemed to have sallied!" says Joseph Stahl.) This process of simply "deeming" vigorous activities to have taken place seems more promising as the years go by.

One of the most elevated things to do during the English summer is to have lunch in the members' enclosure of the All England Club on the opening day of Wimbledon. Lunch there on any day is auspicious, but opening day has about it a particular aura of distinction.

If you enter the grounds of the club at gate five—i.e., the Church Road gate—you have the Fred Perry statue on your right, and the members' enclosure on your left. The members have several places where they can, as some of them put it, "get away from it all," but the actual members' enclosure is where they and their guests have their lunch. It is low and unobtrusive, but if you pass by and glance inside, you will notice that it is also deep and spacious, suggesting comfort, distinction, exclusivity, iced gins, and good food.

At about noon, a number of members always stand outside in the sun, waiting for certain things to happen. In their well-tailored dark suits, with members' badges and ribbons attached, they are a formidable sight. You almost never pass the members' enclosure without seeing someone you know. Basil Hutchins, for example, or Chris Gorringe, or Buzzer Hadingham, or John Beddington. Virginia Wade. Tony Pickard, if Stefan Edberg is not on court. G. L. Ward, perhaps, or G. L. Paish, J. E. Barrett, Barry Weatherill, Roger Ambrose. Charles Swallow, with his sparkling wife, Susanna. Charles and Susanna own the Vanderbilt Racket Club, another impeccable venue for tennis, but on opening day they usually lunch at the All England. Charles as always is tall and distinguished-looking with that fine English eye for a ball that makes you think of cover drives by cricketers like David Gower. Susanna has blue blood and a glint in her eye, and in her beautifully tailored suit looks discreetly elegant and "well stacked" (as the Americans say), although one feels it might be against club rules for any female member to turn up on opening day looking too well stacked.

If he is there, John Feaver may have about him the slightly distracted look that he uses to suggest that there may just be one or two very minor things not quite in place. John is a member of the All England Club committee. If you say to him, "You look a little worried, John," as I once did, he will give the remark some thought.

"Worried?—well, not worried, really, more in a state of—er—limbo, you could say, waiting for—er—several things to, well—er—happen, really. Quite important, some of them. Should all be arranged by now, I suppose—ducks in a row, that kind of thing, but there you are, always the possible slip-up—

could throw things out a bit. Pity if it happens, really."

"Pity if what happens?"

"Fellow I'm waiting for doesn't pitch up. How are you, by the way?"

"I'm very well!"

"Yes. I suppose we all are—or if we're not, we should be. Very well, that is. No excuse, really, if we aren't, is there? Not on a day like today!"

"Any funny things happened lately?" I always ask John.

John has an unusual sense of humour, wry, a little absurd, and so understated that when relating certain stories he often leaves sentences unfinished, for fear, I suppose, that they may only give rise to still further complications as he goes on.

"Funny things?" muses John. "Let's see. Nothing, really. The odd incident comes to mind. Dog ate the neighbour's rabbit, if one can call that—er—funny. Yes. Didn't kill it, actually, only ate it. Already dead, you see, and buried. Our fellow dug it up. Very good at digging, our chap. Didn't really eat it. Just gnawed it a bit. Had to rebury it (me, not the dog). That, and oh, yes, bit of a joke about one of our proposed new sponsors. Branson's lot, you know. Virgin Airlines. Considered sponsoring a women's tournament—Bournemouth, or Brighton, perhaps, somewhere in the south . . . well anyway, bit of a problem with the name—what to call the event, you see. Couldn't decide between the 'Virgin Women's Open,' or the 'Virgin Women's Closed.' Committee got into a bit of a tiz about that. Clearing of throats, rattling of walking sticks. . . ."

In this mood I love to listen to Feaver. "Whom did you say you were waiting for?" I prompt him. One of his bailiwicks is overseeing sponsorship of British tournaments.

"American chap," he says, glancing up and down, "big wheel, corporate stuff, you know, president and so forth, fame, power, money, what we'd all like, really, I suppose. He made it on the—er . . . well, never mind. Anyway, he's a large sponsor, of tournaments, that is—should be here any minute . . . invited to lunch, opening day, Royal Box, tea, etc., Americans love all that—name of Orifice. Yes. Orifice. Paul, actually. There's also a Mrs. Orifice—two Orifices. Orifi, I suppose you could say. I'd be happier with some alternative—Orifeechee, or something a bit Italian perhaps, but, well, no, nothing for it, Orifice it is." He glances at his watch. "Should be here by now. Everything laid on . . . hope the rain holds off. . . ." He goes off to check up on something. Conversations at Wimbledon are so often fragmented by unforeseen interruptions that they sometimes carry on for days.

Or John MacDonald, perhaps, with a little time on his hands. ("Not a lot. Meeting someone for lunch at one!") Bournemouth, 1959, I think. You caught glimpses of an indefinite young New Zealander, playing somebody, somewhere, winning or losing, you weren't sure, but gradually recurring here and there, Hurlingham, Paddington, Nottingham, Scarborough, perhaps, and finally, materialising and becoming J. MacDonald (NZ)—with a low-key, furtive sort of game that was dangerous and hard to beat—the kind you had to watch out for in the draw. Later John got involved with pro tennis, Lamar Hunt, Owen Williams, the Handsome Eight, the WCT, etc., and ran major things, still in his quiet way, until he became Johnny Mac, a permanent part of the scene.

DIARY NOTES, WIMBLEDON, 1991
(OUTSIDE THE MEMBERS' ENCLOSURE)

Today Johnny Mac recalls the time that we went to a ball in Bournemouth. (Now they have players' parties, but then some of the tournaments had balls.) At that ball, without either of us knowing it, John took a fancy to my partner and I took a fancy to his, and we both made covert plans for later on. John warms to his story as the memories return:

"After the dance we stood in the foyer with the two girls, and you said, 'What shall we do now?' and I said, 'Well, I'm tired. I'm thinking of an early night,' and you said, 'Funny, so am I,' and we both said, 'See you in the morning, then,' and we went off to our rooms, and no sooner had we got inside than we sneaked out again. Except that we'd both arranged to meet each other's partners at the same coffee bar, and we arrived dead on time and caught each other red-handed. I'll never forget what you said: 'Well, John,' you said, 'it looks like from now on we've got each other over a barrel!'"

His girl had been tallish and dark and mine had been small and blonde, and after we had swopped it was vice versa.

"Let's go and have a drink to that," I say (now, not then) and I go with him into the members' enclosure, where it is not in the least difficult to get a drink.

After lunching at the Last Eight Club, you usually check to find out what matches are going on, and then work out which ones to drop in on, and whom you are likely to find watching them. Directly in front of the club are courts fourteen to seventeen. Usually, though, you turn left and walk down past the

Lawn Tennis Association offices (where you might bump into Sandilands or Trickey), the International Tennis Federation offices (where you might see Lord Babcock or Doug McCurdy), the museum and tea lawn (where you might meet almost anybody), until you arrive at the Fred Perry statue, where you turn right and proceed past the members' enclosure (where you might continue your little chat with Feaver).

Here you have two options—you can either squeeze down the alley alongside courts five and ten to show court thirteen (near where Abie jumped the fence), or go on down the south concourse, threading your way through the crowds waiting at the main entrance for glimpses of the stars. Anywhere along this concourse you can turn left down the alleys between the courts. During the first week, though, these alleys are jammed with spectators, for the courts abound with interesting and sometimes great matches, and the players are right there beside you, sometimes as close as a yard or two away.

If you don't turn left down the alleys and just keep going, you find yourself beside show court two. On the left is the board with the schedule of matches and results, and on the right is the referee's office and the entrance to the players' lounge and restaurant. Here, a big decision must be made—whether to go into the players' lounge to see who is there, or to continue drifting down towards courts six, seven, eleven, and twelve, and end up at McCormack's tent, just in case the walk has made you feel a cup of tea coming on.

The players' lounge is quite another world. Here, suddenly, the superstars become ordinary teenagers again, carrying their trays of food and chatting with their friends, parents, coaches, etc. Sabatini and Graf are taller than you'd think, and also Agassi, while Sanchez is smaller. Krajicek is not nearly as intense as he seems on court; Sampras and Courier are college kids in T-shirts. Also, the lounge is where all the players' agents make their deals, so you see a lot of them in their suits and ties huddled in corners having conversations. Go up the stairs and onto the balcony and you can look out over courts two to thirteen, and just make out the scores—Masur is leading against Gilbert, Jennifer Capriati is beating Pam Shriver, Sandon Stolle is struggling against Wilkinson. (Somewhere, Fred will be watching!)

Finally, it's time to leave because you've arranged to meet somebody somewhere, and nowhere does time fly as it does at Wimbledon. So you go back down the stairs, and just as you have gathered momentum around the little backwater behind court two, you get to court six and find Fred Stolle furtively watching his son Sandon playing his match.

"Just like all the German mommies and daddies, Forbsey," he says, with a wry smile.

"How's he doing?" I ask.

"He's playing pretty well," says Fred. "Does a few stupid things, though. Funny thing is, I see him doing all the stupid things I used to do when I was a kid, and then, when the match is over, I feel like saying to him, 'How could you be so bloody stupid?'"

Parents in tennis! Seeing themselves suddenly famous— watching their children with avid eyes. Only today on the players' balcony I overheard a worried parental voice saying to some coach, "Well, we've got him through whining and tanking, and now we're into choking, anger, tantrums, and trying to avoid earrings . . . that kind of stuff! We haven't started winning matches yet. Oh, no! Why would we think of winning matches? . . ."

When Abe Segal and Betsy Nagelsen arrive out of the crowds it is time to go to Mark's tent after all. But on the way there, you realise that Ferreira is about to play Becker, so you change direction and for the umpteenth time that day. . . .

Afterwards, when the shadows get long and the courts are all but empty, except perhaps for a few mixed doubles, each with its little cluster of enthusiasts, you make your way back to the Last Eight Club again. You have to be back in town by nine. A taxi? The train at Southfields? Perhaps someone will have a car. . . . Tonight is the night that Marchese makes his three kinds of pasta at McCormack's house in Chelsea. "It's tradition," says McCormack. He's becoming more and more intent on tradition. Things that happened before must happen again. Anyway, Cino's pasta carries the touch of a master chef, but you still have to get there (and not forget the umbrella . . .).

And if today is Saturday, then tomorrow must be Sunday. The middle Sunday of Wimbledon. A day that was always filled with such simple relaxation. The players would all go off to Bisham Abbey in busses for lunch and tea. Now, though, you may just take it easy. Lunch at Windsor, perhaps, or in the country at Wolpe's house. Or Kerzner may phone from his great estate at Ibstone. If all else fails, some small pub by the side of the Thames where you may recall other Sundays from another life. . . .

DIARY NOTES, LONDON, 1968

Let me tell you about Abie's fateful Sunday. There'd been talk around Wimbledon for days about a party. Lynchie's party, word said. Some great house on the Thames, food, champagne, women. The middle Sunday of Wimbledon. Very exclusive, only the "in" crowd invited. Twiggy will be there, almost for sure, not to mention Terence Stamp, Sarah Lawson, maybe even Shrimpton. Harry Fowler, of course. London's gone crazy. Tramps, Arethusas, the beat of the King's Road, women burning bras, models in miniskirts. The very air one breathes is full of lust, and Lynchie, being in show business, personifies the mood.

Of course Abie wouldn't dream of finding out the exact address—oh, no! He knows exactly where Lynchie lives, before Ray Moore even tells him.

"What do you think?" he says. "That I don't know where the Thames is?"

"It's quite a long river, Abie!"

"Listen! Go tell that to the idiots who need road maps and guide dogs!"

So on Sunday morning off he goes, driving his rented van along the Thames until he sees a lot of cars parked outside a house that has "music comin' out the front door." In he goes, and they give him a glass of champagne and he starts chatting to a few people, one of them a girl, Mish, her name is, short for Alicia, yes, she's been to Wimbledon, are you the Abe Segal?—Sure I am! Who else? How many Segals can there be? Etc., etc., then more champagne, and eventually he'd better find old Lynchie and tell him what a great party it is, so he

stops one of these real London chaps wearin' a scarf around his
neck and he says to him:

"Where is Lynchie?"

"Who is Lynchie?" the chap wants to know.

"The guy who is givin' this party," says Abie.

"My dear chap, I'm giving this party!"

"Are you sure you're givin' this party?"

"Was last time I checked, old chap."

"Well, you're definitely not Lynchie!"

"I'm not even nearly Lynchie! Pity, in a way . . . !"

"One of us is at the wrong party," says Abie.

"Well, now that you're here, old chap, have another glass
of champers!"

Abie had finally left the party still determined to "find that
idiot Lynchie." Somewhere in Battersea he took a wrong turning and motored up a ramp into the bus depot to find himself
surrounded by hundreds of red busses. And reversing back
down the ramp he was stopped and questioned by the traffic
police.

"'What were you wanting up there, sir?' they ask me.

"'I was just checkin' up on all these busses,' I tell them."

The red-handed capture led to the unearthing of a file
marked "A. Segal," which carefully listed the multitude of
parking offenses that Abie had committed during his twenty
years of driving hired cars in London traffic.

"We've been waiting for you, Mr. Segal," said the depart-
ment head. "You're a wanted man!"

"A wanted man!" Abie had told me later, liking the sound

of it. "I had to appear in the Old Bailey, and Claude Lister came along to advise me. An old bloke in a grey wig reads out everything I've done wrong. 'Your Worship' they keep callin' him. If I add up all the sentences, I figure I can get about twenty years!

"'How do you plead?' he wants to know.

"'Guilty, Your Worship,' I say. (Boy, was I guilty! Even Claude said I was guilty.)

"'Have you anything to say?' he asks me.

"'Nothing, Your Worship,' I say, 'except if that's what can happen when you park in the wrong place, I'm glad I didn't commit murder!'

"Cost me a hundred quid, Forbsey, and it was cheap at the price!"

17

A B R U S H
W I T H I T A L Y

This morning we take a map of the city and walk, stopping at last for coffee on a small piazza with galleries of marble and a limestone fountain flowing with water as pale as white wine. Sunlight and water! A youth leans against the fountain playing a flute and the woman at the café table beside me has this panel of blue-black hair that falls over a skin like burnt sugar. She closes her eyes to the sun and lazily smokes Italian cigarettes. We drink our coffee and time comes to a standstill until we get up and keep on walking towards the tennis courts.

The Italian Open, played at the Foro Italico in Rome, is now run by Cino Marchese for the Mark McCormack organisation. Cino is the archetypal Italian *magnifico*, the kind of man who stands out in any crowd. Tall, a tanned face, a head of

243

distinguished white hair, and the kind of sartorial style that can be achieved only by certain Italians—suits of, say, beige and copper, sea blue shirts, silk ties, and the right kind of shoes. A sort of *capo de tuti capi* of tennis, Cino has been involved with the game as long as anyone can remember. He gives me his usual warm welcome and on this spring morning in Rome, with the flags lifting on the breeze, the white sunlight, and the dark blue sky, the Foro Italico is full of promise.

"Ciao, Gorrrdon! *Comesta?*"

"Hello, Maestro! Lucky! Lucky to be back in Rome! And on such a day!"

In its own way, the Foro Italico has the same one-of-a-kind aura about it as a Roland Garros or a Wimbledon, and was once regarded as the "fifth" of the world's great tournaments. On its sunken courts with their marble terraces, their statues, and their cypresses, great players have played great matches, made more dramatic by the slowness of the red clay and the fervour of the Italian crowds. Now, as with all the old tournaments, modern things are encroaching. Great bleachers have grown around the centre court, there are billboards, and, to Cino's disgust, fast-food outlets have been installed. He is fervent about both Italy and its foods, and he regards junk food as one of the world's evils.

DIARY NOTES, FORO ITALICO

Today I came upon Jim McManus in the locker room, furtively eating a hamburger.

"Sorry about this," he said.

"I don't mind," I replied.

"Weller Evans and I were dying of hunger," he explained, "so we bought hamburgers. Weller finished his, but I thought I would take mine to the balcony above the courts and watch the tennis while I ate it. But Cino suddenly took it out of my hands and threw it over the balcony into the garden.

"'You can't-a eat that here in-a my tournament!' he said sternly. 'Here you must eat-a the pasta like in civilisation!'

"Then he pointed to the fast-food place and said that the only reason he put it there was to show the Italian people how badly the American people ate." After he left, Jim had to sneak off to buy another hamburger, and eat it in secret.

"Cino never comes into the locker room!" he said.

If anything, Rome has become even more chaotic than I remember it. Lovely as it is, the whole city seems in need of repair. Plastic bags lie everywhere, and the streets are thick with traffic and diesel fumes. I had forgotten about the way Italians drive their cars—one hand on the horn, one foot hovering between gas pedal and brake. Cino sums it up thus:

"To-a normal people, a red traffic light is a law. To-a Romans, it is an *opinion!*"

He gives me a slap on the shoulder and some tickets for the centre court. And after watching Yannick Noah for a while I go down to court six and sit under the pines where, thirty years ago, Jean and I sat one day while we divided between us the lira notes they had given us as "expenses." The old pines are still there, and the pine needles lie on the gravel and smell of a resinous Mediterranean summer. The back courts of the Foro Italico haven't changed at all. Even the old groundsmen

245

drench the courts with the same plumes of spray that used to worry Warren Woodcock while he served.

In the jargon of tennis players, Abie and I "played Rome" on several occasions without having any effect on the final day's matches. After the first few rounds our amusement had to come from eating Italian food and exploring the city. One day in May of about 1957 (my notes are undated), we arrived to find that Abie had to play Joseph Asboth of Hungary in the first round. I had to play Edison Mandarino of Brazil, and Art Larsen had to play an Englishman called Tommy Anderson.

It was Abie who'd told me of Art Larsen, and at first I'd thought that he was exaggerating. "What you got to understand, Forbsey," he said to me, "is that nearly all Americans are a bit weird. But there is a big difference being weird and being crazy. And this Larsen is definitely crazy!" He went on to tell me how Larsen's psychiatrists, after analysing him, had to see their psychiatrists, and that one should thus be careful about spending too much time with him. "Not only is he crazy, Forbsey. He drives other people crazy, too. You wait and see. Why do you think this Herbie Flam can't sleep unless he takes pills and sticks cotton wool in his ears? He's been travelling with Larsen, that's why!"

Abie himself had also travelled with Larsen. Given half a chance he could talk for hours about him—about his strange habits, his superstitions, the eagles on his shoulders, and his superb touch on the tennis court.

And he was right. Larsen was crazy. Gloriously and sublimely crazy in a way that for years delighted his fans and his fellow players all over the world. He did constantly have to tap things, he did often get stuck in his clothes, or in doorways, or while changing ends on the tennis court. He did have an eagle sitting on his shoulder that only went away if he kept his shirt collar clamped between his teeth; and he often talked to his friends on the courtside during his matches, not only between, but actually during, points—a sort of running self-commentary:

"Now watch this, Big Abie. Here's the dropshot. Here's the lob. Now he'll be expecting the dropshot. So I go deep, see? Watch this guy start running in when he should be running back!"

His commentaries seemed to have no effect whatever on his concentration, enabling him to play some of the most beautifully cerebral tennis while at the same time having a little chat. There was no fear in Larsen—only this total absorption in playing tennis. On form and in the right mood, no living person could do more with a racket and a ball than could he.

In his book *Tennis My Way* (published after his Wimbledon and Roland Garros victories in 1950), the great American player Budge Patty listed the players whom he considered to be "the world's ten best players" of the day, stressing that his choices were based purely on his own experiences in playing. His list is as follows, from one to ten:

Frank Sedgman; Arthur Larsen; Ted Schroeder; Jaroslav Drobny; Herbert Flam; Eric Sturgess; Gardnar Mulloy; William Talbert; John Bromwich; and Ken McGregor.

He obviously set aside those players whom he had not played, such as Jack Kramer, but nonetheless, the position of Larsen on his list was significant. Patty also quoted Larsen himself on the reasons for his strange habits:

"One day, in a particularly rough air raid during the war" (related Larsen), "so many of my friends were killed all around me that it was a miracle I came through all right. I figured I must have done something that day that brought me luck, so I remembered everything I'd done, how I'd dressed, which shoe I put on first, what time I had breakfast, etc., and for the rest of the war I followed my lucky routine. After the war my superstitions stayed with me in tennis. If I win a point with one ball, I have to use it again for the next point. When changing sides I must cross on the opposite side to my opponent; if I pass the umpire, I must touch him. I have to tap the baseline before receiving serve, and then not step on it between points. I have so many superstitions now that I forget some of them, and that worries me."

Whenever we arrived at any tournament, the first name we would look for on the draw sheets, after we'd found our own, was that of Art Larsen. Best of all was if Art was drawn to play against people like Don Candy or Warren Woodcock, or perhaps Beppe Merlo or the Italian stone-waller, Fausto Gardini. Such matches were, as Abie used to say, "better than a three-ring circus."

But back to Rome. Both Abie and I believed that we were better on clay than the other was, so that it became a matter of honour who could win the most rounds in Italian tournaments—events that, in addition to the slowness of their courts and the sly behaviour of some of their players, also presented a whole range of other distractions, mainly to do with their umpires and linesmen, and the noisy habits of the partisan spectators.

"Play Italy for too long," Abie used to say, at frequent intervals, "and a man can end up lookin' like this!" and he'd demonstrate a Groucho Marx walk, looking backwards over his shoulder with the same maniacal facial tics that had scared the old umpire at Hurlingham.

Both Asboth and Mandarino were good clay-courters, but it was Asboth who was the more sinister opponent. He was older, for a start, with a weather-beaten look and an eerie Eastern European inscrutability—as fit as a fiddle, as steady as a rock, and with the patience of Job. And yet he was the kind of player whom other players felt they shouldn't lose to. Especially Abie.

Thus it was that he put on an air of great nonchalance when he regarded his draw, asking himself things like, "How tough can an old guy like that be?" several times, and going on to mutter that there was no need to worry and that he could "have him for breakfast" any day of the week.

"He's tough on slow clay, Big Abie," said Mervyn Rose mildly, in the players' coffee bar, a remark to which Abie had in principle to reply: "And what do you think that I am on clay paralysed or something?" which nobody dared respond to, although Woodcock did raise one eyebrow very slightly.

And there was, of course, no doubt about it—if ever clay was slow, the clay at the Foro Italico, soaked as it was by the mighty hoses of the garlic-eating Italian groundsmen, was about as slow as you could get.

"You stay on the baseline, you fall asleep waitin' for your serve to come back!" Abie used to say. But rushing the net was even worse. When heavy Pirelli balls were added to the equation, things came to a virtual standstill. Oh, yes, sure, there was plenty of time to get to the net. That wasn't the problem. What was the problem, was what to do when you got there!

Net-rushing is a fluid and mobile science. You don't really rush the net. In a way you stalk it. From the time of serving to the completion of the volley combinations, the flow of movement must be instinctive and continue until the winning volley is hit and the point won. If you come to a standstill, you are lost—and on clay, because it is so difficult to end the point, standstills among net-rushers are not uncommon.

Now the young players simply power their passing shots either for winners or for errors; but then, when points went wrong, it was much more evil: You served. They returned low and angled. You volleyed deep, hoping for a kill on the next stroke. They returned again, lower and more angled. You volleyed again, more desperately. They ran it down, and it was at this stage that a working knowledge of the Uncertainty Principle became vital. With each volley you seemed to get increasingly bogged down, your legs getting wider apart, the gaps on either side of you becoming bigger, your opponents having more time to make their shots.

Such were the gloomy thoughts that used to go through our minds when we contemplated the courts of Rome and saw names like Asboth looming near us in the draw sheets.

Larsen's opponent, Tommy Anderson, was one of those priceless tennis worshippers for whom the game was simultaneously an obsession and a way of life. At the same time he was a player who, no matter how much he played, never got any better. You could go to the Hurlingham Club on almost any summer morning and you'd find Tommy there, practising. If there was no-one around, he would produce a basket of balls and practise his service. Toss, swing, hit; over and over, the same action, the same serve, as eternal and unchanging as the expression on his face when he contemplated the inevitable results of his efforts. In major tournaments he was a godsend. No-one ever lost to Tommy. The most that he ever expected of himself was to put up a good show.

"He could make a living hiring himself out for first-round matches!" Abie once said. But in Rome that year, it was Larsen who had to play Tommy, and Abie who had to play Asboth.

Larsen, meanwhile, had been playing exhibitions in the New York area, and was thus a day or two late for Rome. Being Larsen, though, he was forgiven. With him, lateness was a minor problem. His actual arrival on the scene was the thing that tournament referees worried about.

After his New York matches, Larsen had drunk a few beers to cool off and then forgotten to change his clothes (something he quite often did), boarding the plane at the last minute in his tennis gear and arriving in Rome somewhat rumpled but ready to walk straight back on the court. At the Rome airport he simply ordered the taxi to take him directly to the tennis courts.

Where he had met and taken into tow the robust blonde female companion who accompanied him, no-one could say. Larsen's seasons of activity in this regard were so varied and surprising that the other players used merely to watch and wonder in silence. Thus it was that when the taxi pulled up at the Foro Italico, the first to emerge was the robust blonde, followed by a travel-stained, ready-to-play Larsen, who hurried straight off to the tournament referee to sign in, leaving his friend and his luggage in a heap in the players' coffee shop.

Could Signor Larsen play on court four in half an hour, the referee anxiously wanted to know? Sure, kid, that would be no problem, he replied. Anytime would do. Straightaway, if they could find his opponent. And of course they could. Tommy Anderson had been waiting eagerly for two days to play the famous Larsen, practising at every opportunity. His game was as ready as it would ever be. So Larsen went back up to the coffee shop to fetch his rackets, only to find when he got there that his blonde friend had disappeared. So he temporarily forgot about his match and set off to find her.

On court three, meanwhile, a match of great drama was in progress between Abie and Asboth. The score stood at two sets to one for Abie, but with Asboth leading 4-1 in the fourth. The final outcome was thus obscure, and Abie was having a lot to say about the habits of the Italian linesmen, who (he felt) were not only having trouble seeing, but who also kept coming and going, apparently to have their lunch. This troubled Abie, who had never gotten over an occasion during a match in Naples when a linesman had unwrapped a large salami sandwich and begun eating it when he was about to serve for the match at 6-5 in the final set.

"Listen, buddy, you don't mind if I serve while you eat?" he'd said, but the linesman had simply ignored him and munched away.

"With my kind of luck," he'd complained to me afterwards, "my opponent's return misses the line on match point and the guy can't call out because his mouth's full of salami! Jesus Christ, Forbsey! These Ites can drive a man crazy!"

DIARY NOTES, ROME

After Abie's match today, when he'd finally cooled down, he gave me the following account:

"It's two sets to one for me, Forbsey" (he says), "and he's up a break in the fourth. But things are just startin' to come together for me—the linesmen have finished their lunch, the groundsmen have stopped sprayin' water, the sun's moved over so I can see to serve, and I'm leadin' thirty-fifteen. So what do you think happens? This Larsen comes down those marble stairs tappin' things like Fred Astaire and he runs straight onto my court.

"'Hey, Big Abie,' he shouts, 'did she go past this way?'

"'Did who go past this way?' I ask—like I really care at that stage who the crap's just gone past.

"'A big blonde with knockers like this!' he says, and he starts to show me how big they are with his hands.

"'Can't you see I'm playin' Asboth?' I ask him.

"'Sure, Asboth,' he says. 'No problem. Just play him short and long. But I'm trying to figure out what's happened to Brenda.'

"'And I'm trying to hold serve while you want a conversation!' I say to him. 'I mean, Jesus, Tappy, can't you just frig off?'

"'That's not very nice, Big Abie,' he says, but he gets the message.

"So off he goes to look for Brenda, and it's still thirty-fifteen and my serve, which I immediately drop. So you think that's the end of the story, Forbsey? No way. We get to two-one in the fifth and I'm still tryin' to hold my service. Next thing I know, Larsen walks on the court next door to play Tommy Anderson.

"'I found Brenda,' he says to me. He's so excited that when Tommy Anderson spins his racket for the toss, he says to him, 'You serve, you take side, you take whatever you want, I'm ready.'

"'Don't you want to hit up?' asks Anderson.

"'I already had a hit in New York,' he says. Then he walks over to my court and he says to me, 'Hey, Abie, what's your score?'

"'Two-sets-all, two-one for him,' I have to tell him. With Larsen, what can you do? For him, two-sets-all is no problem. Meanwhile my concentration is going one way. Next thing he walks even closer to me and he says, 'Listen, Big Abie, with this Asboth all you have to do is play him short and long. I keep telling you that. Now listen. I'll show you. I'll play this guy of mine the way you should be playing Asboth. Just watch me, buddy, and you'll know exactly what you have to do!'

"The next thing I know, I see Tommy Anderson running all over the place after lobs and dropshots, and Tappy is saying to me, 'This is what you have to do, see, Abie. Short and long. Like this, see? What are you hitting so hard for?'

"You think I could concentrate out there, Forbsey, with

all that crap going on? No chance. So I lose the match six-two in the fifth, and here I am, drinking a cup of coffee! 'Jesus Christ, Tappy,' I say to him as I walk off the court, but that doesn't stop him beating Anderson about love, love, and love."

In Rome that year Ian Vermaak, Trevor Fancutt, and I shared a large room overlooking the Piazza de Asedera. In the small streets nearby there were restaurants festooned with great hangings of homemade pasta and smoked hams. You could eat yourself stupid for five shillings, and afterwards, on the piazza, you could buy freshly baked caramel custard in little china dishes.

That was also the year that we hired Lambretta scooters to beat the Rome traffic. I'd never ridden a scooter in Italian traffic before and came close to panic several times before I got the hang of it. Having done so, however, we became as free as birds. The city shrank to comfortable proportions and we were able to explore it, thoroughly and happily, even picking up two Australian girls who were hitchhiking their way around Europe, and showing them the catacombs. ("Yeah, the catacombs," said Abie. "Like you two know such a friggin' lot about the catacombs!")

DIARY NOTES, ROME

After dinner tonight, Fancutt, Vermaak, Abie, Jaroslav Drobny, and I walked along the Via Veneto, looking at the shops. Finally we stopped in front of a shoe store. Abie was very impressed with the Italian shoes, but Drobny, who had seen the size and shape of Abie's feet, gave a snort of laughter.

"They don't know about such shoes in Italy," he said. "If you want shoes you have to go to the docks where they build the boats."

This of course didn't please Abie, who immediately bet Drobny a dollar that they would have a pair of shoes to fit him. We all trooped into the shop and Abie had to put his foot on a footrest and have it measured. We all contemplated it while the shopkeeper got out his measure. When he opened it wide enough to measure Abie's foot, the end of the measuring device came off its rail.

"You see!" said Drobny. "They can't even measure you up!"

"Fifteen!" muttered the assistant, looking very grave. He disappeared into the back of the shop and returned eventually with a large shoe box from which he took a mighty pair of moccasins that made the neat shoes in the window look like miniatures.

"Oh, boy! Drob's right," said Trevor. "We'll be able to row across to Sicily."

As usual, when Abie took off his shoes to try on the new ones, he had no socks on, and there was this great foot in all its glory, toes going all over the place, lumps and bumps sticking out the side. The shopkeeper stepped back with a rattle of Italian.

"He says you need socks," said Drobny. Socks were produced and there was more Italian.

"He says you must buy the socks," said Drobny.

So Abie bought the socks and finally, with the help of a shoehorn, to everyone's surprise Abie's foot disappeared inside the shoe. Being of soft leather, however, it at once took on the shape of the foot, losing nearly all its Italian character and looking like all Abie's other shoes, except more shiny. But Drobny took a dollar out of his pocket and handed it over.

"It was worth it!" he said happily.

Later that night I told Abie that he had amazing feet and that maybe when he died he should leave them to mankind.

"Listen, Forbsey," he replied, "if mankind needs my feet, it's in a hell of a bad way!"

Perhaps it was the scooter riding in the Italian traffic that did it. Or perhaps the scooters in combination with the slow clay courts. Whatever the cause, I did some quite weird things at night in the big *pensione* room that, on that occasion, I shared with Trevor Fancutt and Ian Vermaak. Weird and mysterious, you could say, because for the first few nights I never woke up, so no-one could really explain it.

The first morning, when Ian went to his cupboard to get his clothes he couldn't find some of them, and it was only after some searching that they were found quite neatly packed into Trevor's suitcase.

"What's my stuff doing in your case?" Ian asked Trevor, not unreasonably, but Trevor couldn't tell him.

"I don't know how it got there," he said. "Must be the maid."

The next morning I found my own clothes packed away into Ian's suitcase. When we confronted the Italian chambermaid, she looked blank. On the third night nothing happened, but on the fourth, we were all awoken by a mighty bang caused by the three suitcases falling off the top of the cupboard where they had been stacked. Worse still was that when the light was finally switched on, the person standing amongst the fallen cases was me.

"Oh, boy!" said Trevor, which was what he always said when things got out of hand. "So that's it."

"I know nothing about this," I said curtly but hopelessly. My first instinct when realising that I had been caught out in one of my nightmares was to deny everything.

"You know nothing about it!" said Ian. "Like you knew nothing about it when the Mau Mau came to get us that night in Kenya."

He had me there and he knew it. I'd caused such havoc that night that I still cringed at the very thought of it. Ian and I had played the Middle Eastern circuit—Beirut, Istanbul, and Athens, and then, thoroughly dehydrated by the Mediterranean heat, we'd stopped over for a night in Nairobi at the famous Norfolk Hotel before going on safari on the farm of a friend in the hinterland of Kenya at a place called Nanyuki.

It was bad enough that in the dead of night in the Norfolk I'd had a to-the-death struggle with the mosquito net over my bed, ending up with the whole thing collapsed on top of me and Ian's startled face looking down at me as I lay tangled in the meshes.

"I dreamed I was suffocating," I explained feebly. It was impossible to describe the feeling of instantaneous terror that swept up out of nowhere at such times. I could not understand it myself. Nor could I explain the incident that took place the following night on the farm in Nanyuki—an incident that made my skirmish with the mosquito net look positively tame.

The farm belonged to a settler called Segar Bastard. It was a huge spread on which his great herds of Friesian cattle grazed amongst the zebras and kudus and Thomson's gazelles. Segar and his wife, Dell, were wonderful hosts. We'd arrived in the late afternoon and Segar showed us around in the gathering sunset. Everywhere there remained signs of the Mau Mau terror. The farmstead was ringed by a great dry moat filled with hundreds of wooden spikes instead of water. Great hedges of thorn circled the cow crawls, the windows of the buildings were fitted with bars and bolts, and Segar still carried a Webley and Scott army-issue .45 revolver in a belt holster, although he said it was no longer necessary.

"It's been over for more than two years now," he explained, "but I don't think that we will ever be able to forget"—and he told us stories of the long and anxious days and nights when no-one could be trusted, when the thought of a knife in the back made the flesh crawl, when the darkness was filled with dread and the warm African moonlight was no longer friendly, but cold with treachery.

Dinner was served at a long and massive table—roast venison with farm vegetables and great pitchers of tropical fruit juices. There were at least ten other guests, I remember—Ian and I were playing an exhibition match at the town club the next day, and Segar's friends had gathered for the event. Tired from travelling, we turned in early. Our room was the last one at the end of a long passage, equipped with two comfortable but collapsible beds over which hung the inevitable mosquito nets.

"Don't suffocate," Ian advised me as he got into bed.

"Not tonight," I replied, "I'm too tired."

Some time in the middle of that night I awoke with the most acute feeling of pure fear and the sound of many feet moving. My bed was nearer the window. Stealthily moving the mosquito net and drawing aside the curtains, I looked out. The shadows in the moonlight were alive with Mau Mau. I set aside the drapes and, slipping out of bed, crawled over to Ian's bed on all fours. Cupping my hands round my mouth, I put my lips to his ear and said quietly but frantically, "Mau Mau! Hordes of them!"

"Where?" he wanted to know.

"Out there!" I said, pointing to the window and giving his bed a shake to emphasise the gravity of the situation.

The shake caused his bed to collapse with a crash, which, together with the news I'd given him, seemed to galvanise him into action. He leapt up and ran stealthily down the passage like a sort of pyjama-clad Paul Revere, banging on each door, putting his head inside, and saying "Mau Mau! Hordes of them!" before going on his way to the next door.

In no time at all, the entire household was gathered in the passage in various stages of disarray, loading pistols and shotguns, trying to find flashlights and remember half-forgotten emergency drills. I, meanwhile, having done my part, had gone back to bed and fallen fast asleep—or rather, it is true to say, continued sleeping, as I had never really woken up.

But in the passage, apparently, there was a lot going on.

"Stay clear of the windows!" ordered Segar. "Everybody lie low and keep calm. Now, then. Where are they?"

"Out there," said Ian, pointing.

"How many did you see?" asked Segar.

"I didn't see any," said Ian. "Forbsey saw them. He said there were hordes of them."

"Hordes of them?" asked Segar.

"That's what he said. He seemed very sure of himself."

"That's very odd," said Segar. "Where is Forbsey?"

Forbsey, of course, was in bed, sound asleep, and not at all happy to be woken by Ian's shaking.

"Where are they?" Ian asked urgently.

"Where are who?" I wanted to know.

"The Mau Mau. You said you saw hordes of them."

"Are you sure I said that?"

"He wants to know if I'm sure he said that!" said Ian. There was much more conversation, of course, and eventually even some shaky laughter. Outside, the moonlight was quiet and serene. I stuck to my air of injured innocence for a while, but knew that it was hopeless. I'd done it again. So that when Ian confronted me that night in Rome surrounded by fallen suitcases, he knew that I didn't have a leg to stand on. For some reason it had been my week for packing things away in the night, and I knew it.

We're staying at the Hotel Ambasciatori on the Via Veneto. After the tournament we are to spend a week with Mark and Betsy McCormack at the Villa d'Este, and that, together with Cino Marchese's knowledge of the restaurants in Rome, should satisfy our cravings for Italian food for some time to come.

The Foro Italico has hardly changed—you can still stand

on the balcony and look down on the courts with their harvest of topspin groundstrokes. And the little café overlooking court one is much the way it used to be when Larsen left his bags and his robust blonde there. Even the coffee machine is probably the same.

On the courts, though, there are different players. Guillermo Vilas, now a shadow of his former self, losing to Pimek. Chesnokov versus Svensson. Yannick Noah beating Pistolesi, the groans of the Italian spectators mixed with grudging cheers for Noah's magnificence. He leaps superbly to bury overheads that bounce high into the crowd then grins through the gap in his teeth. Meanwhile Nystrom is losing, inexplicably, to Diego Perez, and suddenly I sense Richard Evans beside me, making notes.

"Perez," he murmurs. "Huge in Uruguay. A big fish in a small pond. After all," he says suddenly, brightening up, "when you think about it, life is really just a series of ponds! You have merely to decide which one it is best to live in!"

We move towards the centre court, discussing the ponds of life, and there Becker is losing to Emilio Sanchez. He screams at himself in German with such fury that one feels he may actually hurt himself. His two selves are locked in furious argument.

"Why does he get so angry?" I ask Richard. "You would think that in his position—very young, very rich, the whole world's hero—his two selves would easily be able to reach agreement!"

I thought momentarily of our own lives on the circuit, the modest *pensiones*, the cheap restaurants, the constant concern about money and the future. "He should just enjoy the game,"

I persist. "What more could he possibly want?"

"He doesn't enjoy losing to Sanchez," says Richard, typically, and again I marvel fleetingly at the levels of life on earth. The beggar by the river, the boy playing his saxophone in the subway, the clerk on the bus, Becker losing to Sanchez. Are all their yearnings of the same intensity, only at different levels? Does the saxophone boy get the same thrill from the ten-dollar bill that suddenly appears in his upturned hat as Becker gets from his winner's cheque?

Back at Mark McCormack's tent there is lunch in the sun under breezy umbrellas with Kerry Packer holding court, talking sporting records and statistics with Richard while McCormack presides, making the odd note and sometimes a mild correction or two—no, it wasn't the semis that someone lost in, it was the quarters, and yes, Ben Hogan had in fact won that year, but only after he'd shot a six on the eleventh in the final round. All three of them are walking encyclopaedias with effortless sporting memories that they seem able to call upon at will.

Mark McCormack and Kerry Packer are staying at the Hassler Hotel. There is something compelling about these quintessential hotels. Life led on the highest plane of style and comfort. In cities where he does not actually run homes, staying at such hotels has become one of McCormack's hobbies. In Paris it will be the Crillon. In Hamburg, Vier Jahreszeiten; in Hong Kong, the Regent; in Miami, the Grand Bay; in San Francisco, the Stanford Court. And so forth. The trick, it seems, is to live in them as casually as one would in any ordinary sort of place—to simply make use of them, to order a hot dog and throw one's coat across a chair. Cost, of course, needs to be kept an eye on.

Packer has the penthouse that overlooks the whole of Rome. When the sun sets over the city, waiters in white uniforms serve champagne on the huge terrace. Drinking it you feel temporarily superior, taking pity on the lesser mortals fighting everyday life and traffic in the streets below. The orange sunset softens the tiled rooftops.

Packer, of course, is born to this life. He is a big man with a confidence in himself so complete that he wears it with total comfort, like an old pair of shoes. No frills or fancies. He's tough and wise and understands the value of things—a plate of pasta, a tennis game, a television network, an offering of stock. And he seems able, above all, to put into proper perspective the inevitable "I"—the eternal, ever-present ego that seems so much a part of all such elevated people, and that some of them handle so badly, inevitably spoiling the magnitude of their achievements.

Afterwards, at the restaurant Il Moro, carefully selected by the resourceful Cino, we are served Italian food in the Italian way, enveloped by everything to do with Italy. Good restaurants are for Mark both a hobby and an enduring passion. There is hardly a city in the world where he cannot lead you to a really good place to eat. He loves the process of selecting—first the restaurant, and once there the meal itself—almost more than he does the eating.

"If I were to tell you," he might say, "that tonight I will take you to a place that will have your most favourite fish dish in the whole world, what would you say to that?"

He has the knack of setting scenes, posing questions in a way that makes you look at familiar things with new eyes. For example, once, when Abie announced that he was embarking on the project of coaching for one year a promising young star whom he thought had great potential, Mark listened carefully, and then said to Abie:

"Now if the father of this player was sitting in his favourite bar, having a drink with his best friends, and they asked him how many weeks his daughter's new coach was going to spend with her in the next twelve months, what answer do you think her father should give to his friends?"

And put this way, even Abie was forced to give attention to the question.

Now, in the restaurant Il Moro, when the bow-wave of waiters descends upon us to take our order, Mark says to Cino: "Tell them to bring to us what they would bring to their own father and mother if they came to eat at this restaurant!"

Well, that is good enough for Richard, Frances, and me. There are few things more pleasant than being at one of the best restaurants in Rome in the company of people whom the restaurant owners like!

FOOTPRINTS IN

MANHATTAN

DIARY NOTES, U.S. OPEN, 1992

I'm at Flushing Meadows doing TV commentary with Drysdale—"alongside him," as they say here in the U.S.A. Usually, Fred Stolle is alongside Cliff, but for South African TV, I have taken over.

"Which is just as well," says Cliff, "because I'm tired of all the horse manure that Fred talks." Had Fred been present he would no doubt have replied, but he is elsewhere, so Cliff's statement goes unopposed, which in a way annoys him. He would prefer to hear what Fred has to say in defence.

At about two o'clock today I got hungry, and just as I was wondering what to do I came across Ian Froman (an ex–South African now living in Israel, tournament director and founder of the Israeli tennis programme) in the players' lounge and found that he was also hungry. So we went along to Slew's Place (a bar and restaurant named for "Slew" Hester, the founder of Flushing Meadows) and ordered a hamburger, fries, and the lightest beer they had. When we had finished eating, the bill came. It was for about thirty dollars, and we were discussing how best it should be settled.

"I'll pay it," I said.

"No, I'll pay it," said Ian.

We had just decided to play matches to see who would pay when Cino Marchese swept up to our table in his magnificent way and stopped for a moment to murmur something in Froman's ear before sweeping on again.

"Do you know what he said to me?" asked Ian. "He said that he thinks that Andrei Medvedev would be prepared to play in my tournament for the very special fee of $75,000. But he a-needs a lot of other-a things"—he imitated Cino's way of speaking—"because he has to fly for a-many hours, and-a the coach, and-a this, and-a that, so we talk-a later, but you have him if you want him, but maybe! hey? Not yet-a for sure."

"Do you want-a him?" I asked Ian.

"If-a I can afford him," said Froman, "then I want him!"

"Then you should invite him if he-a pay for our hamburgers," I said.

"You mean, offer him $74,970?" asked Froman thoughtfully.

"$74,965," I said. "You might as well add the tip!" and we looked at each other and shook our heads and smiled.

It is a clear morning and as the plane descends towards the eastern seaboard there are glimpses through the clouds of the Manhattan skyline with the sun glinting off its glass towers.

No matter how often I arrive here, I am always moved by the first sight of New York—an uneasy lifting of the heart, for in the subconscious the place is too big, the pace too fast, the people too quick, the challenge too never ending. For a moment I am sorry that the journey is over—would like another hour of peace in the quiet white sound of the cabin to finish my book.

But we land, disembark, yawn, prepare to take the strain. At customs a uniformed woman draws me aside. I haven't properly completed the customs declaration form, and she wants to know whether I have any live animals or farm products.

"No," I reply firmly.

"Any foodstuffs?"

"No."

"Any plants, soil, birds, or snails?" and she taps the customs form again. If Abie were with me he'd say, "What's happened to our snails, Forbsey?" and begin looking through his things. But I am very correct.

"No," I say, and glance around nervously for any sign of dogs. In Miami, earlier that year, I had been waiting for my bag to come through and they'd had sniffer dogs. A beagle had sniffed at my ATP Tour carry-on bag then suddenly placed his paw on it and looked up at his handler with soulful eyes.

"Empty it out," the man had said, and amongst the socks and combs and toothpaste had come a beautiful red apple that I'd taken from the bowl in the lounge at Frankfurt, in case I got hungry in the night.

"That's a plant," the man said. "Where you from?"

"South Africa," I replied, adding hastily, "but this is a German apple!"—hoping that a first-world country of origin might make it seem less deadly.

"I don't much care where it comes from," he'd said. "It's a violation."

"I'm very sorry. I'd meant to eat it on the plane. I could still eat it now," I'd said hopefully, but he was not amused and after giving me a warning he'd picked up the apple by its stalk and put it in a plastic bag. At Kennedy Airport, though, on this particular morning, they don't have dogs.

You are never welcomed to New York. You simply arrive. The taxi drivers throw your bags into the trunks of their yellow cabs and you find yourself galloping along the undulating Van Wyck Expressway with its distinctive intersections—Rockaway Blvd, Union Turnpike, Queens Blvd, Long Island Expwy, over Queensboro Bridge and into Manhattan, the familiar East Side apartments, the River Club, the UN Plaza Hotel on Forty-Fourth and First. The sidewalks of New York!

I had first gotten to "know America" at a young age. Childhood in our one-ant town could not have been a more simple one; glamour and excitement existed only in our dreams, and our dreams were nearly all of America, amplified once a month by the old movies they showed in our town hall. Abbott and Costello and the Marx Brothers. The great musicals. The evil gangsters in *Kiss of Death* or *The Big Heat.* The first westerns. *Fort Apache; Stagecoach; Jesse James!* For us, America was gunsmoke and horses clattering in canyons, guys with felt hats and machine guns, dolls with platinum blonde hair, silver palm trees, white grand pianos, chorus lines, and liquid dance floors over which flew the shining shoes of Fred

Astaire. Every American girl had legs that never ended; every song we sang, every image in our minds, came from America; and in the centre of America was New York.

When I first went there in 1962 to play the U.S. Open, my vision held together perfectly when, from the window of the plane, I first saw the staggering Manhattan skyline. But at close quarters another New York had quickly emerged, and I wrote about it in my diary with angry disappointment:

DIARY NOTES, NEW YORK, 1962

Where are the chorus lines? Where is Gene Kelly? Just these endless city blocks, where the glamour moves away from you like a mirage. It's always somewhere else—above in the glass canyons, or farther up the street amongst the lights and neon signs. Around you the pavements are falling apart, the streets potholed and black with oil; the manholes breathe vapours and the garbage lies everywhere. I came looking for dreams and found a town that has lung cancer and athlete's foot!

But on another day it was better:

At Rockefeller Center it is all light and music and the smell of hot bagels. The great buildings march away down Sixth Avenue; in front of the Time-Life building the Ninth Street Stompers are playing jazz, the thin crackle of their trumpets carried upwards with the pigeons. "Beale Street Blues." In front of the band a small boy holds out his hat.

Slowly I was to find that neither city was real—not the one that had lived in my mind, nor the one that I found when I first arrived. The real New York was yet another city, probably the most indefinable of all cities, and not one that you could easily get to know.

DIARY NOTES, 1995

At the Oyster Bar at Grand Central you might have the grilled mackerel and at Smith and Wollensky on Forty-Ninth Street you might have the prime New York rib, and they'd be quite different, but both essentially Manhattan. And where else but on Lexington Avenue would you find "Lily's Backroom Restaurant and Bar at the Roger Smith—the Great Little New York Hotel"? Or: The Gotham Bar and Grill; Paparazzi; Nobu; The Fashion Café; The 42nd St. Eatery; carveries, dineries, beaneries! You could spend a lifetime eating in this city and you would still leave almost everything untried—would still be searching for that elusive dish that would enable you to say, "This is the one! This at last is New York City!"

To my surprise, on almost my first day there in 1962 I discovered that the city had an honest heart. Finding that my childhood compulsion to go "up the Empire State Building" was shared by some of the other players, I organised a small party consisting of Fred and Pat Stolle, Sandra and Lowell Price, Roy Emerson, and Rene Schuurman, and up we went. From the gallery at the top we marvelled like children at the pure geometry of Manhattan—a thousand planes and verticals, with the wind flinging skeins of low cloud against the architecture and sunlight catching the glass panels. All around us were the names from our movies—Battery Park, Brooklyn, Staten Island, Broadway. Here, high above the streets, the New York of our dreams was much easier to find.

It was only after we descended and found a drugstore that served milkshakes that I discovered that my leather money clip was no longer in my trouser pocket. By that time I had been on the circuit for almost five months, and the clip contained all the money that I had received as "expenses" during the tour—sterling, marks, francs, dollars, even some krona and guilders—in total about twelve hundred dollars, which I had carefully saved up against my return to South Africa and the expenses that I knew had built up while I was away.

One talks of panic! What with the despair and confusion that filled my mind, it was some time before I became aware of Fred Stolle shaking my arm.

"Forbsey, listen, what did your money clip look like?"

"A leather folder," I replied mechanically, and added, "but what does it matter, Fred? This is New York! It's gone, and I'll never get it back!"

"I think I saw one of the uniformed attendants in the [Empire State] building pick something up that looked like a wallet," said Fred.

We hurried back to the building, and I remember my new despair at the milling crowds. But Fred peered about and suddenly said, "That's the guy, there!" and we surrounded him and asked him whether he had found a leather money clip. He looked at us with cold, impassive eyes.

"What kind of a money clip?"

With growing excitement I described the clip and the

various notes it contained. There were many other questions, but finally the supervisor was called, a safe opened, and my precious money laid down on the counter before me.

The miracle was complete. I felt like a man suddenly acquitted by a grand jury, and fervently thanked Fred for his remarkable powers of observation.

"I could kiss you a hundred times!" I said.

"I'd rather have a hundred beers, Forbsey," he replied. I am still paying him back.

During that U.S. Open in 1962, the players were all accommodated at the Vanderbilt Hotel down in the Thirties, and I shared a room with Cliff Drysdale and Donald Dell, in accordance with the conditions of my invitation: free accommodation (shared) including breakfast, lunches in a tent in the grounds of The West Side Tennis Club, and seventy-five dollars per week for expenses. You had to buy your own dinners and pay for your own laundry.

Rod Laver, bidding for his first Grand Slam, had his own large room higher up in the hotel, and got his dinners and his laundry free. He also got five hundred dollars per week, which I wasn't supposed to know about. But we'd shared a room as guests of a rich American family during the U.S National Doubles in Boston the week before and I'd scared him so badly with my dreams that he'd told me confidentially (documented in *A Handful of Summers*).

DIARY NOTES, 1992

My room in the UN Plaza Hotel overlooks the gardens of

the United Nations Building, the borough of Queens, and the airplanes rising from La Guardia and melting into the haze. A barge moves on the oily, grey waters of the East River and as it passes, its tugboat gives an important little whoop. In this city even the tugboats have egos! I put my suitcase on the bed and begin to unpack, while the air-conditioned room hums softly to itself. On the streets below the lights change (WALK—DON'T WALK) and the yellow cabs nudge each other round the blocks.

Now, in 1995, we stay in the very heart of town—The Grand Hyatt, to be exact—right over Grand Central Station, where you sometimes sense the throbbing of trains. There are quieter hotels, but in a way the Hyatt is New York, and it is also the USTA hotel; midsummer; August. The U.S. Open, just beginning. At the Hyatt, if you need the subway you just head on downwards. Strange to think that here, now, if the mood takes us, we can actually Take the A Train and go to Sugar Hill way up in Harlem.

On this very first evening, though, with the edge just coming off the heat of the day, to get the feel of things we stroll west on Forty-Second Street. The boy, Jamie (our son), thirteen yesterday, is on the in-line skates he has bought with his birthday money (the first thing we had to do) and is weaving in amongst sidewalk crowds. Franny (his mother) watches with a frown while she holds onto her handbag. ("Aren't they supposed to snatch things in New York, Forbsey?")

Past the library and Bryant Park on our left, the handsome Grace Building, RadioShack, and Gymnasium, where we bought the skates, and turn right at Times Square where all the currents of the city meet, Herman's Sports, Nathan's Hot Dogs, the Manhattan Chili Company; Broadway with its glitter—Sardi's, Joey's, RKO Cinema, the Lyceum Theatre, Roy Rogers, the Marriott Marquis, hot and tired and grand, with the teeming sidewalks, the novelty shops, the Roxy Deli, the man playing his metal drums, the beggar on the pavement, the girls in the doorways, watching, watching. . . .

Past the Palace Theatre we wander, the boy on his skates (he wants to buy posters), past Harry's Hamburgers and Cooper's Coffee House, and finally, to escape the heat and pressure of the sultry afternoon, turn into Forty-Seventh Street at Maxwell's, Sbarro Pizza, Dish of Salt, and sit at the window of a coffee shop and look out.

5:55 P.M. Hot and still. The people going home with dogged steps, the salesman with his samples, the office girls, the director in his shiny suit (tie loosened at the neck), the woman with her old string bag—now on this corner, Forty-Seventh Street and Sixth, but going on to other corners, other avenues; stop at a bench to tie a shoe (it came undone at Thirty-First and Lexington), and then go on. We drink our Lipton's raspberry tea and watch the people going home, then go out and join them (hot city air), and walk back to the hotel, through the revolving doors, into the cool flatness of the great lobby, on to the elevators, and up into the quiet room.

Every half hour there is a bus that takes the *"non joueurs"* out to Flushing Meadows—inching its way through the city traffic, laboriously crossing the river, and traversing the faceless streets of Queens while you idly chat away and the boy reads out the signs: "3 Bee Auto Sales, Martha's Vineyard, the Deer Head Diner, Pizza Sam." People busy trying to make a buck, I tell him, not so easy on these streets. At last Shea Stadium appears, and after some final twists and turns, we reach the USTA (United States Tennis Association) National Tennis Center at Flushing Meadow Park, home of the U.S. Open Championships.

When the U.S. Open was held at The West Side Tennis Club in Forest Hills, as it always used to be, the tournament had about it much of the same spirit of place as, say, Roland Garros or Wimbledon. The matches were played on grass courts, and you did not talk of playing "The U.S. Open," but rather of playing "Forest Hills."

The venue at Flushing Meadow Park is a restless place, existing midway between a fairground, a campus, and a public park. There is very little grass. The court surfaces are hard, the centre court is massive and impersonal, and there is a lot of concrete construction, with walkways and iron railings, billboards and fast-food kiosks. But a few encouraging trees still grow out of the concrete paving; there are flags, tents, and awnings, and, above all, a curious sense of energy, the heartbeat of excitement so typical of American sporting events.

DIARY NOTES, 1992

From the commentary box high above the Flushing Meadows centre court I watched Jim Courier play Andre Agassi in the quarter-finals. I am becoming an expert on Courier\Agassi matches! Alongside me, emitting his usual flow of airy information, Cliff Drysdale seemed unmoved by the tennis on the court below; but in my opinion, a grand battle was taking place. The medium-paced, even surface of the hard courts gives the players confidence, producing the most effortless and spectacular stroke making, with all the usual mental undercurrents. After their previous matches, points had to be proved, egos defended all over again. The second set reached a state of almost agonising perfection before Agassi won the tiebreaker.

"Am I imagining things," I asked Cliff during the pause that followed, "or was that just about the best set of back court tennis that I have ever seen in my life?"

"What do you mean, 'back-court tennis'?" said Cliff. "That's how you have to play in this league, Forbsey. That's what tennis has become. It's not beautiful, but it wins matches."

"I think it is beautiful in its own kind of way," I persisted, reluctant to let my excitement go down the drain. And yet after the match, in the press room, when I went on about the stunning quality of that set of tennis, some members of the press didn't agree with me.

"It was mindless tennis," they cried. "A contest of animal strength boring and repetitive." In fairness to them, they were not claiming that either Agassi or Courier was, in fact, boring or mindless. It was just a pressman's way of making a point. But it again set me thinking.

Were they right? Was it, in fact, boring tennis? Had I really enjoyed it, or was I simply riveted by the sheer power and precision, a technique that, because I had never mastered it, filled me with awe?

"It had to be good tennis, Cliff," I insisted. "They hit more
great shots in one rally than I used to hit in a whole match!"
"In your whole life!" replied Cliff, brutally.

On the way to the media centre the next morning I pass
the practise courts and pause to watch Pete Sampras. The sight
of his clean, effortless strokes takes me back to a day in
Manchester, England, during the first tour I ever made. I had
been searching for the court that I had been allocated when
suddenly I came upon Lew Hoad and Ken Rosewall hitting up.
Young as I was, I knew instinctively that I was watching something momentous. "Of course! That's it! That's it exactly!" I
whispered to myself—and now, watching Sampras, I get that
same old feeling.

On a nearby court Nick Bollettieri is watching over a young
Russian girl no more than ten years old. The same sun-creased
eyes that watched such players as Agassi, Courier, Monica
Seles, Aaron Krickstein, and Jimmy Arias now observes Anna
Kournikova.

"You're very good at giving players big forehands, hey,
Maestro?" I say to him, and he laughs.

"Today you need a big weapon," he says, his husky voice
confidential, as though I am the only one that ought to know—
then nods towards Anna. "Mr. Forbes, you are watching a
future champion. She has all the shots. Now she must learn
to use them in competition. In a few more years, who knows
how good she will be?"

Standing beside him I see the child with the tennis strokes
of an adult, the fervent eyes of the parents. I imagine the

eternity of tennis strokes that must still be hit, and for a moment I wonder again at the dedication necessary to create a modern tennis champion. "Is it worth it?" I get asked over and over, and the answer is always "yes"—for in this modern world crowded with young people searching for somewhere, is it not a good thing for a child with a particular talent to follow her star?

DIARY NOTES, 1995

In the concourse between the centre court and the players' lounge I am suddenly taken in a bear hug that shatters the happy daze that the Courier\Chang match has left me with. It's Roy Emerson with the same grin he used in 1963.

"Thought you were being mugged!" he says.

"Yes."

"I hear you and Abie played the seniors at Wimbledon last year," he goes on.

"Yes."

"And you were pitiful. Pitiful!"—as though one "pitiful" isn't enough.

"Yes."

It had been Abie's fault. It was he who had accosted Chris Gorringe at Wimbledon that year and virtually insisted that he and I be invited to play, one last time. "Before we turn into waxworks," he said, and Chris was too nice to tell him to "go take a jump," which is what he should have done. "We are already waxworks, Abie," I said dubiously. "Those guys are younger than us and very good. We'll get killed." But Abie said that I was talking crap, and that it was grass, and did I remember how well we served on grass, and I said yes, but . . . and he said, listen, Forbsey, how bad can it be?—and for once he was wrong. It was very bad. Jan Kodes and Alex Metreveli ran rings around us and we got only three games.

"Pitiful," *says Emerson again, beaming at me.*

"Have a heart," *I protest mildly, then to change the sub-ject I ask him whom he is playing with in the U.S. Open vet-erans' doubles.*

"Horny Tom," *he replies.*

Tom Okker, the great Dutch player of the seventies, had earned this nickname by roaming the tennis tournaments of the world and apparently arousing irresistible surges of lust in the hearts of virtually all the women who ever crossed his path. "From eight to eighty," said Emerson.

"Is it true," *I ask Roy, "that you and Fred [Stolle] once played against Freddie de Jesus and Mike Kreiss, and when the umpire announced the match he'd mispronounced the names, calling out: 'Emerson\Stolle versus de Jesus\Kreiss' and you turned to Fred and said, 'Could have a problem here, Fred'?"*

"Quite true," *says Roy. "And here's an even funnier one—about when Fred and I played against Horny Tom and Mark Cox?" (a once-famous British player), "Did I ever tell you that one?'*

"No," *I say.*

"Funny story," *he goes on. "We got into a tie-break in the* *first set, you see, and the old umpire, who was a bit doddery, started to call out the score, 'one-zero, Emerson\Stolle! Two-zero, Emerson\Stolle!' Then they caught up and he called out, 'Three-two, Cox\Okker!' There was a bit of a murmur in the crowd, and when he called, 'Four-two, Cox\Okker,' people began to laugh. Fred went up to him and suggested that he change the order of the names, and he was so embarrassed when he realised what he'd done that on the very next point he got it wrong again and called out, 'Four-three, Okkers\Coc.' Got a bit of a laugh, that did! Horny Tom!" And he chuckles away at the memories.*

Following the example set by Wimbledon, they now have a Last Eight Club at Flushing Meadows, except that in a typically American declaration of independence it is called the *Final* Eight Club. During the pauses in our commentaries I sometimes make my way there for a cup of tea. Although for me Flushing Meadows is without memories, here in this breezy marquee with wicker chairs and iced tea the memories are revived by the people whom you might find inhabiting the place. Dick Savitt will be there, Victor Seixas, Hamilton Richardson, Billy Talbert, perhaps, and Gardnar Mulloy. All the Australians. Only yesterday I saw Don Budge talking to Bobby Riggs and wondered whether they would remember a windy Tuesday afternoon in Queenstown.

At ten this morning, though, the club is deserted except for Mervyn Rose, Australian star of the late fifties, and at present the coach and adviser of Arantxa Sanchez-Vicario. He has just prepared his charge for her match and escorted her to her court, and he is drinking a Bud Lite before going out to watch her play.

"What did you tell her today?" I ask, dropping into the chair beside him.

"One thing at a time," he says laconically. "You tell any of these young players two things and they'll forget one of them!"

As a player, Rose was a master contestant. Few other players would have been able to make so much of a game that, though brilliant, had its limitations. Thinking back I see only an angular, left-handed service, oblique volleys, and some wild-looking groundstrokes, yet he'd won both the Italian and the French Opens in the same year and you didn't do that unless you really could play—even if you did have the knack of talking your opponent into a state of bewildered stupefaction as artfully as Mervyn seemed able to do.

Now, reflectively drinking his beer, he talks no more of Arantxa Sanchez-Vicario. The sight of me has reminded him of Abie, and the thought of Abie has reminded him of an Australian player from the outback called Pat O'Kane, whom Abie played way back in 1957. Or was it 1958? He doesn't remember when, but it was in Rome. Anyway, O'Kane was ambidextrous, had two forehands (one on either side, didn't know what a backhand was, never hit one in his life), and Abie played him for four sets. After he finally won the match, he said to Rose: "Holy hell, Mervyn, I kept trying to come in on his backhand but he always ran around and hit a forehand!"

"He doesn't have a backhand, you stupid nit!" Rose said, and even now he chuckles away, seeing Abie struggling to come to net on a backhand that didn't exist. Which reminds him of something else that Abie did:

"I played him once," says Rose. "In Scarborough. In the wind. Big serve, Abie had. Had to be careful if he really got it working. Better to knock him off his perch before he settled down. We hit up, then he remembered we hadn't tossed for serve, so he spun his racket and called out 'Rough or smooth?' and I won.

"'I'll receive,' I said.

"'Are you crazy?' he says to me. 'You can't do that!'

"'Why not?' I ask.

"'Because all you've got is a serve,' he says to me. 'What exactly do you think you're going to use for returns?'

"'I receive better than you receive, Big Abie,' I said to him.

"'Jesus Christ, Mervyn!' he says, 'the last time I saw you make a return was two years ago in Barcelona!'

"So we start the match and on the very first point he serves this big swinging thing to my backhand. It's a bad grass court and the wind's blowing a gale, but I take a swing at it anyway and the ball comes off the throat of my racket and falls over in the corner near the net. Abie just stands there and he says to me, 'What kind of a fucked-up spitball is that, Mervyn!' and he goes up to the umpire and says we should start the match over again.

"'Why?' asks the umpire.

"'Because Rose wasn't ready,' says Abie.

"Then he goes back for the next point, still thinking about the first point, and you know what happens when you do that...."

The story dies away with his chuckles. He thinks he won

the match but the result doesn't matter. More important is the fact that, for a moment, he is back on a bleak grass court in Scarborough, young and strong, outwitting Abe, and looking forwards to the beer he will have after the match and the jokes he will tell the dark-haired American girl he is meeting that evening for coffee in the little bar of his small hotel.

DIARY NOTES, 1995

McCormack's New York office is on the corner of Seventy-First and Madison, and this morning I had to go there for a meeting. Traffic jammed solid, so the subway to Sixty-Eighth, and then a short walk. On Sixty-Ninth Street I come across two old men busy loading garbage bags into a great van— pavement piled with bags and this superb New York jogger approaching, female, thirty-ish, shining bodysuit, legs, head-phones, glowing with vitamins, a bounding stride that carries her clear over the garbage bags. The two men and I regard her receding figure.

"Look at dose buns!" says the one old man.

"Concentrate on de garbage, Joey," says the other. New York is full of "Joeys."

The bus transportation waits outside the hotel but the boy, Jamie, wants to take the subway. Tokens for $1.25 and gusts of hot air as you go through the turnstiles. "Take a seven," the woman said, "down two levels," and down you go, getting hotter and hotter, answering the boy's questions. Yes, the trains come quite quickly, yes, they take you right to the tennis, no, they don't break down, this is America, they know about trains, we just have to follow the signs. Jackson Avenue, Queens Plaza, no, the trains go under the river, not over it, the boy looking at the map and the woman near the map telling me that she has never missed a U.S. Open, see, her son lives in Woodside and works for the utilities, and after the tennis she always drops in and has a cup of cawfee with him, every year, see, it's right on the way, and now they have this cute son who sure would like to be a champion like Sampras, what did I think? Lowery Street, Lincoln Avenue, the boy asking, will he have a proper pass, will he get to see Agassi close up, and the woman telling me she remembered when Jimmy won, there would never be another Jimmy, he played for the people.

The journey takes only twenty-six minutes, with about twelve stops: Bliss; Woodside; Jackson Heights; Corona; and, finally, Shea Stadium. We disembark shoulder to shoulder with the fans. We have already decided that tennis fans from different parts of the world behave differently. The British, the French, the Italians all have particular habits. Americans, and especially New Yorkers, are no exception. They are, in fact, perhaps the most singular of all sports watchers.

They seem actually to participate rather than to spectate. Nowhere else do fans get closer to the game—study the statistics, choose their heroes, and follow their progress with such fervour. Some even dress the part in designer outfits—Nike, Adidas, Fila, Ellesse. The boy is wide-eyed. The kids walking beside us in their Agassi T-shirts carry rackets and balls, and for today, anyway, they *become* Agassi, fighting to get a glimpse of him arriving at the courts, watching his matches and calling out things like "Go, Andre! Let's do it!" while holding their rackets with two hands. ("Can I have an Agassi outfit?" says the boy.) For here in New York of all cities, because it is so big and impersonal, and because fame and fortune seem so near and yet so unattainable, people need at least to have their dreams.

In between dreams, of course, they talk and eat. They are, after all, New Yorkers, and every New Yorker is an expert and always hungry. Fame may be hard to find, but expert views are quite another matter, and they emerge much more easily between mouthfuls of fast food—cheese nachos, nuts, pretzels, bagels, ice cream—anything will do to keep up comment and opinion. Climb into the bleachers, sit there and listen, and you will find a quite new way of watching tennis.

Today in the forecourt of the players' enclosure a great press of fans waits patiently to see Andre Agassi appear for his match against Stefan Edberg; while in the corporate marquees the business mongols and their guests sip champagne and help themselves to shrimp.

"The match is about to start," someone says.

"Agassi\Edberg? Oh, sure. And then maybe we'll just catch a set of the Sampras match and then take the limo back to town."

"Howard has tickets for the Met, and before that we have cocktails at the van Lorenz's. Kinda late, huh?"

"So we take a rain check on Sampras. . . ."

"I guess. We get to see him in the finals anyway."

"Gloria, you ready to go?"

"In a minute, honey. I'm just communicating with Iris

about Saturday."

"Oh, hi, Dexter. What's this about Morgan J. Ramsay getting a pink slip? Kinda puts a different spin on the Sherwood-Lewis deal, right? They say the big guys in the board-room are bouncing off the walls! Hey! Agassi's up a break. You want to go watch three games?"

"I don't care to go all that way! No sooner we get to the box it's time to leave. . . ."

And outside, in long lines, the fans wait.

DIARY NOTES, 1992

Our commentary box is situated alongside the press gallery high above the centre court. The gallery is a long, ter-raced room littered with stationery, ideas, conversations, sta tistics, paper cups, laptops, and the particular little bundles so precious to each individual—private notebooks, records, references—personal things they use to help them write their stories in their own special way. This eternal search for news! Somehow each one will meet his deadline—find somewhere the small inspirations, the little quotes, the new angles and innuendos that appear the next day to give the fans another image to add onto their dreams.

I have never been a pressman, but I have come to regard this singular breed with the greatest respect. There can be no more demanding job than the constant production of creative thoughts to meet nagging deadlines. The never-ending search for something new to say with the same old set of words. The hours of waiting, with half-full coffee cups, statistics, the incessant chatter of television screens. Waiting—for the match to end, the rain to stop, the play to recommence. Waiting—companion most of all to their own private thoughts.

No two pressmen have ever been the same, yet in each there are measures of the observer, the wit, the cynic, the oracle, and the naughty schoolboy. And in each there is often a certain wistfulness, as though he knows that he is destined only to witness and to document the deeds that he himself in another life may just have done.

The U.S. Open is the last Grand Slam event of the year, and as it ends there is always a reflectiveness in the air. Another year almost gone, a new champion emerging, an older one about to fade away. Today, Steffi Graf will play Monica Seles in the finals of the women's singles. Every so often destiny serves up the perfect sporting occasion. Graf, at twenty-six, already a legend, arguably the greatest stylist and athlete tennis has ever known. Seles, the protégée, the tennis machine, the child, who was busy taking over the world of tennis in her own particular way when one of the most bizarre incidents ever to occur in any sport stopped her in her tracks. Now, at twenty-two, after two years, she has returned, has reached the final of her first Grand Slam with all the magic of her unique two-handed strokes still intact.

It is our last day, and for the occasion we will abandon the bus and the subway, ride to the tennis in McCormack's dark blue limo, and watch the match from his courtside box—a lifestyle that, says the boy, he could easily get used to. A last lunch in the players' restaurant, and then we go out into the sun of the centre court to witness at first hand what turns out to be the greatest women's tennis match in the history of the game—or so one believes when time and again the flow of strokes reaches and maintains an almost impossible perfection.

DIARY NOTES, U.S. OPEN

After the match we will take a last walk around the outside courts to watch the juniors. The boy will want his last ice cream. And in the Final Eight Club Mervyn Rose will want to reminisce one last time about the finals of Rome and how he and Don Candy teamed up to beat Nicola Pietrangeli.

"No way I could beat him in Rome on my own," he says. "Up against the whole of Italy, you see! Had to have a plan. Pietrangeli liked to have a massage during the ten-minute break if the match went longer than three straight sets. So I figured I had to win one of the first three sets and then get Candy onto the massage table during the break. So I scrape the second set, and as I lose the third I signal to Candy, 'Get on the table,' which he does, so that when Nicki gets into the locker room he's got nowhere to go!"

"Told Nicki I had a bad back," says Candy, who is listening. "'Can't serve with a bad back,' I told him. 'Have to play a big mixed doubles!'"

"Candy couldn't serve with a good back," Rose has to interject, although he risks losing the thread of his story. Sure enough, Nicki got mad and Rose won the championship in five sets.

"Nearly got put in jail," he adds, remembering.

The turning of the wheel! Tomorrow, Sampras will defeat Agassi in the men's final and move a step closer to the immortality that awaits him. We will leave Manhattan, feel again its irresistible tugging at our sleeve, board the plane, watch the city lights fade into a New York sunset, and sit in the cabin of the big jet with the flush of sound in our ears and the darkness outside.

AGE SHALL NOT

WEARY THEM

DIARY NOTES, MIAMI, 1992, LIPTON'S
INTERNATIONAL TOURNAMENT

Today at Butch and Cliff Buchholz's tournament I sneaked into the locker room amongst all the stars and changed into new tennis gear for a friendly game on the back courts. J. Wayne Richmond (of the ATP Tour) and I against John Feaver and Steve Devoe (tournament director of the U.S. Open). It suddenly became very serious when it emerged in idle conversation that they actually expected to beat us. We played on one of the American clay courts, and for a while I served well and J. Wayne's somewhat perilous game held together, while both Feaver and Devoe showed signs of being mentally unprepared for the match.

Devoe has this immensely high toss-up on his serve and everyone gets a bit tense waiting for the ball to come back down. When I asked him why he tossed the ball so high, he said that he felt he had a good smash but a bad serve, so the idea was to make his body think he was smashing and not serving. "If I toss the ball high enough my body thinks it's a smash," he explained.

"Things are pretty bad when you have to lie to your own body!" I told him.

"Do you suppose I could get my body to think I'm only hitting forehands?" J. Wayne wanted to know, and Feaver, who had just arrived and was suffering from jet lag, said that the match was unfair because his body thought it was still playing on grass!

At John and Anne de St. Croix's house in the quiet Johannesburg suburb of Inanda, there has been a tennis school that has continued for over thirty years. John has recently turned sixty. As a young man he had a Rosewall-like backhand and was said to be a devil with women. Now he has aged in a distinguished sort of way and, with his greying hair and beard, has assumed all the qualities of the definitive doyen. He has a slanting sense of humour that tends to leak into even his most profound remarks, and a Walter Mitty–like mind that enables him to be anything from Fred Astaire dancing with Ginger Rogers, to Don Bradman scoring a century against England.

John's court is set into a leafy garden and is overlooked by a thatched pavillion, with a bar and chairs for viewing. One of the walls of the pavillion is decorated with the broken rackets that, over the years, have been hurled in anger, accidentally hitting poles. There is also a "Bagel Board" that records all the sets that various doubles pairings have lost to love—three columns with the cryptic headings:

WHO GOT IT.   WHO GAVE IT.   WHY?

The reasons in the WHY column are very brief, e.g.: "Suffering from jet advance"; "Rigor mortis set in"; "Rest in peace"; "The impossible dream"; "Gone fishing"; etc.

"Giving a bagel" at the de St. Croix school is the cause of the most exquisite and undisguised glee; getting it is a fate worse than a fate worse than death.

At 2:30 on Saturdays and 9:30 on Sundays the players arrive and begin to remove sweaters, apply ointments and athletic supports, and gingerly test movements in certain joints and muscles. The activities of the previous night are often discussed—mostly dealing with the aftereffects of foods and beverages, but sometimes branching off into other activities. Wheeler, for instance, now fifty-eight and a bachelor, has been seen with a voluptuous Italian woman and thus needs to be questioned. Lidgey is testing the latest Prince "Thunderclap," Bowring's elbow is sore, and de Bruin's plumbing is starting to play up. . . . There are many ifs and buts. Finally, with everything more or less settled, the first set commences.

DIARY NOTES, INANDA, 1992

Today the honoured guest at our school was Graham Lovett, ATP Tour board member, tournament director, entrepreneur, and stager of international events. Graham plays a fast and robust game, with a tendency to leap up and kill high balls. It took some time before he realised that he was playing in a school where blinding pace has long since been replaced by subtlety and cunning, so that at first he found himself leaping too soon, coming back to earth, and having to leap again.

The penny finally dropped when he was aced by Brian Lidgey. Not only was it one of the smallest aces in living memory, it was made even more surprising by the fact that it was an underarm second service, the toss-up of the first service having gone sideways through the open gate of the tennis-court surround.

Ever since being one of South Africa's top juniors, Lidgey has had confrontations with his toss-up. It takes place to the side of his body and incorporates a circular, anticlockwise motion of the arm, so that the direction of the toss depends upon when the ball is released. If the release is too early, the ball goes to the right (and thus, in extremus, through, for instance, an open gate). If it is too late, it goes to the left (and could, theoretically, pass through a gate on the other side of the court).

After years of trying to control said toss-up, Lidgey has finally given up, and now applies Heisenberg's Uncertainty Principle, trying only to predict the most likely direction and velocity of the toss, while simultaneously preparing to hit the ball wherever it goes. Latest developments include a very early backswing, the theory being that the racket head will not be caught unprepared.

"The downside," says Lidgey, "is that if the backswing gets any earlier it will have to take place at changeover, or between points while the balls are being collected."

When the theory fails, Lidgey (with a short, bitter laugh)

serves small underarm cuts, and it was one of these that had surprised Graham Lovett.

"You're surely not going to count that?" he cried.

"We don't mess about in this school!" said Lidgey, less concerned about the brotherhood of tennis players than the prospect of avoiding a bagel.

"You fellows have very unusual habits," said Graham.

"We're cunning as closet rats," said Lidgey, comfortably.

DIARY NOTES, INANDA, 1993

Today the following events took place, in this order:

1. *I served a first ball to Gerald Berkowitz.*
2. *He hit a feeble, high return, which I was about to knock off.*
3. *A bird flew across the court.*
4. *The return hit the bird, deflected over my waiting racket, but fell inside our court.*
5. *The bird flew on, unharmed.*
6. *Berkowitz claimed the point.*
7. *I requested to know the rules concerning flying birds.*
8. *Basil Wheeler said that it depended upon the status of the bird: Was it a spectator, an official bird, or just a casual flyer by?*
9. *Owen Williams (guest of the week) said that he remembered a time at the Philadelphia tournament when a ball had deflected off Marilyn Fernberger and been allowed. "But she was an official bird," said Wheeler.*

Finally we all decided that a let should be played, but Berkowitz said he was going on appeal.

"You should appoint Joseph Stahl," I advised. "He will argue that the bird be deemed to be null and void."

These notes are intended to show that tennis can be enjoyed later on in life. Not only has veterans' tennis become very popular, it is also now well organised internationally. Unlike in golf, it has settled itself into a sort of two-tier system of competition. At one level are the ATP Tour alumni members, grand masters like Laver, Rosewall, Newcombe, Stolle, Roche, Emerson, Drysdale, etc., along with the relative newcomers like Borg, Connors, Nastase, the Gullikson twins, and Eddie Dibbs. These players keep to themselves in an exclusive circuit designed to retain the aura of distinction that surrounded their youth.

At another and even more active level are a far larger group of players—*"non joueurs,"* in a sense, who have a deep love of tennis and who, in later life especially, have worked very hard at their games and their physical conditions. Most of these players lack the complete mastery of the grand masters, but such is their consistency and fitness that the tennis they play is very effective. In nearly all countries of the world there now exist comprehensive veterans' tournament networks, where the spirit of enthusiasm is arguably more vibrant than in any other area of tennis.

DIARY NOTES, BARCELONA, 1992

I'm on this bus in Barcelona with a lot of other "alter

kackers" playing in a competition called "The Potter Cup." It's a forty-five-and-over International Club team event— a sort of Davis Cup for geriatrics, which for some reason the players are getting into a bit of a state about. Today, even for the practise matches there were tremendous goings-on— captains' meetings, protein breakfasts, team talks, etc. In the locker room was a great array of things like high-technology knee guards, bandages, liniments, pills, special gadgets for reducing vibration in the elbow, slow-mag anticramp tablets, etc. The U.S. team members have the very latest wide-bodied, lightweight rackets that make my old graphite Wimbledons look like objects taken from an archaeological dig!

No-one has yet come up with an antipanic remedy, though, and being old doesn't mean you don't get nervous. If anything, age makes it worse! Nervousness, exhaustion, and lack of practise— any minute now one of my bedroom walls will fall over!

Anyway, we're all on this bus. Across the aisle from me is the venerable old Jean Borotra, now ninety-four and virtu- ally on his last legs, although I suppose we're all a bit anxious about the state of our legs. In front of old Jean is Bob Abdesselam, seventy-something, then there's me, fifty-eight, next to me Sergio Tacchini, fifty-three, and just behind us, Pat Cramer and Graydon Garner, both forty-six-ish. Fore and aft, other heads are visible above the seats, the hair upon them in vari- ous stages of colour and density.

We're all very grateful for the presence of old Jean, because he makes everyone else on the bus feel young. He sits there quite peacefully, looking out of the window with weary old eyes, and one wonders what goes on inside his head. He's seen *it all, done it all so many times before that I don't suppose he even cares exactly where he is—Barcelona, Rome, Athens, Madrid, they must by now all be the same. One city is much like another—if the Eiffel Tower appears, it's Paris, if Big Ben drifts past, it's London. So long as at the end of the day you've got a bit of supper and a nice soft bed.*

Last night at the Real Club de Tenis, the International Club of Spain entertained us to a gala dinner, and afterwards the chef produced a grand cake he'd made in the form of a tennis court, complete with lines, umpire, and two people playing singles. Needless to say they were both on the baseline, as it was a clay-court cake, not at all the kind that you would rush the net on—a slow, red clay-court cake, with a surface of caramel, coffee, sprinklings of cinnamon sugar and a little brandy. Typically Continental. If the tournament had been on grass, in England, at, say, the All England Club, it would have been a fast, green grass-court cake with a lemon-flavoured surface, and one of the players would have been up at net, knocking off a volley!

After the dinner, the captains of the various teams all crowded round the cake to be photographed. They gave old Jean Borotra a mighty knife to cut it with, and the only way he could do it was by holding a backhand grip!

The International Tennis Club was founded in England in 1924. Its colours are steel grey and pink, and its seal contains the four Latin words *Benevolentia* ("Goodwill"), *Aequitas* ("Sportsmanship"), *Virtus* ("Courage, bravery"), and *Amicitia* ("Friendship"). In 1929 Jean Borotra formed the I.C. of France, to be followed in 1931 by the I.C. of U.S.A. and The Netherlands. There are now twenty-eight I.C. clubs throughout the world. Jean Borotra remained the honorary president until his death in 1994.

Initially membership was restricted to players who had played for their countries. In the halcyon days of the true amateur, membership was considered a signal honour, and the aims of the club resounded with the highest ideals of sportsmanship and the purity of amateur traditions. The Potter Cup (an event established by the tennis aficionado Jim Potter) is still regarded as one of the world's most prestigious team events. Both in 1992 and 1994, I found myself on the South African team, and as usual I kept notes.

At eleven in the morning, the Barcelona airport is a blaze of dry, white light; inside the glass terminal building the unmistakable smell of Spain—a blend of coffee, perfume, heat, dust, tobacco, and something else that seems to come in from the outside through the glass walls, something to do with the palms and oleanders, the dark cypresses and the mountains that shimmer in the haze near the sea. I clear customs and sit in the back of my taxi with the smell of distance and diesel coming in through the window on the hot, dry breeze.

The taxi finally drops me off at the Apartamentos Victoria. The others have already arrived and are having lunch in the sun. Cramer, Wolpert, Garner, Mandelstam, Koep, and Berkowitz, good men, all, and true. Patrick Cramer is our biggest gun, having in his day reached the quarters of Wimbledon, and won such divers events as Lee on Solent, Kansas City, and Bloemfontein.

DIARY NOTES, BARCELONA, 1992

The Real Club de Tenis! We played Davis Cup here in about 1959, but the memories of these clay courts surrounded by their hedges of clipped, grey cypress are almost gone—the merest shadows, which return somewhat when the old groundsman unfurls his hose with a flourish and sends out showers of water that slake the clay and lift hot scents of resin from the cypresses.

We sit at lunch and have a strategic team talk before our first practise, looking anxiously at our draw. A first round versus Luxemburg is encouraging, but then we play the Americans, who are seeded number one! The list of names that Juan Tintore (the organiser of the event) has sent us bristles with American vigour: Jody Rush; David Nash; Larry Dodge! Even Charlie Hoeveler, with his selection of cuts and slices, looks sinister.

"They're all as good as shit!" says Patrick Cramer, who now lives in the United States and knows them all. He has these singular phrases that he comes up with. "All six of them, good as shit, but what the heck, so are we!"

It's all very well for Patrick. He is a lusty, strapping forty-six-year-old who has life by the scruff of the neck. He is waiting for his main course, and as he talks he dips slabs of warm, Spanish bread into a bowl of golden olive oil, puts them in his mouth, chews with relish, and washes the mixture down with beer. You can virtually see the vitamins flowing into his veins.

"This bread is insane!" More Cramer usage. When things

get too ecstatic, they become insane. "We're going to have to pressure them from the first point," he is saying, "serve big, hit heavy. . . ."

Garner and I watch him with some envy. He's a bachelor, for a start, and while he eats and talks about the way he thinks we should play the Americans, fragments about the latest women in his life infiltrate his diatribe—fragments triggered by the shape of the dark-eyed waitress who brings the mugs of beer. "Those hooters are insane!" he remarks. Hooters. "Reminds me of Judy . . . they're good as shit," he says again (the Americans, not the hooters), "all down the line, good competitors . . . I should have asked her to come over with me—what a body she has . . . even their number five, guy called Dodge, very steady, doesn't miss a ball . . . problem is, at my time of life, hooters aren't everything. Must have a brain, too . . . we're better at doubles. Brain, brain, brain. Vital. Hooters just pass in the night . . . their top guy, Nash, is an athlete, too. Big serve, big volley, moves well . . . the stuff he does"—another of his phrases—"the stuff he does is tough as shit!"

The rest of us move uneasily in our chairs. Such talk creates minor clangs in all our souls. We feel a little pale and wintry, while Cramer has his Florida tan. To make matters worse, our practise courts are situated between the Americans and the Italians. On the one side the blazing American intensity, on the other the swarthy Italian players merging with the fine clay and gradually turning red as sweat mixes with the dust that creeps into their socks and up their legs.

We beat Luxemburg and then have a great battle with the Americans, whom we also beat in the tie-breaker of the last match of the tie. In the semifinals, the Italians are quite another matter. We lose to them, and for a while I am transported back to the days of Pietrangeli and Sirola, and the Davis Cup match we lost in Florence. The difference is that then, it mattered terribly. Now, we played a game of tennis, enjoyed the heat and the excitement, and will enjoy as much the lunch that waits on the tables underneath the plane trees.

In 1994 I persuaded Abie to play for our team and, amongst others, made the following notes to show that his age had not wearied him:

The clock has been turned right back! My friend Segal, now over sixty, finds himself once more locked in battle against one Santi Giancarlo of Italy. Overhead, a hot Spanish sun, and underfoot, damp, red clay. Two old warhorses still sweating it out! Somewhere in the third set, at some critical point (in this heat all points are critical), Giancarlo hits a very deep shot that Abie would give his soul to call out, but that just seems to nick a bit of white off the line. Abie looks at the mark, says nothing, but draws around it the familiar semicircle that the young players use these days to emphasise that balls have just missed lines.

"I was hoping," admits Abie with a grin, "that the umpire would see what I did, take it for granted, and just call it out! Instead, what do you think? The idiot gets off his chair to come and see! He looks down at the mark and I look down at the mark.

"'But the ball was good,' he says.

"'I know,' I say to him. 'I just wanted to show you what a

good shot it was!'"

And so, you see, even Abie has stayed very much the same.

20

THE LIGHT AT THE END OF

THE DAY

Jean's early habits never changed. Later in life, whenever she packed for a journey, the first thing she decided was which books to take along. One book was never enough. There had to be several, all of them tucked into her carry-on luggage, and all of them small books.

"I'm not great on thick books," she once told me. "I'd much rather have three thin books than one thick one. Gatsby would never have been Gatsby in a thick book, would he?"

When I left on journeys and she dropped in to say good-bye she would often bring a book for me to take along. Once when I was leaving for a business trip to Europe, the book she tucked into my open briefcase was called *Sea and Sardinia* by D. H. Lawrence. The date was July 1983, and it was the last book she ever gave me.

It was about a journey—a simple one made by Lawrence and his wife across what was then a primitive Sardinia, and I

think I know why she gave it to me. (There was a special reason
for nearly all the books she lent me.) This particular book was a
kind of warning against excesses—a reminder about the times
in life when, say, a cup of hot milk and a piece of bread might
be the most important things of all.

I still have the book. It is well worn by now, its bookmark
is still the torn-off Swissair boarding card (flight SR 0621), and I
take it with me on all my journeys as a sort of home comfort, a
rabbit's foot that never changes no matter where I go. The opening lines read:

> Comes over one an absolute necessity to move. And
> what is more, to move in some particular direction. A
> double necessity then: to get on the move, and to
> know whither.

I have come to know them off by heart.

One last journey, then? The night flight to Frankfurt is a
simple one. Dinner, a glass of wine, a page or two of reading,
half the movie perhaps, and then dozing to sounds of darkness
and space; suddenly, the grey woods of a misty Germany, with
glimpses of the Main through streamers of winter fog. The run-
way is still wet from the night rain. The big jet bumps, brakes,
and rumbles to its mooring past the silent rows of U.S.
warplanes.

Above all, Frankfurt airport is a gateway to other places.
Oslo; Ismir; Ljubljana; Pisa; Karachi. The boarding signs flash as
you walk towards the customs and baggage halls. Somewhere

there will be a small bar and a cup of the dark German coffee (which you really ought to have when you arrive in Frankfurt)—somewhere in the *Ladengalerie* with its elegant shops: Zimmerman, Otto Klein, der Freizeitmode, Gotta Golf, Tabak—an *Apotheke* where a big blonde girl is trying out perfumes, a very big girl, in lederhausen, with strong, white, well-shaped legs and all the robust winter sensuousness of an Oktoberfest with beer. She sprays the perfume on her wrist, sniffs at it, then holds her wrist to the nose of the young man who is with her, watching him intently and laughing at his reactions.

Signs pointing downstairs say BAHNHOF and suggest train journeys through winter woods, past villages on rivers: Bad Homburg, Langen, Neunkirchen; you browse briefly through the images of some other world where perhaps you may have walked, wrapped up in coat and gloves; a soft felt hat with feather in its band; *Kaffee und eine Sahnehaube*, in some other life that at some other time you might have lived. And while you hand your passport to the customs guard and wait for your bag to appear on the conveyor belt, a memory that has lain about in the corners of your mind suddenly solidifies:

HAMBURG, 1962

I had been asked to play an exhibition match at some club in the suburbs. Mixed doubles, of all things. The club has this team that wins the league, and one woman player who is supposed to be very good, etc., etc., and I would get two hundred deutsche marks for my pains. So I said yes, I would, and ended up playing with the woman, who turned out to have a big topspin forehand and a big serve and smash—altogether a big woman—some kind of field athlete, they said.

"Like a ten-ton truck, Forbsey!" In my mind I could hear Abie's voice as I walked on the court. "You should be playing men's doubles, not mixed!"

She and I had won our matches, and after our victory we celebrated with the champagne that the president of the club opened. They gave me my two hundred DM and she showered and washed her hair, leaving it to tumble dry like a bundle of hay. We were pleased with ourselves and laughed a lot.

"Forbey, you have touch of visard!" she said, more than once. "You are genius wis vollee"—of which I'd had plenty—setups, mostly, because of her big forehand returns.

By the time we'd left the club it was dark. The taxi rumbled over the cobblestones, and when we finally arrived back at the hotel it was quite late, so we'd gone up to my room. The radio was playing Brahms and she found a Mars bar left over from England on the dressing table and ate it at once, which seemed to do the trick.

Crazy woman, this large stranger. She was so bonelessly feminine that I forgot all about her big forehand and her blonde, unshaven underarms. Fortunately Abie didn't know, or he'd have had something to say about me consorting with a ten-ton truck. He would also never have believed that I'd found the combination of her size, her topspin forehand, the 4711 cologne she wore, and the Brahms very unusual. For Abie things have to be as easy to do and instantly rewarding as sinking his teeth into the Mars bar. He doesn't have time for combinations.

"That guy Brahms of yours," he once said, "could easily

have been a genius, but it sure takes a hell of a long time to find out why."

As I leave the baggage hall the welcome from the ATP Tour arrivals desk ends the reverie. This is, after all, the tennis event of the year. Everyone who is anyone in tennis will be present. Brand-new Opel cars wait outside. They are driven by students from the universities, and on the way to town the young driver tells me of the new, united Germany. It has been a great cultural coming together, he says, but now, jobs are scarce. He will probably be a teacher. Or perhaps (wistfully) an architect, which is ze chance he really wants, if only he could . . . (the rose garden! the rose garden! I say to myself, and urge him to be an architect).

It is raining as we turn onto the Autobahn and the wind is almost a gale, rattling the rain against the windshield. Slowly the city materialises—neat, grey German streets—Zeppelin Allee, Kaiserplatz, Berlinerstrasse, and, finally, the Arabella Grand Hotel. My room overlooks a quiet *Platz*—a cobbled square with plane trees cut low, a fountain, a gift shop, and a restaurant with toy ducks called Entenhause—all so thoroughly German that I stand at the window for a moment and stare. Again the spirit of place! Bad Neustadt. Bad Homburg. The Rhine! The girl in Baden-Baden with the dark hair who led the town tours, whose breath smelt of sweet corn and whom Abie said was a hell of a guide. . . .

The ATP Tour World Championships are held in the Festhalle in Frankfurt every November as a culmination of the year's tournament schedule. The event is superbly staged and epitomises all that is new in tennis. Opulence, luxury, perfection—all that money can buy! In the lobby of the hotel, the usual signs of tennis. Ivanisevic with Bob Brett, Muster's loping walk, a glimpse of Pete Sampras's dark head, managers, coaches, agents, suppliers, the ATP Tour guys, Miles, Scott, Richmond, Evans et al., and the ever-cheerful ATP Tour women, Silvi, Lesley, Robin, Annie Adams. . . .

This state-of-the-art tennis machine! In every corner a meeting, in every conference room a forum. Faxes, phone calls, messages; will-do, can-do, have done, no way, maybe, the fluid world of words and deals, meetings in passages, promises made, promises broken, rumours, hearsay, fact, fiction, a world built on the shifting sands of losses, victories, computer points, and the whims and fancies of young superstars who shelter in their suites and seem sublimely unaware of the furor necessary to support their deeds.

In the great media room of the Festhalle the world's best sports analysts work in functional luxury. Discussions, comparisons, the clicking of machines, and the murmur of languages. Gianni Clerici, Peter Bodo, Gerald Williams, Frew MacMillan. Any minute now will appear the unmistakable visage of Bud Collins, writer, speaker, teller of tales, fellow of tennis. Wherever distinguished tennis is played, there you will find him, moving about in his mysterious way, and you'll talk to him and he'll tell you things. But after he leaves you will always feel that he knows much more.

If ever a tennis tournament has reached the dizzy heights of show business, this is it. At the Festhalle they're putting on the finishing touches. The most luxurious carpets, seatings, boxes, flowers; the flags of the nations. You can't move without getting offered a glass of something. In the centre of everything, in all its glory, our latest GreenSet Trophy court—for this event a luminous blue. Finally it has the perfect speed and texture, firm but not hard, malleable but not sticky, comfortable under-foot, the ultimate playing surface. Lee Frankel is very pleased. Will I hit a few shots on it to try it out, he wants to know?

"Here? Now?" The vision of my ancient game in all this splendour is hard to conjure up. "Don't you think my shots are too—well—old-fashioned, I suppose?"

But there are not many people around and so I put on my warm-up and wait for Bob Brett to finish his session with Goran Ivanisevic. While Goran is packing his bag, Bob hits a few shots to me. It is a lovely court, firm, soft, with flawless bounces. The lighting is perfect, and of course there is no wind, so it is very easy to stroke the ball smoothly back and forth. When Bob has to leave, Mary Carillo wants to hit a few—Mary, dark and slender, who used to be a touring pro and who is now one of the top TV commentators, working at this event with Drysdale and Stolle. She is dressed in black slacks and a white men's dress shirt ("I bought it on a sale"), and in this hand-some outfit she plays her elegant, logical tennis.

"What do you really think of these top young players?" I ask her when we have to hand over the court to Edberg and Pickard.

"Oh, they're very good, of course," she says. "The best there ever were. And they're nice young guys. But they do tend to God it up a bit."

God it up! And I am aware again that I am of another generation.

In the ATP Tour courtside boxes, with Ian Froman and Charlie Pasarell, I watch Agassi returning Becker's service.

"Did you see *that*?" asks Froman. Agassi has just stepped into one of Becker's first services with his double-hander, taken it on the rise, and hit it back past Becker before he could so much as move.

"It did happen very quickly," I agree.

"Well, just so that you know, that shot took place on the side where our *backhands* used to be!"

"If you could hit a backhand like that, would you feel inclined to God it up a bit?" I ask him.

"If he could hit a shot like that, he would build his own private synagogue," says Pasarell.

DIARY NOTES, FRANKFURT, NOVEMBER 1994

We are dazzled by this tennis! How many times in the past have I not watched great concert pianists or violinists, ballet dancers or opera singers, and been filled with admiration at the technical perfection that they regard as merely the norm—the very least they need in order to do proper justice to their art. Why then, I would always ask myself, are tennis players not able to achieve this same perfection? Why do they sometimes make such simple errors? Are the skills so different? Is it really so much harder, say, to serve every first ball into the court, or to never miss a forehand drive, than it is to play a

Beethoven violin concerto, or dance the lead in Swan Lake?
The questions have always stayed unanswered in my mind.

Now, watching the world's top eight singles players practising and playing under the perfect conditions of the Festhalle
in 1994, I sense in the attitude of the players a quest for just
such perfection. There are almost no unforced errors. On the
contrary, I watch tennis of a standard so high that it overlays
the memories of previous great tennis matches with new ones
of even greater matches. And then a strange thing happens.
As I sit watching the tennis, I find the very perfection for
which I always searched becoming the norm, and I find myself
sifting through the successive rallies of perfect strokes for those
few that are superperfect!—that, like certain passages in the
Beethoven, make the flesh tingle with delight.

In our courtside box, Ian Froman and I look on and talk of
this new perfection. Agassi is playing Bruguera, and the tennis
they play exactly suits our conversation.

"What do you think, Forbsey?" he says at last.

"I was thinking about the old sand court that we had on
the farm," I reply, "and our old wooden rackets strung with
catgut, and our canvas tackies, and the manure, and the little‾
explosions of dust that used to come up when we served near
the lines."

"That it should come to this," he says.

"That it should come to this!"

There is another silence.

"But have we not seen enough brilliant shots for one
night?" I ask him after a while. "After all, it's still only tennis!
Should we not perhaps go up to the Champion's Club and have

a glass of champagne?"

"Why not?" he replies. "I am sure that on the way there we will be able to think of something we can celebrate!"

It is November—another year is nearly at an end, another tournament is reaching final stages that have about them, as final stages always tend to have, a slight air of sadness. The end of something. Yes, there will be a new beginning; tomorrow, perhaps; but we have grown to like this time; this place; why then must it pass so soon?

EPILOGUE

Dearly Beloved,

That's all for now. Time to call it a day. We've watched some tennis, visited some old haunts, chatted to a few people, drunk a little wine. And now this journey is all but over. Of course there is still Jenny's question that needs to be answered—did we, or did we not, get anywhere? The other day I asked Abie and he said, "Sure we did. We got everywhere!" Well, let's agree with Abie. Let's say that we managed to find the passage, opened the door, and walked in the garden! And that the sun was out, and the roses were in full bloom.

And because old T. S. helped us to begin this particular journey, perhaps we can persuade him to help us end it.

> We shall not cease from exploration
> And the end of all our exploring
> Will be to arrive where we started
> And know the place for the first time.

Now what about that cloudy glass of wine? As Froman says, there must be something we can find to celebrate!

Ever yours,
G.